THE AMERICAN IDEA RENEWED

SUDDEN CHANGE MEDIA

THE AMERICAN IDEA RENEWED

Edited by James Kemp

Speeches by Jack Kemp on America's leadership in the world, economic growth, freedom, dignity and opportunity, and the competition of ideas; *Reflections and Proceedings* from the 2014 Kemp Forum on the Future of the American Idea at Lincoln Cottage; and *Marist Opinion Poll* on Americans' views of the American Idea.

The American Idea Renewed

Edited by James Kemp

Copyright © 2016 by The Jack Kemp Foundation

ISBN 978-0-9971609-0-1

All rights reserved. This book or any portion thereof may not be reproduced or used in any manner whatsoever without the express written permission of the

    Jack Kemp Foundation

    1200 New Hampshire Ave NW, Suite 800

    Washington, DC 20036

Printed in the United States of America

PREFACE

The American Idea is both a birthright and an obligation. Like President Lincoln and the Union he led 150 years ago, citizens of the United States are the providential heirs of a "nation, conceived in liberty and dedicated to the proposition that all men are created equal." As with every generation before us, our calling is to find the wisdom to carry forward that great experiment in democracy.

Jack Kemp, who always called his party the "Party of Lincoln," took that calling to heart. He used to say that the American Dream is the human dream given a chance and a place to happen. He believed that America is exceptional because, unlike any other, this country grew out of a compelling idea: that freedom and human dignity are universal values that apply to all people everywhere.

In these pages you will find a selection of his speeches, some published here for the first time, on America's leadership in the world, economic growth, freedom, dignity, opportunity, and the competition of ideas. As they remind us, Dad had a rare ability to devise and promote ideas that appealed with equal force across the political spectrum and across racial, ethnic, gender, age, and socioeconomic lines. In Part II of this book, six modern commentators provide their contemporary reflections on those same themes.

On May 16, 2014, the *Kemp Forum on the Future of the American Idea* met at the hilltop cottage in Washington, D.C. where President Lincoln first penned the Emancipation Proclamation. We hope that the day's proceedings, captured in Part III, reflect the goals to which we aspire at every Kemp Forum:

- To speak to the things that unite us, rather than divide us: freedom, opportunity, growth, compassion, dignity, and hope;
- To embrace the politics of reaching for our better angels, shouldering our civic responsibilities, empowering America to be a moral force for good;
- To promote and defend the virtues necessary to make freedom work and our citizens flourish; and
- To develop and advance wise public policies to enable every American to rise as high as his or her God-given talents will allow.

The Jack Kemp Foundation is dedicated to empowering the next generation of leaders to carry forward the revolutionary idea that gave rise to this new nation. Three quarters of Americans of diverse political persuasions all believe the United States has been and remains a model of freedom and opportunity for other nations (see Marist Opinion Poll in the Appendix). I like to think that when people say, "I am a Kemp Republican" or sometimes "a Kemp Democrat," the American Idea is what they have in mind.

James Kemp, President

TABLE OF CONTENTS

PREFACE
by Jimmy Kemp

PART I

JACK KEMP ON THE AMERICAN IDEA

LEADERSHIP FOR THE AMERICAN IDEA

The Roots of American Foreign Policy
New York, New York – March 29, 1982 13

> "It is impossible to talk about the ideas behind American foreign policy without beginning with the American Idea: what it means to us at home. The American Idea is a certain view of mankind...."

Soldier of the Soul 27
New York, New York – November 19, 1996

> "Let us resolve not that it be an American Century per se— but a Democratic Century for all."

An African-American Partnership 33
Harare, Zimbabwe – July 21, 1997

> "A nation's greatest assets are not the wealth that can be seen, but the unseen potential of the human mind and spirit."

Why America Must Lead 43
Los Angeles, California – February 23, 1998

> "As powerful as we are, our future will not be secure unless we use that power to create a world which honors those things we hold sacred...."

GROWTH, GROWTH, GROWTH!

The Nature and Cause of the Wealth of our Nation 55
Cambridge, Massachusetts – April 21, 1994

> "[T]he technological revolution which will change everything in our lives is dependent upon an ancient moral principle: freedom."

The Economic Growth Imperative 63
Chicago, Illinois – March 11, 1997

> "A contrary view to what has become the smothering conventional wisdom that slow growth not only is inevitable but desirable."

Progress is Not Foreordained 77
Simi Valley, California – February 5, 1999

> "[W]e must establish a comprehensive economic policy based on the ideals of the last lion of this century. I can think of no better monument to the revolution that he started."

A Judeo-Christian View of Economics 87
Colorado Springs, Colorado – April 4, 2003

> "Democratic capitalism has been history's sharpest weapon against poverty, oppression, and tyranny."

FREEDOM, DIGNITY, OPPORTUNITY

America's Religious Heritage 95
Lynchburg, Virginia – November 1, 1983

> "Martin Luther King and Jerry Falwell would disagree on many issues of public policy. But surely on this central idea they are united, as all Americans should be: Democracy without morality, or freedom without faith, is impossible."

Inquiry into the Nature and Causes of Poverty in America and How to Combat It 109
Washington, D.C. – June 6, 1990

> "America is divided into two economies: mainstream (democratic capitalism, entrepreneurial) and that created for the poor (dependency, welfare bureaucracy, social costs)."

Lincoln's Vision of Democracy 121
Gettysburg, Pennsylvania – November 19, 1990

> "Mr. Lincoln…envisioned an America where freedom is inseparable from economic, political and social opportunity, and upward mobility."

A Cultural Renaissance 129
Hillsdale College, Michigan – February 22, 1994

> "I've often argued that economic prosperity will help solve many of our serious social problems, but I've never argued that it is sufficient. An economy and a government have limits set at the boundaries of the human heart. And the habits of the heart are learned in families—shelters for civilized standards and ethical behavior."

What Pro Football Taught Me 143
Washington, D.C. – August 14, 1995

> *"The lesson that stands out above all is that when a team walks onto the field... race, color, religion—all artificial differences—get left on the sidelines, and if they don't, the whole team goes down to defeat."*

POLITICS AND THE COMPETITION OF IDEAS

A Republican Tidal Wave (Address to the Republican National Convention) 147
Detroit, Michigan – July 15, 1980

> *"The American Idea was never that everyone would be leveled to the same position in life. The American Idea was that each individual should have the same opportunity to rise as high as his effort and imitative and God-given talent could carry him."*

Black Americans and the Republican Party 153
Cleveland, Ohio – July 30, 1984

> *"Our party was born out of the struggle for equality and opportunity—the two always went together... But somewhere along the way the Republican Party blundered and strayed...One day millions of black Americans are going to surprise themselves by voting Republican again."*

My Friends, We Have a Revolution to Finish 167
Text of Remarks prepared for delivery to Republicans at Federal Hall
New York, New York – March 27, 1987

> *"The American Revolution is the only revolution in history which did not disappoint its architects. But that productive tension between principles and action must continue to challenge and motivate, to move an energize us today. Ours is an unfinished revolution..."*

The Politics of the Impossible 173
Washington, D.C. – November 15, 1994

> *"Let me share a vision of the American Idea, deeply rooted in the conservative vision of the Founders. Return to people their resources, and they will accept their responsibilities. Return to people power, and they will rebuild the institutions of a free society. Return to people authority, and they will create the moral capital to help renew our nation."*

Acceptance Speech (Excerpts) – Nomination for Vice President 181
San Diego, California – August 16, 1996

> *"Every generation faces a choice: hope or despair—to plan for scarcity or to embrace possibilities. Societies throughout history believed they had reached the*

frontiers of human accomplishment. But in every age, those who trusted the divine spark of imagination discovered that vastly greater horizons lay ahead."

PART II

REFLECTIONS ON THE FUTURE OF THE AMERICAN IDEA

The Idea of America by John Bolton 189

American Prosperity and the American Idea by Brian Domitrovic 192

The American Idea by Ben Elliott 195

Personal Reinvention by Douglas Holtz-Eakin 200

Rediscovering Growth by Stephen Moore 203

Reflections on the American Idea by Peter Wehner 205

PART III

KEMP FORUM ON THE FUTURE OF THE AMERICAN IDEA

OPENING REMARKS 211
Rich Lowry on Mr. Lincoln and the American Idea

LEADERSHIP FOR THE AMERICAN IDEA – Rapporteur's Report 217

Panel: William Kristol, Garry Kasparov, Peggy Noonan, Bob Schoultz

GROWTH, GROWTH, GROWTH! – Rapporteur's Report 229

Panel: Fred Barnes, George Gilder, Amity Shlaes, Deborah Wince-Smith

FREEDOM, DIGNITY, OPPORTUNITY – Rapporteur's Report 247

Panel: Juan Williams, Arthur Brooks, Ron Christie, Wayne Frederick

KEYNOTE ADDRESS 263
Garry Kasparov

SPEAKER BIOGRAPHIES

INDEX

APPENDIX – THE AMERICAN IDEA: A NATIONAL SURVEY

PART I

JACK KEMP ON THE AMERICAN IDEA

Eighteen speeches by Jack Kemp on the subjects of American leadership, growth, freedom, dignity and opportunity, and politics in America; some published here for the first time and printed in their entirety to preserve the historical context that inspired them and the enduring themes they address.

LEADERSHIP FOR THE AMERICAN IDEA

The Roots of American Foreign Policy

Congressman Jack Kemp (R-NY)

Before the Council on Foreign Relations
New York City, March 29, 1982

"It is impossible to talk about the ideas behind American foreign policy without beginning with the American Idea: what it means to us at home. The American Idea is a certain view of mankind ..."

As ranking Republican member on the Foreign Operations subcommittee of the Committee on Appropriations, I can tell you that in making foreign policy, a policymaker is in constant danger of missing the forest for the trees. We have spent a good part of the first fourteen months of President Reagan's Administration in chopping deadwood and planting new seedlings. We have wrangled over appropriations for International Development Association (IDA), over Multilateral Development Bank "graduation" policies, and over military sales credit formulas until numbers and acronyms dance in our heads. In the end, we passed the first foreign aid bill in a long time. After the flurry of activity, it seems more than ever necessary to remind ourselves that our job is not to come up with numbers; we are trying to realize certain ideas, to affect lives for the better here and around the globe. Therefore, it's a good time to ask ourselves, and to make explicit, exactly which ideas motivate and drive our foreign policy.

It is impossible to talk about the ideas behind American foreign policy without beginning with the American Idea: what it means to us at home. The American Idea is a certain view of mankind. It sees each individual as valuable because he or she is endowed by God with life, with unique talents by nature, but their realization is not. Our natural rights must be won at a cost, and maintained by institution. Government must be established to protect the rights of each individual, and the rights of the community as a whole. Beyond this, the proper scope of government is a matter for continual debate. But government itself must be limited so that it does not threaten the rights with which it is entrusted.

Does the American Idea therefore mean that the behavior of individuals should be regulated as little as possible? Far from it. Our political behavior is regulated by the Constitution, which places certain rights beyond the power of even a majority. Our moral behavior is regulated by the Judeo-Christian values which are instilled by family and religion. Out social behavior is regulated by our dependence upon the community in which we live. And our economic behavior is regulated and directed by the rules of just exchange, that is, by the price mechanism. Far from a highly individualistic society, our Founding Fathers envisioned a system exquisitely balanced between the right of freedom and the regulation of responsibility.

Ours is a system which puts the center of decision-making power neither with the individual nor with the government, but somewhere in between—in the family, the church, and the community. It is only the ham-handed efforts of government to overtake more and more regulation of economic, social and moral behavior, which have promoted tendencies toward atomistic and heedless individualism, by cutting people off from their natural roots in the social order.

The American Idea is also the human idea. We know this is true because people around the world naturally choose it, often at great risk, when they get the chance. We do not have to fence our people in, or put them under surveillance, or try to prevent them from embarking in leaky boats for distant shores. Rather, many of our problems stem from the need to accommodate the many refugees from foreign oppression.

After the Second World War, the United States clearly recognized its responsibility as steward of the American Idea and as Leader of the Free World. The policy of containment of Soviet aggression was conceived not merely as military and territorial, but also as economic and ideological. In announcing his Truman Doctrine before a joint session of Congress, President Truman warned:

> *The seeds of totalitarian regimes are nurtured by misery and want. They spread and grow in the evil soil of poverty and strife. The reach their full growth when the hope of a people for a better life has died.*

We must keep that hope alive.

The free peoples of the world look to us for support in maintaining their freedoms. If we falter in our leadership, we may endanger the peace of the world—and we shall surely endanger the welfare of our own Nation.

We established the principle of free determination of government by popular vote in all the liberated territories. We had enough faith in our own democratic political system to establish it in the lands of our former enemies, Japan and West Germany. But we did more. We recognized that a free international order requires institutions to maintain it. With the memories of beggar-your-neighbor protectionism in the Thirties still fresh in our minds, the United States led the world in reestablishing an international system based on a common money, thereby stabilizing exchange rates. We progressively re-established a system of free trade among nations, and abolished capital controls. All of these laid the groundwork for the incredible growth of world trade, and the marvelous stability of the next quarter century.

How, then, can there have been so much doubt about the worth of the American Idea in recent years? How could George Kennan write, for example, that our social and economic system has "nothing to teach the world," and might not be worth defending if push came to shove? "I can see very little merit," Kennan wrote, "in organizing ourselves to defend from the Russians the porno shops of central Washington."

How, too, can the Soviets proclaim the final "crisis of capitalism?" Yuri Davidov, a Soviet commentator on the United States, has argued that American resolve has collapsed because of "a recognition of the failure of the American path of development." That's pretty rich, coming from a nation which has suffered 64 consecutive bad harvests since 1917. It's ironic when you consider that the Soviet Union must rely on American grain to feed its own people.

There are two answers to this puzzle, I think. The first is that, over the years, our military assistance programs were not always coupled with President Truman's original vision that, while there is no freedom without security, the point of security is to preserve the institutions which promote political, economic and personal freedom; in short, to join might with right.

The second, and related reason, is that belief in our own path of economic development was a casualty of the Great Depression. We did not blame the Great Depression on its true causes—the peculiar and dangerous post-1918 monetary system, protectionist tariffs, high tax rates and a general paralysis of prices caused by well-intended blunders. No, John Maynard Keynes told us that our free market is marred by an inherent tendency toward depression. According to Keynes, individuals cannot be relied upon to spend their money, when left to their own devices. So the government must step in, he said, to stimulate and direct investment and consumption.

This notion ravished the American economic profession. Paul Samuelson, whose Ph.D. dissertation had just provided the mathematical framework for Keynesian analysis, wrote in 1943: "Were the war to end suddenly within the next six months, were we again planlessly to wind up the war effort…then would be ushered in the greatest period of unemployment and industrial dislocation which any economy has ever faced." When the Pabst Brewing Company offered a $25,000 prize for the best plan for reordering the economy after the war, neither the winning essay nor any of the also-rans saw any role whatever for the entrepreneur in the post-war American economy. Instead, the essays were a compendium, of measures for central planning, the relief of already existing corporations, and thorough-going management of aggregate demand.

Luckily for us, economists did not yet have the political influence they were to gain by the mid-1960s. And luckily for the conquered nations, the democratic political institutions we forced upon them enabled them to reject our economic advice. Germany and Japan did not perform their economic miracles on the basis of centralized planning, import substitution and capital transfers. At a time when Great Britain and the United States were beginning to labor under such ideas, Germany and Japan were beginning to prosper by heeding the ideas of Adam Smith and the Founding Fathers.

One of my favorite stories illustrates how the West Germans had to defy the American authorities in order to begin their "Wirtschaftswunder." In 1948, Ludwig Erhad was just an obscure professor from the University of Freiburg, who was economic adviser to the provisional civilian government. Immediately following a currency reform which ended inflation, Erhad proclaimed the complete abolition of price controls and rationing, on his own initiative. In fact, he had to do it on a weekend, because the economic advisers from the U.S. State Department were against the idea. The following Monday, Erhad was summoned to the office of the American commander, Gen. Lucius Clay said, "Mr. Erhad, my advisers tell me you have made a terrible mistake." Erhad replied, "Herr General, pay no attention to them. My own advisers tell me the same thing." Erhad succeeded in persuading Clay to let him pursue his idea of the "soziale Marktwirtschaft": the socially responsible market economy.

In Japan, the economic miracle did not begin until 1950, when its Parliament, the Diet, decided to try the original American Idea, not the shoddy post-war stuff we were exporting. They reconstituted the trading companied which had been broken up in 1945, and riddled the progressive tax code we had given them with loopholes to restore incentives. As the economy grew and revenues expanded, the government continued to cut tax rates—every year in fact, between 1950 and 1974.

The rest of the world was not so fortunate. Lured by the resources and expertise of a nation militarily and economically superior to any ever known, the underdeveloped nations came to Washington, D.C., to the United Nations in New York, and to World Bank outposts around the world, to learn the secret of economic growth.

And what did we tell them? Did we tell them the truth—that their greatest asset is the energy and initiative of their people that the secret of a strong nation lies in the liberty and cohesion of its society? No, we told them that a country's wealth comes from its infrastructure. We told them that roads, steel mills and power plants are the secret of wealth and strength. So we advised them to turn over their economies to planners who would direct massive taxation and spending. Control and direct investment, and supervise the tremendous burden of debt which would be necessary to build their infrastructure. For the most part, our advice was followed. The tragic results can be seen throughout the world.

The utterly predictable failure of these policies led many in our foreign policy establishment to the most destructive and paternalistic conclusions. We feared that democratic capitalism, and perhaps even democracy itself, might not be a practical system for the underdeveloped world. That democracy presupposed a strong middle class, because uneducated peasants, given the vote, would simply vote themselves the resources of the tiny productive class. Our thinking degenerated so far that some assumed that all these tiny new countries needed a strong man, a benign dictator who would make wise decisions on behalf of the rabble. In the economic field, the idea developed that those living in developing nations respond to incentives in some perverse way or, in many cases, not at all. All this thinly disguised elitism is a far cry from the American Idea.

For their part, many of the leaders of the developing nations concluded that their failure was due to the "structure" of world relations. Lenin had tried to explain the failure of capitalism to collapse as predicted by saying that the capitalist countries were postponing the day of reckoning by exploiting the former colonies through trade; as these new nations developed, Lenin believed, the contradictions of capitalism would reassert themselves. Instead, after World War II most of the growth of world trade occurred within and among the industrialized countries, and the less developed countries seemed to become more and more marginal. The new idea is that this is so because of some unspecified structural defects in the world economy, which exclude the new countries from a fair chance. The premise changes; only the conclusion that the free international order is somehow to blame does not change.

The main premise of the advocated of this new economic order is absolute scarcity. The Club of Rome, the Global 2000 Report, and the recommendations of the Brandt Commission, all see the world's resources as limited and declining, so that the expansion of production is virtually impossible. Only massive redistribution of wealth from rich nations to poor, we are told, can supply the basic human needs of the world's population.

To establish the absurdity of the supposed dichotomy between North and South, it is necessary only to look at a map. In fact, the map on the cover of the Brandt Commission report tried to divide the world's nations into the developed North and the abjectly poor South. But the dividing line meanders all over the globe, jogging here to avoid Australia, New Zealand and South Africa—all former colonies—and over there leaving Hong Kong, Singapore and other success stories in the impoverished South. The map-drawers see no apparent distinction between Brazil and Upper Volta.

Why is it so hard to draw the line between North and South? The answer is very simple: the line doesn't exist. The scale of per-capita income, however measured, stretches without a break from Sweden to sub-Saharan Africa. Oil rich nations have stagnant economies but report per-capita incomes far ahead of dynamic nations such as South Korea, the Ivory and Hong Kong. Sri Lanka, a nation rich in human potential, has unleashed its own economic miracle through its internal policies. As A. W. Clausen, president of the World Bank observes, the North-South dichotomy "is not very useful because it has tended to create a bipolar concept of world economic dynamics that glosses over—or completely leaves out—a whole series of other elements of economic activity that just do not fit into a rigid 'North-South' dichotomy." I don't have to tell you what a refreshing departure this statement represents.

Perhaps Theodore Schultz, who could be called the "grandfather of supply-side economics," expresses it best: "The decisive factors of production in improving the welfare of poor people are not space, energy and cropland; the decisive factors are the improvement in population quality and advances in knowledge." Those who doubt this would deny 200 years of American history. Consider Nobel Laureate Wassily Leontief, who tried to explain why the U.S. exports labor intensive goods, when volumes of economic theory say that our comparative advantage should rest with technological goods. The answer, once again, is the quality and ability of individual Americans.

The entire issue of scarcity is inextricably tied to attitudes toward the value of human life. The first goal of planners for the underdeveloped nations seems to be to denude them of their most precious resource: people. If resources are absolutely limited, if the economic growth is impossible, as the planners believe, the only way to raise living standards is to adjust the population to the level of resources. The neo-Malthusians tell us that an increase in the population of cattle adds to our national wealth, but an increase in the population of human beings subtracts from it.

This idea, also, can be held only by someone who ignores reality. Most of Africa is sparsely populated, rich in natural resources—and dirt poor. Hong Kong, Singapore and Japan are densely populated, poor in natural resources—and their wealth is rapidly increasing. Because of immigration, Hong Kong has the most rapid population growth in Asia. Yet at the height of immigration, the unemployment rate there remained unchanged. There is simply no economic basis whatsoever for government control of population,

The Reagan administration clearly recognizes the primacy of individuals in the process of "development." Representing the administration at the U.N., Michael Novak said: "While we believe a free system will almost inevitably lead to development, it is up to the individual, acting alone or within a group, to gain for himself that success through his own best efforts. The human community serves individuals by supplying social tissue within which individuals exercise their Creator-given rights to life, liberty and the pursuit of happiness. Social cooperation is indispensable. Individuals must then imagine, create, and act—or nature relapses into silence. Development does not happen. It must be made to happen by active individuals."

The election of Ronald Reagan in 1980, I believe, was a resounding affirmation of the American Idea. Its consequences for our domestic policy are obvious. But this reaffirmation cannot help having far-reaching consequences for our foreign policy as well. First, restoring the American Idea to its proper place in our society will restore the confidence upon which any resolute foreign policy must depend. Second, we have begun to reverse the decline of resources devoted to an adequate defense of our ideas and institutions. Third, we can begin again to export the American Idea —because the idea is right and because it works.

The first major opportunity to do so is now before the Congress. Recently, the president sent us his Caribbean Basin Initiative. At the same time, he requested substantial new resources for aiding our friends in that region in their struggle against Soviet influence spreading from Cuba.

With the U.S. Marines in Cuba, 1986

It is evident that the president thoroughly understands the issues involved and the necessity of moral leadership on our part. In the message which accompanied his request he said:

> *The economic, political and security challenges in the Caribbean Basin are formidable. Our neighbors need time to develop representative and responsive institutions, which are the guarantors of democracy and justice that freedom's foes seek to stamp out. They need to defend themselves against attempts by externally supported minorities to impose an alien, hostile and unworkable system upon them. The alternative is further expansion of political violence from the extreme left and the extreme right, resulting in the imposition of dictatorships and— inevitably—more economic decline, and more human suffering and dislocation.*

Our objective, therefore, is to rebuild institutions which guarantee democracy, a just social order, and free exchange. The events in Guatemala and El Salvador indicate the tenuous position of democracy in many parts of the Caribbean. While we must work with the military governments, whose existence is a fact of life, we must make every effort to establish the principle of constitutional civilian control the armed forces. And we must insist on the primacy of individual rights, and emphasize the steadying influence of the social institutions of family and community.

The main thrust of the president's program is an expansion of trade through a unilateral removal of trade restrictions. To accompany this improved trade restrictions, to accompany this improved trade he proposes to grant investment tax credits to U.S. firms expanding in the region. On the military side, he is seeking sufficient grants and sales credits to allow our friend in the region to arm themselves against Soviet aggression.

I support the president's effort. But I think that he would be the first to agree that, in light of our ambitious objectives, it does not go far enough. The unilateral removal of barriers to trade and introduction of tax incentives are a gesture of good faith on our part that there will be a new direction for American policy in the Caribbean. But the gesture cannot be mistaken for the continuing policy. Our offer of increased assistance must be seen as incentive, not as a substitute, for the establishment of institutions which foster economic and political democracy and free trade.

Nations participating in the Caribbean Basin Initiative (CBI) should be encouraged to undertake thorough reform of their domestic fiscal policies to restore economic incentives for individuals and businesses. Trade in all commodities and manufactured goods should be unrestricted in both directions. And all must recognize that there cannot be any sustained revival of these countries' economies until investors are assured of the safety of their investments from expropriation or expatriation taxes. Also, our assistance programs, military as well as economic, should concentrate on developing human resources: entrepreneurial skills and regional agricultural research in the case of economic aid, and education and training in the case of military aid. But even these suggestions do not address two of the most important disincentives to development in the Caribbean, because these two disincentives now plague the whole world: the progressively growing threat to free trade and stable currencies.

Shortly after I became a congressman 12 years ago, I became increasingly aware that the problems which afflicted my depressed Buffalo-area district could not be solved by local projects. Buffalo was suffering from problems of national scope, which required solutions on a national level. In the same way, the economic problems of the Caribbean cannot be fundamentally solved even by daring fiscal reforms and free trade in the area.

To use a homely example: my brother is president in California of the Coca-Cola Bottling Company. He sells a product which is truly international. A bottle of Coke sold in China uses plastic from Middle East oil; the sugar comes from a plantation in Jamaica; the bottling machinery is precision milled in Ohio; the entire operation is held together at every point by entrepreneurial expertise from a hub in Atlanta. Thus a single bottle of Coke unites the efforts and aspirations of families which may have no other communication, perhaps no conception of the part each plays in the lives of others. But this cooperation is not enabled by some bilateral agreement between the United States and Jamaica, or with Saudi Arabia, or with any of the other countries involved. Such a product is possible only by more or less open exchange with everyone, because the product, and the cooperation it represents, can be threatened by disruption at any point along the way.

The argument for free trade is well established, and so is the argument against protectionism, whether it passes under the title of tariff, quota, "buy American," or reciprocity. Adam Smith pointed out that the material progress of mankind depends on an increasingly specialized and interdependent division of labor. History has proven repeatedly that attempting to disrupt this cooperation is as painful to everyone as dismemberment—which is what it amounts to. Why, then, are we seeing yet again a growing pressure for protectionism, both here and abroad?

What is too little recognized is the fact that the pressure for protectionism more often than not originates in a failure of the monetary system. A common and increasingly integrated market requires a common medium of exchange. Therefore, monetary disorders manifest themselves as disruptions in trade.

Back in the 1930s, protectionist walls were raised to counteract what appeared to be a worldwide orgy of "dumping"—that is, of everyone competing to sell their articles below cost. The protectionist walls were an attempt to keep domestic prices up in the face of this apparently ruinous worldwide competition.

It should have been obvious—but apparently was not—that everyone was dumping, not because of competition run amok, but rather because the collapse of the monetary system was causing a fall in prices. This meant that no one had a choice as to whether to sell below cost. The proper answer was to repair the monetary system. Instead, Congress and other parliamentary bodies insisted on fixing things that weren't broken: raising tax rates and tariffs, and paralyzing wages and prices. This only made things worse, and we didn't emerge from the morass until the Second World War.

Many of the same elements are present today. Ever since 1971, the world has suffered from the progressive disappearance of a reliable monetary standard. Our problems in the steel and auto and agricultural industries, like the oil crisis of a few years ago, are not due to isolated instances of predatory or monopolistic pricing by our trading partners, but primarily by the collapse of the Bretton Woods system and the monetary chaos which has spread since then.

Since I dwelt at the length on specific proposals for monetary reform ten days ago at the Federal Reserve Bank of Atlanta, I won't go into great detail here. I will only stress my conclusion: that domestic interest rates will not come down permanently until the dollar's value is stabilized by the restoration of gold convertibility; and that the threat of an implosion of world trade, with its mounting pressures for protectionism, will not end until the world once again reinstitutes a world monetary standard. Such a standard would presumably be, as it was under the classical gold standard and the Bretton Woods system, a fixed weight of gold bullion. If we do not begin such reforms immediately, we will face the continual double threat of spiraling credit liquidation on the one hand, and rapid depreciation of the dollar on the other. Without an anchor of real value, the monetary system has no tendency whatsoever toward stability—whether it is managed by monetarists or Keynesians. If we do not reform monetary policy, we risk seeing the pressures on our free international order becoming unbearable.

We don't hurt ourselves, and the world, in that way. If we can learn the lessons of the 1920s and 1930s, there is no reason to repeat the unpleasant experience of the period.

Let us fix our sights instead on a different world order: an order in which all nations respect the political, economic, and personal rights of individuals. Where the accumulation of wealth is accomplished by peaceful cooperation and interdependence. Where all people can move themselves and their possessions freely so as to achieve the fulfillment of their talents as God gives them light. And an order in which attempts to disrupt the system become increasingly costly, and therefore, unlikely.

We cannot ignore the fact that the Soviet Union actively opposes this view on mankind and of world order. Therefore, we cannot fail to defend ourselves, our vision, and our like-minded friends around the world. Let us recognize—and eagerly grasp—our terrible responsibility to see that might and right are joined—and held—together.

Soldier of the Soul

The Honorable Jack Kemp

Before the Endowment for Democracy in Eastern Europe
New York City, November 19, 1996

"Let us resolve not that it be an American Century per se—but a Democratic Century for all."

Thank you very much for this award in the name of Raoul Wallenberg, a great hero of mine. In September of 1981, I had the honor of working with Congressman Tom Lantos to pass legislation granting honorary U.S. citizenship to this courageous "soldier of the soul." And thank you to the Endowment for Democracy in Eastern Europe, for whose work in the causes of education and human rights and in so many other endeavors to promote liberty throughout the world I hold a profound regard.

In 1899, Emile Zola, in his famous outcry against the anti-Semitism manifest in the French Army's conspiracy to convict Captain Dreyfus of treason, spoke to the inevitable triumph of truth over prejudice when he said, "truth is on the march and nothing in history can stop it." At the time, the French people were polarized over the controversy which presented them with a moral choice between the life of one man and the reputation of the French Army.

As America approaches the turn of the next century, we face many similar controversies—controversies which challenge us to make a moral choice between political expediency and the inalienable right to liberty. Fortified by the memory of our great heritage and what is occurring at breakneck speed in the world, we can now proclaim, with equal conviction: "Democracy is on the march and nothing in history can stop it." But the task of preserving and advancing this democratic evolution will take truth-tellers, seekers of justice, men and women of honor and courage willing to act on their convictions.

It will take men and women such as Raoul Wallenberg and people like you who form this great Endowment for Democracy in Eastern Europe.

Historically, every form of government or societal structure that refused to recognize the basic human right of freedom has failed. Whether it be the enslavement of the Israelites in Egypt, the persecution of the

Christians in Rome, the oppression of the peasant class by the aristocracy in pre-revolutionary France, the lack of just representation for the American colonies by the British monarchy, the evil of slavery in pre-Civil War America, the abuse of labor in industrial England, the comprehensive manipulation and subjugation of people by the socialist systems of Eastern and Central Europe and in Asia, or the monstrous evil of apartheid in South Africa, tyranny infallibly authors its own epitaph. The oppressed are driven to the point of revolt. The system collapses internally, unable to supply the hope, motivation and freedom that promotes the general welfare of a people and a nation and which respond to the Jewish wish and Christian ideal of freedom as an inalienable, God-given right of all people everywhere and always.

Raoul Wallenberg had the historical honor of being a victim of both Nazi and Communist tyranny. I say an honor because this persecution is the mark of a Godly man, of a liberal man in the classical sense. For there is only one truth, but many lies; one charity, but many forms of envy and selfishness. To stand up for what is good, right and true often, attracts enemies from very different directions.

The world is in a similar situation today, with democracy and freedom being attacked from different angles.

Democracy is on the march, and on the surface, appears to have unstoppable momentum. Just yesterday, Romania celebrated the triumphal election of anti-Communist Emil Constantinescu as president—a fact which, in Constantinescu's own words, signifies that "Romania comes back now to the great concert of a democratic Europe ..." In the Freedom House survey, more than half the people of the world live in countries that are democratic or somewhat democratic. In economic terms, the worldwide trend toward democracy is even stronger. More than 93 percent of the world's trade comes from democratic and partly democratic countries (Alexis de Tocqueville Institution, 1989 and 1996). As a matter of economic and industrial output, communism and dictatorship barely exist, and where their production is rising (Vietnam, China) it is only because regimes are falling all over themselves to "open up to the outside" and establish economic and trade liberalization.

But there are threats to political and economic freedom, to democracy, from without and within. They are not as violent, purposive, or determined as the enemies Raoul Wallenberg fought, and we may thank God for it. But they are serious and important, and if they are more corrosive than aggressive in nature, they may nevertheless poison our civilization if left unchecked.

One is the threat foreseen by Alexis de Tocqueville more than 150 years ago. Tocqueville called this the velvet tyranny of mindless, numbing bureaucracy. It would not outlaw religion, but it would sap the human spirit, and set up a new pseudo-religion, the worship of the state, in place of churches and synagogues. It would not brazenly abolish private property, but it would smother property—and, what is equally important, human initiative—in a well-meaning but deadly array of taxes, regulations, and stipulations.

Lincoln summed up the animating spirit of Tocqueville's velvet tyranny when he described the spirit of slavery in America—and we may regard it as chilling that the terms would have such a resemblance. Lincoln called this the idea of "you plant the grain, you make the bread, and I'll eat it." Lincoln went on to say that we must not rest until this "artificial weight is lifted from the shoulders of all mankind."

In the affairs of the world that Wallenbergcared so deeply about, the force of velvet tyranny is most visible, and certainly most important, in the countries of Central and Eastern Europe. On the one hand, these countries have enjoyed a miraculous transformation. On the other hand, they have endured a decline in industrial production and gross output for which it is difficult to find a parallel. Russian, Polish, Czech, and Hungarian output dropped by more than 50 percent in real terms over five years—a record that puts our "Great Depression" to shame.

History teaches that this kind of economic implosion often hastens tyranny, whether it be tyranny of the far left or the far right. The rise of Nazi Germany was preceded by the Weimar Republic's tragedy of runaway inflation in the '20s followed by democratically-elected Henrich Brunning's economics of austerity in the early '30s. This precipitated Brunning's abolishment of the Reichstag and thus a coalition government in 1933, led by Adolph Hitler. And Soviet Communism grew out of the state-directed industrial capitalism in Russia during the confusion of World War I.

The response of the West to today's economic threat to democracy has not been encouraging. For more than five years, going back to the Houston Summit, the United States and the West have been presented with one of the great opportunities for creative statesmanship in human history. Instead of seizing it, as we did under Harry Truman, General Marshall, and Western Unification—we have turned it over to the International Monetary Fund.

Today, the top Russian tax rate is close to 70 percent on income from labor, and what little money a Russian worker is left with after this is taxed through high value-added, excise, and other consumption taxes. The same is true, by the way, in Hungary, Poland, the Ukraine, and the rest of Eastern Europe. The tax rate on some types of labor and business activity is over 90 percent.

No wonder wages today are less than 38 percent of Russia's entire economy—a situation which has driven one of the most talented peoples in the world underground. Again, the pattern is nearly identical in Hungary and other countries. (In OECD countries, wages typically account for more than 60 percent of national income.) The people who have done some of the best reporting on the true Russian tax burden, a newsletter called Emerging Markets Wntd1 down in Washington, have managed to cull these data out of the ridiculously secret International Monetary Fund (IMF) memoranda and staff reports that go by top officials there every few weeks. But it is only by months and years of tireless digging that they've been able to uncover what should be public knowledge: how the U.S. and the West are spending, or rather misspending, the billions in annual "aid" to Eastern Europe.

Somehow, the IMF and the West—which should be leading a sweeping Russian tax, monetary and trade reform—remain numb to the urgency of bringing economic growth to the new democracies. Do you know that two years ago, the IMF insisted that Russia increase its taxes by 4.1 percent of gross domestic product (GDP) in one year? To put this in perspective, both the Bush and Clinton tax increases that attracted such displeasure in the U.S. in the last five years were less than 1 percent of GDP, and these at least were not piled on the back of a crippled economy.

This is not a partisan issue. It goes back to the Bush Administration, when we encouraged the same mind-numbing austerity as is being applied to Russia, Hungary, and Poland today through the IMF's conditionality agreements and Article N process. In 1993, I joined with the late Ed Muskie, George Soros, Senator Joe Lieberman, and a group of nearly three dozen other leading Americans of both parties to urge the president to take the fate of Russia out of the hands of the inept and incapable economists at the IMF and devise a serious, direct program of Western aid and trade to bring economic growth to the emerging democracies of Central and East Europe.

The post-Cold-War peace must not become another Versailles settlement of pain and austerity. America and the West must see that they cannot afford to send the common reply, "it isn't our concern." We must dedicate ourselves to the opposite spirit, the spirit of liberal optimism and open trade with the East. And we must resolve to include Eastern Europe and Russia at the table.

I am reminded of a famous cartoon from Wallenberg's time, in which Russia, Germany, and Hungary were at the front end of a ship that was rapidly taking in water. The ship was labeled, "The World Monetary Crisis," and the year was about 1927, as the first signs of protectionism and deflation were making themselves felt. In the back of the ship were three men labeled France, Britain, and the United States. They watched with interest and a little bit of sympathy as the men bailed furiously in front. But they were not concerned. "Awful leak," said one of them. "Yes, awful," said another. "Thank goodness it's not in our end of the boat."

Today, democracy is doing much better, but the burden on us is that much higher. We have a tremendous opportunity to secure the fruits of the Cold War victory: to build a stable and prosperous Eastern and Central Europe; to guard Russia from a new form of tyranny—economic tyranny.

Indeed, we are bound by the awesome responsibility that comes with our own freedom to guard the rightful freedom of all people.

Raoul Wallenberg had a profound understanding of this moral imperative. He refused to accept the awful conclusion that we needn't be concerned about others, or that there is "nothing we can do." He did not believe the unpragmatic counsel that we can ignore the front of the boat because it isn't our end. His life was an incarnate assertion of the equal and opposite imperative—the democratic imperative, the assertion of Rabbi

Hillel, the New Testament, and Hebrew Scripture, that we are our brother's keeper, and our neighbor's brother.

As President Reagan said during the Rose Garden ceremony conferring honorary American citizenship upon Wallenberg, "[A] man makes at least a start on understanding the meaning of human life when he plants shade trees under which he will never sit. Raoul Wallenberg is just such a man. He nurtured the lives of those he never knew at the risk of his own."

Visiting a synagogue in Moscow, USSR, July 1983

What better example to look to as we challenge ourselves to respond to the needs of a changing world—to plant the trees of shade, succor and democratic successes under which we might never sit, but which will surely shelter our children and grandchildren in the 21st century.

Let us resolve not that it be an American Century per se—but a Democratic Century for all.

An African-American Partnership

The Honorable Jack Kemp

African African-American Summit
Harare, Zimbabwe, July 21, 1997

"A nation's greatest assets are not the wealth that can be seen, but the unseen potential of the human mind and spirit."

It is a great honor to be speaking at the Fourth African African-American Summit, as it was an honor Sunday evening in Pretoria to be able to meet president Nelson Mandela and so many other distinguished African and African-American leaders. This summit truly marks the first week of the 21st century for Africa and U.S.–African relations.

Much of Africa is growing dynamically today—growing economically, politically, socially and most of all in the attention of the United States and the world. Shifts toward political and market liberalization are revitalizing and energizing the continent. And we see a new generation of leaders, implementing democratic reforms, expanding economic growth, and unleashing the human spirit that will help bring greater stability, prosperity, and democracy to African nations. Problems and challenges abound, but the potential of both human and physical resources are enormous.

Many of Africa's leaders are with us, like President Museveni of Uganda and his colleagues, who have revived the East African Community and brought trade liberalization and renewed economic growth to Uganda and the region.

We have the spirit of Thabo Mbecki, who rejected the cramped goals of mere subsistence and African recovery or Western aid. It is not enough, as he has said, for us to work for "African development," We must seek nothing less than an "African Renaissance."

And we have the great Leon Sullivan, whose memorable words I quoted all over the world and most recently in my testimony before the Ways and Means Committee of the United States House of Representatives on behalf of the African Growth and Opportunity Bill, championed by Congressmen Crane, Rangel, McDermott, and Payne, to encourage African development, self-reliance, and free trade. Reverend

Sullivan said, "The desire of men to improve their living conditions and to be free, is universal. That desire must be nurtured and inspired by new projects of hope and new programs of opportunities. New leaders must spring up like strong oak trees stretching across the land." That's what this summit is all about: the universal desire of mankind to be free and to improve his standard of living. Leon Sullivan is the bridge between America and Africa; between white, black, colored, and, indeed, all peoples.

But with so much accomplished in a post-colonial and post-Cold War Africa, may I suggest that the time is at hand to build on this achievement. Africa's progress is considerable but it has not yet reached enough people. Too many in Africa are unemployed, undereducated and living in poverty. Though political stability has improved for much of the continent, some African nations are still plagued by political unrest. And though economic growth is healthy, development is slowed by remaining political and economic barriers which hinder Africans from reaching their fullest God-given potential.

By removing those barriers, we can build an even stronger, more prosperous, more democratic Africa, a community of nations mutually benefiting each other, secured and sustained by a broad-based economic growth, trading openly with the rest of the world. In that spirit, I am pleased to be here today to learn and to discuss some means that might help catalyze Africa's own efforts to grow and build. And to suggest some ways in which America might assist this endeavor, not in a paternalistic sense but as a true partner of this great continent.

Let me begin by saying that official thinking in the United States about Africa has undergone a major paradigm shift. Trade and investment issues have clearly jumped to the top of the agenda thanks both the Republican Party and, more specifically, the members of Congress I mentioned a moment ago. While economic aid and humanitarian assistance remain essential tools in coping with Africa's inevitable crises, policy makers have determined to utilize other methods to encourage and support economic and political reforms underway in Africa. The private sector is the key element in the policy debate.

I was pleased to be at the White House on June 17th, when President Clinton said upon the introduction of the administration's Africa initiative: "If we all persist at this, if we keep working at this, then people will look back at this moment as a pivotal one for Africa, for America and for the global community. The members of Congress of both parties who have shown such leadership in this effort have recognized that a prosperous, democratic America in the 21sth Century needs a prosperous, democratic Africa."

I couldn't agree more. This bipartisan spirit marks a new day for U.S.-African relations on the eve of a new century. Together we must make it the century of democracy.

But, with all due respect to the individual leaders assembled with us today, it is not our wisdom, or the limited wisdom of any leader, that will bring prosperity to Africa. It will be the people themselves. A nation's greatest assets are not the wealth that can be seen, but the unseen potential of the human mind and spirit. Africa is rich in resources, but her greatest resources are not in the ground; they are in the hearts, minds, and talents of her people.

And, in order for people to flourish and prosper, they must be free. The most important tool, the essential tool for building and developing any economy is freedom—not only market freedom but civil and religious freedom as well.

Freedom is the mainspring of all human progress. It is a fundamental principle of democratic capitalism that prosperity, wealth and opportunity can only be created by people freely exercising their talents and potential. The more people are able to exchange and transact freely with others, the more they are able to reap directly the benefits of their hard work and enterprise, the more their energy, genius, innovation and ability will come to the fore. This is the seminal message of democratic capitalism's triumph: growth is the product of individual effort, where the link between effort and reward is both preserved and promoted. I call this capitalism with a "human face," a safety net under the poor with a ladder of equal opportunity for all.

It means preserving the value of people's money, not cheating them out of their savings through devaluation. This will encourage people to save and invest.

It means defending property rights through the rule of law, so the people need not fear the confiscation of the fruits of their labors. This will encourage production.

It means taxing solely to raise revenues for the legitimate needs of the state, not to punish wealth and success in order to promote so-called egalitarian ends by forcible redistribution. This will encourage people to pay their fair share and allow them to be charitable without resentment while working hard to improve their standard of living.

It means preserving the competition of the marketplace at all levels of enterprise, resisting the impulse to protect big business and state enterprise at the expense of young entrepreneurs who ultimately create most new wealth and new jobs. This will encourage people to take risks.

These are the timeless truths Adam Smith laid out in 1776 in his Inquiry into the Nature and Causes of the Wealth of Nations. They are timeless and transcendent principles which can be enhanced by the African-American free trade and investment initiative.

Notwithstanding the fact that some forces of protectionism and isolationism still exist in both Africa and the United States, the democratic ideas we are talking about today have already gained ground in many African nations. It is obvious that some African countries have been able to achieve significant economic growth in recent years.

I cannot help but notice some common themes in the policy mix of African countries enjoying strong economic growth: (1) reasonable tax rates, particularly on personal incomes, that allow individual Africans to flourish and prosper; (2) stable monetary and exchange rate policies; and (3) balanced policies on foreign investment with a focus on privatization and economic growth as the solid foundation that is the ultimate magnet for investment.

Now we can encourage other African nations to follow in the footsteps of these countries. As more countries implement growth-enhancing policies—cutting tax rates, stabilizing currencies, putting checks on regulation, privatizing government holdings and monopolies, dropping tariffs and other trade restrictions—those nations and the continent as a whole will prosper.

But the opening of African markets should not stop with individual, national economies; it should extend to trade among African nations and with the rest of the world. As I've mentioned, there is a significant progressive initiative in our Congress to liberalize American trade with Africa, one upon which President Clinton has elaborated. We must aim for its full implementation by the first day of the new century.

I believe, however, that a somewhat more ambitious approach may be possible, and would capture the imagination of entrepreneurs, dreamers, and builders on both continents.

The initiative, I believe, can come from Africa. And in a great sense, it has. The East African Community, with its progress toward tariff-free trade and, soon, even a common passport, is only one example. In the South of Africa, the Common Market of Eastern and South Africa and the Economic Community of Western African States have formed other trading blocs. I am hopeful that we could soon see one great common market for Africa trading openly and freely with the whole developed world.

It is in Africa's interest to rapidly expand these friendly trading areas, and it is in America's interest to achieve trade liberalization with a growing and prosperous Africa, just as the world gained from this process in Europe and Asia.

The sheer audacity of the proposal would excite the best imaginations in Africa and America. I have, in fact, been participating in an effort in recent months with a small number of African and U.S. officials to develop a proposal along these lines.

But to truly bring the full power of freedom and free markets to Africa, it seems to me that we must first break away from the so-called conventional wisdom of the "international development bureaucracy," and of Western lending institutions that impose austerity and "conditionality" measures. I include several members of the lending collective, but principally the International Monetary Fund, because its requirements of austerity, higher taxes, and exchange rate instability have had such a negative impact on the environment for overall economic growth and development.

The mantra of the "international development bureaucracies" for helping developing nations is incredibly destructive. It goes something like this: people are so poor, so uneducated, so lacking in resources, so primitive in their outlook that recovery and development, if possible at all, will be painful, hard to endure and of such duration that not much can be done except to provide massive injections of government assistance and forcible redistribution of wealth. They would have countries preoccupy themselves with reducing their debt at the same time they entice them to become more indebted by encouraging them to maintain excessively high tax rates and soft money policies.

May I say as a friend, the best debt reduction strategy is strong and consistent economic growth, John Maynard Keynes himself aptly described how a debt reduction strategy that relies on heavy taxation cannot work. He said: "Nor shall the argument seem strange, that taxation would be so high as to defeat its object and that given sufficient time to gather the fruits, a reduction of taxation will run a better chance than an increase of balancing the budget. To take the opposite view today is to resemble a manufacturer who running at a loss decides to raise his price. And when his declining sales increase the loss, wrapping himself in the rectitude of plain arithmetic, decides that prudence requires him to raise the price still more. And who, when at last his account is balanced with naught on both sides is still found righteously declaring that it would have been the act of a gambler to reduce the price when you were already making a loss."

The colonial powers took so much out of Africa but they left their terribly high tax rates. This must be reversed if Africa is to achieve its fullest potential.

Such is the danger in Africa, where many countries have accrued considerable debt by adhering to the misguided council of international lending organizations. But it will come as a surprise to many people in the West that most African countries have no worse a default rate than other sovereign nations. Yet, they pay a somewhat higher rate of interest because of the higher perceived risk of doing business in Africa. The U.S. must help Africa with not only enhanced market access but with debt relief as well. This is what Dr. Sullivan is making as one of his highest priorities for African-U.S. relations.

Clearly a serious plan for political liberalization and economic growth for Africa would help turn around this misperception. It would happen almost immediately, just as the shattered economies of Europe in the aftermath of WW II felt immediate benefit in their stock and bond markets when, in the summer of 1947, the Marshall Plan was announced, and the Bretton Woods monetary system began to be followed made a significant breakthrough—real triple bonanza for Western Europe.

It gave people confidence that European trade and political liberalization was really going to happen; that monetary stability was a reality; and that the U.S. was committed to European growth and reconstruction. A similar growth plan for Africa would create the political and economic conditions for the international lenders—the London Club, the Paris Club, IMF and World Bank—to offer debt relief and to extend new credit on better terms.

In my opinion, Africa will not succeed simply because America sets up more development banks, nor does it require government-to-government grants and massive infusions of Marshall-style aid, especially if that aid is conditioned on adopting the wrong policies such as keeping tax rates high and pursuing a managed-trade policy based on devaluation of the currency. Africa certainly does not need industrial policies to direct economy activity, that is the role of markets. What Africa needs is trade and investment not just aid.

If the World Bank and the IMF want to do something constructive, why don't they loan money to countries to bridge over any temporary deficits that might arise from slashing excessive tax rates and tariffs? It should not be insuperably difficult for the International Monetary Fund to revise its conditionality policies to favor tax relief, stable money, and other pro-growth policies.

Accordingly, I am working with a group of interested U.S. leaders to promote such reforms in IMF policies. I am happy to be joined in this effort by a diverse group that includes Cyrus Vance, William Simon, Bill Bradley, Senator Connie Mack, and Congressman Donald Payne of New Jersey, with whom I work at the de Tocqueville Institute in Washington, D.C.

This is an excellent time for such matters to be discussed, since another quota adjustment is upon us, and is in fact being debated by the United States Congress. I believe a unified African statement, or even significant African cooperation in the form of joint ventures and approaches, would carry great influence in reforming Western conditionality to serve growth and the people of Africa.

As African nations extricate themselves from the restrictive conditions of the IMF and boldly embrace growth, free enterprise, and free trade, development on the continent will accelerate, which will, in turn, attract capital and the interest of foreign investors and businesses. With its recent growth rate of 5 percent, Africa is already drawing notice from foreign investors and businesses. Imagine how many more foreign companies will begin to invest in Africa when it is registering growth rates of 8, 9, or even 10 percent. These were, and are in some cases, the growth rates of several Asian Pacific nations both large and small.

But foreign investors do not need to wait to invest in Africa. For too long Africa has been neglected by American foreign economic policy and Western diplomacy generally. But there are numerous reasons why investing in Africa today would be a sound decision.

In the first place, Africa is one of the biggest investment opportunities in the world, given that the gap between potential and actual output is wider in Africa than in any other region of the globe. In other words, Africa has the greatest potential for increases in productivity in the world at the moment.

And though a quarter century of colonial policies retarded Africa's potential, now the barriers to development are being lifted. The process is just beginning and now needs acceleration.

Accordingly, Africa lived most of the 60s, 70s, and 80s under tax codes designed with very little concern for domestic development—in some cases, designed to perpetuate low-wage, commodity-based production. In 1991, the average top tax rate in Africa still exceeded 50 percent.

This is twice unfortunate and ironic since—given its abundance of human potential—Africa needs more than other countries to retain skilled labor and reward effort. As well, given the level of political and other risks involved, it needs to promote higher after-tax rates of return to labor, capital, and investment than in the secure, developed countries.

In recent years, though, the country-average highest rate of taxation in Africa has declined by nearly 8 percentage points. The rate of taxation at a per-capita average income has fallen by 7 percentage points. In my opinion, tax reform that lowers tax rates and simplifies the system will lead to more not less revenue. As U.S. President John F. Kennedy said, "it is a paradoxical truth that tax rates are too high today and tax revenues are too low and the soundest way to raise the revenues in the long run is to cut the rates now."

African development is becoming freer and significantly more democratic. Recently, the Alexis de Tocqueville Institution adapted the Freedom House annual freedom rankings into a 100-point scale. On that scale, the average African country stood at just 16 points in 1985. It improved to an average of 31 by 1995, and according to the latest rankings, is getting close to 40. (Zero equals least free regime, 100 equals most free regime.)

Most important is the improvement in some of Africa's investable debt and equities markets. These improvements are on a par with those of Latin America and Asia, and comparable to the improvement in Eastern Europe—all areas that have enjoyed significant bull markets in debt and equities in recent years.

Africa has solid assets in the competition for capital, and not just its natural and human resources. One is a record of steady monetary policy: From 1970 to 1990, Africa's continental inflation rate was virtually indistinguishable from that of Asia, and a fraction of the level of annual price increases in Latin America.

But though market conditions and economic factors are reasons enough, there is also a broader reason to invest in the rapid development of Africa. The democratic, economic revival of Africa marks the beginning of an open international relationship that will be mutually beneficial to Africa and her partners in trade, business and diplomacy. This is the genius of economic freedom from which every nation can benefit: no country succeeds at the expense of another. Everyone benefits from their neighbor's prosperity. It is the common ground on which to build a stable international community.

That is why the Free World should be taking note of Africa: because there are no limits to growth in our world—just frontiers waiting to be opened. If other nations, and especially the United States, encourage those economic pioneers who cross those frontiers—with policies that favor enterprise over planning, sound money over devaluations, growth over austerity—it will play a leading role in the advance of freedom, peace and prosperity in our world.

Freedom is already on the march across the African frontier. Now, it is up to Africa and the United States in partnership to nurture the seeds of democratic capitalism that are taking root—" African solutions to African problems." The same principles which brought prosperity to America, to post-World-War-II Western Europe, Asia and other democratic nations will work for Latin America and Africa as well. We can all look forward, in the not-so-distant-future, to an Africa that is brimming with human endeavor, opportunity, abundance and hope.

As Rev. Sullivan expressed at this conference two years ago: "If we work and move and plan together," he said, "Africa can do anything any other parts of the world have been able to do, and in a short period of time. It is my hope and prayer that African countries and companies will come together to help make this happen, using principles of democracy, corporate responsibility and human rights, a bright new day lies ahead."

Why America Must Lead

The Honorable Jack Kemp

World Affairs Council
Los Angeles, February 23, 1998

"As powerful as we are, our future will not be secure unless we use that power to create a world which honors those things we hold sacred..."

Right from the outset, let me confess to you that I'm trying something new today. I know you probably came here expecting to hear me deliver a rousing pep talk about the flat tax, or the gold standard, or maybe a sermon on why politicians in high places should keep at least 50 percent of their campaign promises. If so, I'm afraid I'm going to have to disappoint you.

Today we're going to talk political philosophy. To butter you up a bit for what might be a trying experience, let me say that I passed up several opportunities in the last few months awaiting the right time and place. Today is the right time, this is the right place, and this prestigious forum is the right audience.

What I hope to inaugurate here today is a series of discussions, through the course of this year and next, about the choices the American people must make in order to ensure the well-being of the United States and the American way of life in the 21st century. These are complex choices for all of us, arising from the fact that we are now alone, uncontested as the sole leaders in a unipolar world. There is no book of instructions on how America should lead in the world. We have to write one and now is a good time to begin.

Perhaps the best place to start is to examine how we came to be the world leader in the first place. Interestingly enough, although American power and influence played the decisive role in the major struggles of the twentieth century, the United States was not the initiator of those cataclysmic events.

In every case, we were called upon to defend and protect those threatened by oppression and tyranny ... and in every case American leaders were sustained by the unwavering support of the American people, who wisely understood that events far from home played a substantial role in our own survival and our own future. We were not involved at all in the decisions that led up to the first World War. Not one bit.

History will show that we made some major policy blunders that helped bring on the Great Depression and indeed the Second World War – particularly the insanely protectionist Smoot-Hawley Tariff Act of 1930 and the overwhelming isolationism of that whole decade. At the time, though, we were not aware of our power and influence on world affairs and were largely absent from the international scene as the world careened toward a Second World War.

And, though we might have played our cards better with the Soviet Union after that war, we certainly didn't start the Cold War—they did.

Rather, every time we have exerted our influence and power in this century, it has been in reaction to the inability of others to contend with the aggressive and evil intentions of their fascist and communist adversaries.

And because we accepted these challenges so successfully, it is often said that the twentieth century has been the "American Century." It truly has been a time in which American ideals of freedom and democratic government prevailed over totalitarian beliefs, finally bringing a benign peace to the world and hope for the future.

It was a successful outcome, a time when mankind made incredible advancements, but still it was a century of war and turmoil and economic depression for much of the world. I believe not only can we improve on it, but we must, in order to be true to our highest ideals.

My vision is that the twentieth century would be but a prelude to a new century founded on American ideas and precepts and rooted in America's lasting, democratic values—a century in which the achievements of yesteryear will pale by comparison. This is what I'm waxing philosophical about—the possibility of a golden age of liberal democracy, peace and equality of opportunity, not only in America but throughout the world.

In thinking about how if America is to lead, we will have to avoid being trapped in the false dichotomy that currently characterizes the discussion of America's role in the world—a dichotomy that distorts and unnecessarily limits our vision of what that role should be.

First, we hear suggestions from some that the United States should simply yield its power, trusting its fate to the collective will and judgment of a more powerful United Nations and other international bureaucracies like the IMF, the World Bank and the World Trade Organization (WTO). If America is really serious about democracy, so the argument goes, we should have no problem binding ourselves to the decisions of an international majority.

Second, we have the isolationist, what the media likes to call the "nativist," view that America should retire from the world scene, and withdraw behind protectionist barriers, in order to tend to the myriad problems that have beset our society during these last decades of wars and periodic economic privations.

Ironically, though these two views are diametrically opposed, they arrive at the same result; that is, they contemplate little or no role for American leadership in the world, opting instead for an abdication of our moral responsibility to lead.

But these views represent the extremes, and, of course, those of us here in this room and the vast majority of the American people are not at the extremes. I hope we can agree that the uncomfortable equilibrium resulting from the countervailing pull of these two extremes is still preferable to either view.

But that equilibrium cannot long persist, nor should it. If we are going to draft an architecture for the coming American Century, these competing forces have to be taken into account and composed.

But in the meantime, we must watch out for a third, potentially more dangerous development. In the midst of our deliberation we have recently developed a rather ambivalent posture toward world affairs—reacting to world events on an ad hoc basis, dabbling in the world's affairs when it suits our mood or our politics. We intend to keep silent on what should now be done with the world, but we continue to announce that we will intervene on our own motion in any circumstance or series of events which we find threatening . . . or interesting.

As we listen to all of these opinions on America's future role, and more alarmingly, ponder the assumptions which support them, thoughtful people must be given pause.

Quite simply, America must lead. The United States cannot abdicate, we cannot withdraw from the world and we cannot simply dabble in its affairs.

Let me take on these arguments one by one. First, it is a gross mistake to assume that relinquishing power to the United Nations would constitute a giant step for democracy. The United Nations is not a body representative of people, only of governments. As such, it has no standing as a democratic body. The idea that sovereign powers should be yielded to an international body of elitists that could by majority vote decide what was best for the world, unreviewed by public opinion, would constitute the greatest loss of freedom in the history of the world.

Empower America co-founder and former U.N. Ambassador Jeane Kirkpatrick, 1994

And besides, the notion that a United Nations with expanded powers could administer over a lasting peace in the world is an idyllic one at best. The United Nations was formed in a second American attempt to provide a forum for the countries of the world, so that disputes could be solved more peacefully and wars avoided. But today, that noble purpose has been undermined by political forces—notwithstanding the trip of the U.N. General Secretary to the Middle East.

Nor does it make sense to yield more power to the United Nations, thinking it will mean less responsibility for us. The day would not be far away when some action was taken which we clearly could not abide.

Without our support, and financial backing, the United Nations would soon collapse, thus ending its present limited value as a global forum. Far better to withhold these new powers in the first place than agree to any charade of world government. My guess is that if the people of the world could vote by secret ballot, they would reject the idea of giving their own representatives power at the expense of the United States. They are seriously looking up to us, I believe, for guidance in how to make the coming century one of harmony and prosperity.

But this is all the more reason why we must also reject the other argument in the dichotomy. We cannot simply withdraw from the world, living a life of self-indulgence behind closed borders and trade barriers in an ill-fated effort to protect American jobs. We cannot hope to assure our well-being and national security by superior military might alone. Nor would building a fortress America relieve us from any responsibility for what happens in the rest of the world.

Even those who express such daydreams know they are impossible, that they are genuinely an anathema to an American spirit that tells each of us that the rest of the world sent its best people to the New World, hoping to someday learn from our experience how they too can succeed as we do. Mankind did not struggle over all these millennia to see America—the nation of nations—finally get to the top, only to find us pulling the ladder up and resolving to keep the rest of the world in its place, underfoot and outside our borders.

The benefits of being an American accrue to us individually, not communally. Crucial to the experience of enjoying these benefits is that fair competition is maximized, initiative rewarded and human beings encouraged to dream, and make those dreams come true. Even if we could do it, Americans don't wish to live in a protectionist world where choices are limited; mediocrity encouraged and the individual diminished. Without choice there is no freedom; without the risk of failure there is no chance of success.

Neither the country the isolationists would create nor a world governed by a United Nations would be an America as we have known it or would want it.

The third approach to our future—dabbling here and there and ad hoc responses to crises real or perceived—is the one I see taking shape in our national political establishment, by which I mean the movers and shakers of both political parties. This power core seems to have it in mind that it can be isolationist one day and internationalist the next, depending upon U.S. interest as they define it at the moment. They would have us indulge in whatever whim we might feel at the moment. They can be found citing our lack of interest in what happens to the world when we don't wish to act and citing our "grave national interest" or our U.N. Security Council obligations when we see a chance to intervene profitably. This is a strategy without a policy, a posture that would lead us down the path of imperialism and inevitably cause much of the world to conspire against us.

Can we say our reluctance to examine our future role in the world more positively stems from the fact that we never sought the kind of ascendancy which we presently enjoy? Perhaps. Unlike the great empires of the past, American has never really wanted imperial power. We know our country is special. We intuitively understand that Lincoln was right in saying America is the last, best hope for mankind.

My own guess is that we have been reluctant to map out or role in the world because we assumed or hoped the future would take care of itself, without our worrying about it. That is proving not to be the case. The Cold War is over, the Berlin wall is down and Apartheid is dead. Stock markets and bond markets are bustling in Beijing and Moscow and records are being broken on Wall Street every time you turn around. But suddenly comes a huge downdraft in Thailand and we are watching a trapdoor open up below the Tigers of Asia, a great sucking sound as capital disappears down a black hole somewhere in the Pacific. Now there are people in Nevada traipsing around with anthrax, perhaps looking for a way to end the short history of civilization. And there is Saddam Hussein and the Palestinians and the Bosnians and Serbs.

The future is not taking care of itself, it is showing up in most unexpected and even threatening ways, and it is spoiling our Sunday afternoons at the ballpark and giving us bad dreams at night.

No question about it, ladies and gentlemen. We cannot afford to let the future take care of itself. We have to think this through. Otherwise, as the prophet warned, the people will perish for lack of vision. Clearly, we need a new rationale or policy to explain our actions. We need a new compact with the American people which sets out our goals and explains our actions in the context of achieving those goals. And particularly, we need a vision of boundless opportunity of which the whole world can be a part.

Winston Churchill said "In victory, magnanimity." By this I'm sure he did not simply mean the country that comes out on top in a competition should be a good sport and buy the next round of drinks. Rather, Churchill advises us that there are two ways for those who lead to stay in the lead. One is by conniving to keep all potential competitors weak, kicking out at those who seem to be climbing up close. The other is by sharing the secrets of our success with them so magnanimously that the pyramid grows and lifts us even higher.

Dare I say everyone in this room agrees with Churchill that we want to stay in the lead by being so good at that historic assignment that those below will fight off any contenders who seek to displace us. It is in that spirit that I have for several years been calling for reform of the International Monetary Fund, which has over the decades since it was founded in 1944 gathered up its own kind of Evil Empire.

I'm sure that its boss, Michel Camdessus, is a loving father and grandfather, but his record is the worst record of a financial institution in the history of the world. He can't help it. It is in the nature of the institution, which was co-opted by the world's most powerful bankers 30 years ago. It served the purpose of our power brokers during the Cold War, handing out money to this country or that dictator, to keep them in line. It has now become an international menace.

Three years ago, almost anyone with one eye in Washington could see that the IMF helped engineer the peso devaluation in Mexico, so its friendly supporters at the banks could cash in. The people of Mexico looked up to the United States and hoped through the North American Free Trade Agreement (NAFTA) agreement that we could finally protect them from the periodic monetary devaluations that are creatively arranged to keep poor people in their place.

But open trade without a sound international monetary arrangement can easily be destabilized by an international bureaucracy like the IMF, willing to use extortion to foster beggar-thy-neighbor currency devaluations. How tragic that it takes so little effort by so few international bureaucrats to cause such so much pain and suffering. Does anyone doubt that the Asian currency crisis that has hit the Pacific rim so hard was at least encouraged by Michel Camdessus and his associates at the IMF? This is why I said on CNN a few days ago that if it were up to me, I would not give one dime, one nickel, one cent to the IMF—which is asking our taxpayers for $18 billion—until it changes its policies and top personnel.

Clearly, we have to figure out a way to improve the performance of the IMF, totally reform it, or abolish it altogether, because the people of the world do see it as our agent. The world does not need a lender of last resort for banks and corporations to save them from currency meltdowns like we have seen in Asia.

What the world needs is a stable monetary regime that would prevent currency meltdowns in the first place. The greatest threat to worldwide economic stability today is the international monetary arrangement of floating currencies in which no currency is linked to a stable anchor and all countries are being encouraged to used currency devaluation as an economic policy instrument during times of economic duress. In the same way, we must adopt a strategy for dealing with ruthless and unpredictable tyrants like Saddam Hussein, that does not inevitably corner the United States into blowing Baghdad to bits, or sending young men and women into harm's way.

When I heard last night that the Secretary General of the United Nations was returning from Iraq with a deal, my first reaction was great relief. Then, I began to listen to the news reports in detail, and some of that relief turned to uncertainty as it became clear that we do not really know what is in the agreement. But I do know, we must have a strategy that provides for and accommodates the use of force as a final option but does not create the circumstances that necessitate its use from the very beginning.

In 1990, I assure you I was among the most enthusiastic supporters of President Bush in his conduct of the Gulf War. I was in his Cabinet. What made it easy for me to be enthusiastic is that Iraq's neighbors supported our demand that he get out of Kuwait. What distresses me now—and I think what upsets the young people in Ohio and Minnesota who criticized the president's team last week—is that Iraq's neighbors do not want us to use force. They want us to use diplomacy.

Until this past weekend, the president seemed to be saying that diplomacy would fail and force would be required. Iraq appeared to believe that we had absolutely no intentions of ever lifting the sanctions as long as Saddam remained in power. And rightly or wrongly, they believed that our demand for unfettered and unlimited access to the so-called presidential palaces was merely a pretext for escalating the conflict. Based upon previous statements by our Secretary of State one can concede that such an interpretation was at least possible, not only by the Iraqis but also by the rest of the world.

We all hope that the diplomatic solution the Secretary General is bringing back will give us unfettered and complete access to every square inch of the country. But we should not delude ourselves into thinking that even with such access, we could ever prove a negative. Thus at some point in the near future—after we have reached a reasonable level of comfort through a successful inspections process—we must be willing to lift the sanctions and rely on deterrents to insure that any weapons we may have missed will never be used.

Let's face it. We have Saddam in a box, the so-called presidential palaces. We have begun the end game, and Saddam is cornered. He is taunting President Clinton, trying to goad him into making a horrendous mistake. The president, I fear, has been playing into Saddam's hands. He has demanded that Saddam acknowledge his ultimate checkmate and resign from the game immediately or else Mr. Clinton has threatened to tip over the chess board in frustration and let the pieces fall where they may.

A great nation does not rush to the use of force, particularly with insufficient information. A great nation, led by great statesmen, exhibits self-restraint, self-discipline and the patience to play out the diplomatic mission to its conclusion.

Yes, Saddam Hussein is a ruthless dictator, but we did clean his clock in the Gulf War, and his neighbors now believe he is not an immediate threat to them. Our onward rush to make 100 percent sure that every inch of Iraq is clean of weapons concerns me greatly because it sends a signal to the world that America is undisciplined, acting not from a position of strength but out of fear, or perhaps duplicity. The entire Arab world and the entire Islamic world of 1.4 billion people may very well take our bombing campaign as a sure sign the United States will use its supreme power petulantly to crush anyone who refuses our dictates.

These are the unintended consequences of ill-considered use of force. If there is to be order in the world, and the long hoped for peace which should come from it, such an event cannot occur without the most powerful and wealthiest country making plain when it will act and when it will not. If America is to have good friends and close allies in the future, it will be because others see that we have a plan, that we are sincere in trying to accomplish it and that it seems to be working. We must find the confidence and consensus among us, to agree on that plan and execute it.

To me, America is a country whose destiny has yet to be fulfilled, whose people stand ready to support its leaders once new goals can be set and the means for obtaining them envisioned.

But perhaps most important is the business of deriving a lasting and durable peace with freedom, a project which has so far eluded the ingenuity of man.

The absence of war is not peace; such a peace is only possible through development of a shared, worldwide economic and political system, based on individual freedom, the rule of law, the defense of human civil rights (including the right to property) and capable of providing the boundless opportunity for all the world's people to realize their God-given potential.

How do we do this? Believe me I do not have all the answers, nor even half of them. As I have today, in the months ahead I shall be exploring with groups such as yours my own views on what course America's leadership should take. I would hope that others will give their views as well. Admittedly, there is much work to be done on the domestic front and much that bothers the people about the condition of American politics.

But unless we can adjust our vision to the world scene, and convince the people they can have confidence in America's guidance on how to address the world's problems, nothing we do here at home will have the lasting value we all want.

As powerful as we are, our future today will not be secure unless we use that power to create a world which honors those things we hold sacred: human life, individual freedom, faith, family, democracy and equality of opportunity for all.

Throughout our history, each generation of Americans has assumed the burden of making a commitment to what was best for their country. They fought and died in wars, gave willingly of their abilities and money in order to preserve our unique way of life. Such a commitment must be made by this generation of Americans so that history will record that the great American experiment in giving freedom didn't flunk its final test.

GROWTH, GROWTH, GROWTH!

The Nature and Cause of the Wealth of our Nation

The Honorable Jack Kemp

Arco Forum – Kennedy School of Government
Cambridge, Massachusetts, April 21, 1994

"[T]he technological revolution which will change everything in our lives is dependent upon an ancient moral principle: freedom."

Congressman Boulter, students and alumni of the Kennedy School of Government at Harvard University: Thank you so much for your warm reception and for the opportunity to once again meet with so many leaders—and future leaders—in government, business, and politics throughout this state and our nation.

I have chosen to focus my remarks tonight on The Nature and Cause of the Wealth of Our Nation. Too often in our descent into the policy minutia of budget and trade deficits, fiscal and monetary policy, we overlook the broader and bigger picture.

Experts spend endless hours perfecting econometric models to forecast GDP figures and interest rate projections, but neglect to consider how "wealth" is created, how jobs come into being, and "how the world really works." They frequently debate statistics like the national savings rate, but show little interest in learning how entrepreneurs turn their ideas into new products, new businesses, new jobs, and new wealth.

They talk about building a government-sponsored National Information Infrastructure, to use my friend Al Gore's phrase, but fail to understand that government regulation has already fallen behind what MCI, TCI, McCaw Cellular, GTE, General Instruments, the Bell companies, and countless other leading U.S. companies are already doing or would like to do if they weren't regulated out of trying.

The ongoing Information Revolution will influence our lives in ways we can hardly imagine ... and that government bureaucrats can never hope to anticipate or duplicate.

Built on the silicon, fiber optics, and microprocessors that comprise the foundation of the new Information Age, this is a revolution as profound in its implications as our evolution from an agricultural to an industrial economy. In a speech at the Harvard Business School, George Gilder, the author of Microcosm, summarized it this way:

> *The new information technology is not merely a tool to increase the efficiency of the current industrial order. It is a force transforming all markets and industries, revitalizing their cultures. The telecomputer will change the business environment far more than television did 40 years ago. Indeed, the telecomputer will rival automobiles in its influence and, in a sense, will compete with them.*

Before Adam Smith first articulated the system of natural liberty in 1776, the wealth of nations was measured by the amount of gold each country could horde. Today, the causes of the wealth of nations are being multiplied in ways that not even the great architect of democratic capitalism could conceive.

First, as Gilder reminds us, we are in the process of being released from the restraints of physical resources.

This liberation is symbolized by the silicon chip. Next to oxygen, silicon is the most abundant substance on the face of the earth. Its supply is as endless as the desert. Yet the development of the semiconductor will create more wealth than all the gold, oil, or gems we could ever extract from the ground.

Second, we are in the process of being released from all the old constraints on information and its dissemination.

When all the books in the entire Library of Congress can fit on a few high-density computer tapes, the world has changed. Satellite dishes no bigger than a dinner plate can instantaneously put us in the middle of events occurring in every corner of the globe. All the bureaucracies of command economies will never again be enough to stop the liberating flow of information and ideas.

The paradox of this moment in history is that the technological revolution which will change everything in our lives is dependent upon an ancient moral principle: human freedom. And the cause of freedom can only be served by a liberal-democratic political system and an economy based on entrepreneurial capitalism, private property, and sound money.

The key, then, to creating wealth and prosperity is allowing people freedom—freedom to work, to save, to trade, to own property, to take entrepreneurial risks, knowing that they will be rewarded for their efforts.

Our greatest assets are not the wealth we see around us, but in the potential which is unseen in the economy of the human mind. It is the minds and talents of a free people—not their material resources—which is the source of all wealth.

Sir Winston Churchill once said, "The empires of the future are the empires of the mind." This manifest destiny of the mind is the greatest liberating force in history. It is transforming the global economy. And it is also rendering impossible any great nation's withdrawal into a protectionist cocoon.

With fiber optic cables now winding their way over continents and under oceans, flashing ideas and dollars across borders at the speed of light ... with the cost of computing power dropping so rapidly that we can envision the day when computers are as common in homes as telephones or VCRs ... a Second Industrial Revolution, the Information Revolution, is underway.

Today, technological innovation accounts for more and more of value added. The market value of Microsoft Corporation now rivals that of General Motors, though Microsoft has only a fraction of GM's annual sales. This reflects the market's judgment that more so than ever before, wealth inheres not in physical capital and raw materials—not in factories and freeways, oil and gold—but in the talent, intellect, and creativity of people. Today, both literally and metaphorically, hardware is cheap, software is priceless.

Just a few years ago, politicians worried that America was falling hopelessly behind Japan in the development of High Definition Television. But, as Forbes magazine publisher Steve Forbes has pointed out, HDTV was based on obsolete technology. While the Japanese and the Dutch were spending $3 billion over ten years perfecting out-of-date technology, one U.S. company, General Instrument, transcended HDTV with a $40 million investment.

Intel and Cyrix—one huge, the other small—dominate the microchip market as Japan scrambles in vain to catch up. The best and brightest bureaucrats at Ministry of International Trade and Industry (MITI) were no match for one entrepreneurial company. Today, Japanese leaders openly worry that Japan will be relegated to the status of "subcontractor" to America's innovative, high-tech firms.

The implications of this revolution are staggering to many, unsettling to some, and incomprehensible to others. Unfortunately, the Clinton administration seems to be served by a disproportionate share of that last category. This sets up a political battle that will determine much about America's economic future.

An economy based on entrepreneurial capitalism is the only system capable of responding to the dynamic challenges of the worldwide market of the 21st century. Government planning and industrial policies cannot succeed in high technology markets where the premium is on innovation rather than administration. But these realities seem to be lost on President Clinton's economic team.

Listen to Labor Secretary Robert Reich. He has declared an end to the "myth" that "the little guy who works hard and believes in himself" will succeed in America. He claims that we have entered an age of "collective entrepreneurialism," the greatest oxymoron since "managed competition."

Collective entrepreneurship—what an absurd proposition! Can anyone imagine some "National Entrepreneurship Committee" supporting the dreams of a college dropout—even if he was a Harvard dropout—who wanted to displace IBM as America's technological leader? That's the story of Bill Gates and Microsoft.

Can you imagine this national bureaucracy helping the man who sold his mother's furniture to raise $400 so he could start a magazine and escape poverty in Chicago? That was John Johnson who built a publishing empire that includes Ebony and Jet magazines.

The Clinton Administration's theory prefers the collective over the individual. Planning over initiative. Industrial policy over market competition. Entitlement capitalism over entrepreneurial capitalism. And government subsidies for targeted businesses over lower tax rates on both labor and capital.

The president's basic approach is publicly justified by his appeal to our desire for "security" and an end to risk. A powerful political appeal—but also what Ted Forstmann of Forstmann Little in a recent speech at Pepperdine University called "a false promise and a fool's gold."

Before embarking on this path, America must step back for a moment and recall what is at stake. The words of Tom Paine are as true today as when our nation was founded: "Those who seek security at the expense of freedom end up with neither."

The elimination of risk will not bring security ... it will bring stagnation. Risk is the source of all innovation. It is the precursor to every new enterprise that is launched and every new product that is brought to market.

Discussing tax legislation, 1982

The story of successful entrepreneurs is almost always the story of failure after failure overcome by sheer determination. Our economic policy should be designed to encourage not stifle risk taking. We need to reward the successful entrepreneur while recognizing that true freedom requires having the freedom to fail, but to pick yourself up and try again.

The Information Age is bringing a new dynamism to global economics, forever shattering the idea of "blissful isolation." As Columbia University economist Robert Mundell says, "The only closed economy is the world economy."

The global market system registers events on every part of the globe, adjusting prices instantaneously to account for a new tariff in the U.S. or a tax cut in Hong Kong. Capital moves across borders, pausing in one place only as long as it offers the highest possible rate of return, ready to depart as quickly as it arrived.

The arrival of the Information Age requires political leaders to finally jettison the zero-sum ideologies of the past, when economics was still "the dismal science." There are a series of bedrock principles that I believe will define success or failure as we enter the new millennium. Nations which practice these principles will prosper; nations which don't will stagnate or decline. The principles include:

- A policy of free trade to expand existing markets and break open new ones to U.S. goods and services.

- A currency that is sound, stable, and honest so that interest rates can come down and savings and property are not confiscated through the corrosive effects of inflation.

- A tax system where rates are low and economic growth and upward mobility, not redistribution of wealth are the primary goals; one that rewards, not punishes risk-taking, investing, and working.

- A fiscal policy that restrains the encroachment of government upon private enterprise caused by spending and regulation.

- And a welfare system that rewards working, saving, and marriage instead of punishing productive human activities.

We stand at a critical, but exciting crossroads in the history of our nation and the world. The Information Revolution is well underway. America's inherent entrepreneurial spirit has put us on the leading edge of this revolution and the eyes of the world are on us.

But the question remains: Will America adopt the policies which will allow us to maintain and indeed build upon our advantage in technological innovation? Or will we, in a futile attempt at "security," abandon our traditional strengths and adopt policies that will put us on a path toward mediocrity. Will we allow the American Dream to be renewed in our nation's inner cities so that the poor can escape poverty; or will we allow the socialist, Third World welfare system to expand the "underclass?"

At this remarkable watershed in history, we must not miss the chance to begin an era of lasting peace, prosperity, and boundless opportunity by realizing all the blessings of freedom through free markets, free enterprise, and free trade for all.

The Economic Growth Imperative

The Honorable Jack Kemp

Conference on Economic Growth
National Association of Manufacturers (NAM)
Chicago, Illinois, March 11, 1997

A "contrary view to what has become the smothering conventional wisdom that slow growth not only is inevitable but desirable."

Thank you Jerry, for inviting me to keynote NAMs Conference on Economic growth during your world-class trade show, National Manufacturing Week. My remarks today are an abbreviated version of a more comprehensive statement of the growth imperative argument which will appear as a chapter in the forthcoming book The Rising Tide, edited by NAM's own Jerry Jasinowski. So Jerry, let me put in a plug for your book and encourage everyone to pick one up when it hits the bookstores. It will represent a welcome and urgently needed contrary view to what has become the smothering conventional wisdom that slow growth not only is inevitable but desirable.

Of course, the apologia for slow growth is seldom put so bluntly. As so frequently is the case today, language is mangled in Orwellian fashion to make something abnormal appear to be normal—another instance of what Senator Daniel Patrick Moynihan termed "defining deviancy down" or put less scholarly, "dumbing down expectations." In the case of the economy, I call it "dumbing down prosperity."

Today's economic growth, which is decidedly substandard by any historic measure, is dubbed "moderate growth" by the low-aspirations crowd. Languid and sluggish by standards of the 1980s, today's economy is christened the "Goldilocks economy"—not too hot, not too cold but an economy that is just right."

How is it that in 1992, candidate Bill Clinton could characterize an economy growing "only" 2.7 percent a year with 2.7 percent inflation (as low as it had been then in more than a decade) "the worst economy in 50 years," yet today he calls an economy that averages no better than 2.5 percent growth a year with inflation not dramatically improved at 2.1 percent "the best in three decades?"

And, don't be fooled by the stock market. Since President Clinton took office, the Dow Jones Industrial Average has increased an average of 22.6 percent a year. During Ronald Reagan's "7 Fat Years," the Dow went up an average of 26.2 percent a year. Whether pontificating on "ethical standards" or pronouncing on the economy, the Clinton Administration appears to be life imitating art, more specifically an old Marx Brothers movie: "Who are you going to believe, me or your own two eyes?"

With Senator Bill Bradley (D-NJ)

Ladies and Gentlemen, believe your eyes. It is not better than it appears, and what you see is all you are going to get until something is changed to raise our expectations, elevate our aspirations and change reality.

THE HISTORIC RECORD GROWTH

Since the end of World War II, the American economy has produced incredible prosperity for most of its citizens despite the fact that throughout this same period the economy has operated under the growing burden of government. The government extracted an increasing share of the nation's resources from the private economy to satisfy the spending appetites of special interests, allowed the currency to deteriorate to help foot the bill and increasingly intervened into the free enterprise system with regulations in a well-intended but self-defeating attempt to fine tune markets toward a better result.

In the first half of the 1980s, President Reagan's economic program of tax reduction and regulatory relief brought a valuable but temporary respite from the growing burden of government. By 1986, however, the stage was being set for a permanent, policy-induced economic slowdown when a number of extremely anti-growth tax provisions were incorporated into otherwise commendable tax reform legislation.

These tax-policy errors were compounded immeasurably when Present Reagan's economic program was abandoned at the close of the 1980s, and the federal government embarked on a spending spree and a tax and regulatory binge. A huge tax increase in 1990 combined with excessively tight monetary policy and accelerating regulatory actions to knock the economy off its long-run growth path into recession.

In 1993, the economy's fate was sealed when tax rates were raised again in the largest tax increase in history. At this point, the accumulated dead-weight burden of bad policy made it impossible for the economy to rebound back to its long-run growth path. By this time, the accumulated weight of anti-growth policies had created a policy-induced, permanent (until policy is changed), economic slowdown.

Some experts say the economic downshift is inevitable; this is as good as it gets; it's not so bad; get used to it. I say, baloney.

Since the end of the 1980s, many leaders in both American political parties became captivated by economists and a few prominent members of the business community who believe to the very depths of their souls that economic growth cannot proceed much faster than 2.5 percent a year; that to attempt to achieve more rapid growth would produce inflation; and that our first economic priority should be to balance the budget. Ladies and Gentlemen, you know better, and you know why.

HOW GOVERNMENT RETARDS GROWTH AND LIMITS OPPORTUNITY

When government grows too big, it becomes a net drain on the private sector and slows economic growth. There is substantial empirical evidence indicating that when government saps more than 20 to 25 percent of the nation's output, the economy's ability to grow is significantly reduced.

In the United States, all levels of government combined spend about 33 percent of gross domestic product annually. The federal government will spend about 21 percent of GDP this year. A proportionate reduction in government at the federal level to bring overall government spending more into line with maximum economic performance would require federal spending to fall into the neighborhood of 15 percent to 16 percent of GDP.

The federal tax code is also a significant drag on economic performance. Not only does government take too much, its method of extraction is economically destructive. If there was an Economic Protection Agency to watch over the economy the way Environmental Protection Agency (EPA) watches over the environment, the IRS would be labeled "toxic." IRS forms would carry a warning label: "The Economist-General of the United States has determined that the Internal Revenue Code is hazardous to America's economic health and could cause financial devastation to your family."

The National Commission on Economic Growth and Tax Reform, which I was privileged to chair, found that our current income tax system is economically destructive, impossibly complex and overly intrusive. High marginal tax rates weaken the link between effort and reward, depress productivity and kill jobs. Multiple layers of taxation on work, saving and investment dry up new capital, retard entrepreneurial activity and stifle creation of new businesses. Recent empirical analyses of the dead-weight burden of the current tax code reveal that fundamental overhaul of the tax system could raise long-term growth by one full percentage point or more. But taxing and spending are not the only ways government saps the private sector and slows economic growth.

Government also regulates the activities of entrepreneurs, business managers and workers. It is estimated that annual regulatory costs consume

19 percent of a household's after-tax budget. Between 1963 and 1993, increased regulatory activity lowered the nation's output by $1.3 trillion a year. Without this added regulatory burden, the 1993 GDP would have been 21 percent larger, $7.6 trillion instead of $6.3 trillion.

The empirical record of the 1990s tells the story: Since the end of the 1990-91 recession, the American economy has experienced the slowest economic expansion in more than a century, growing a mere 2.3 percent a year as compared to its 4.4 percent annual average growth rate during the preceding five economic expansions. Over the entire post-war period, including recessions as well as expansions, the American economy managed to grow 3.2 percent a year after accounting for inflation. Not only is the 1990s lackluster in comparison to other expansion periods, it fails even to measure up to the overall performance of the economy including periods of economic contraction.

WHAT HAPPENED TO GROWTH?

There are three main conventional explanations of what happened to growth—all of which are unconvincing. First, it is pointed out that population growth has slowed. True, but decline in population growth cannot account for more than roughly a quarter of the decline in the annual growth rate at most—about 0.3 percentage points.

In other words, the decline in population growth may account for why we might be growing below 3.5 percent but it cannot account for why we appear to be stuck at 2.3 percent annual growth today.

Second, the most frequently touted explanation of the falloff in growth—the observation that productivity growth has declined—is not really an explanation at all but simply a restatement of the problem itself. The question reduces to, "what happen to productivity?" Conventional economic theory seems to have no satisfactory answer.

Lacking a theoretical explanation of the slowdown in growth, economists and Wall Street analysts increasingly have fallen back onto Phillips-Curve mythology where the Federal Reserve Board—with Alan Greenspan playing the myth's hero, Odysseus—must carefully guide the economy through the narrow strait of "moderate growth" between the Scylla of high unemployment and the Charybdis of inflation.

Reality debunks the myth. Inflation, as Milton Friedman has taught us, is everywhere and always a monetary phenomenon. In other words, inflation is caused by too many dollars chasing too few goods, not by too many people working.

Inflation results when government prints too much money or leaves people uncertain about the future value of their currency. Far from being inflationary, real expansion of the economy "soaks up" inflation, creating more goods for the same amount of money to pursue.

If the Phillips-Curve theory were correct, think for a moment how the world would have to work. As economic expansions gain momentum, economic growth will accelerate out of control—the economy will spontaneously begin to grow "too fast" and stimulate inflation. The laws of supply and demand are suspended as everyone in the process is able to pass along rising prices.

The laws of supply and demand do not cease to function. Just the opposite occurs when the market is allowed to operate. The price mechanism acts like a self-adjusting flywheel to prevent the economy from overheating. Developing bottlenecks and scarcities—especially of labor—are signaled by rising prices (wages), which in turn reduce demand for them. Resources are allocated efficiently through the price mechanism, and demand is kept in line with the economy's overall ability to produce.

Why have we gone from an economy that through good times and bad, consistently grew faster than 3 percent a year to an economy that cannot manage to grow faster than 2.5 percent a year during the best of times? The mystery is really no mystery at all: Uncle Sam did it, in Washington, D.C., with taxes, spending and regulations. With all due respect to President Clinton's variation on Ronald Reagan's theme about the role of government: let me be unambiguous.

Government continues to be the problem and it is seldom the solution. It spends too much; it taxes too much; it confiscates our estates; it fails to maintain the integrity of our currency; it takes our property without just compensation; it dampens our spirits by limiting our freedom; it undermines families by sapping parental authority; and it is the cause of poverty and despair in our nation's inner cities. Government requires a complete overhaul.

As a result, today's economy is being forced to operate under an artificial, government erected growth ceiling of about 2.5 percent. For all of his hyperbole, Bill Clinton was much closer to correct in his criticism of economic performance in 1992 than he is in his praise of today's economy. Regrettably, President Clinton gave us a double dose of the same venom that was poisoning the economy then, and he attempts to defend today's mediocre economic performance as a prudent midcourse between two extremes.

I will concede that under the Clinton policy regime, it is without-a-doubt true that the only way we could hope to grow much faster would be for the Fed to stimulate production artificially through a surprise monetary inflation. But the president poses a false choice between today's slow growth or inflation because he refuses to consider the third choice of removing the growth ceiling.

The good news is that today's slow economic growth has nothing to do with the economy's intrinsic ability to produce or any inherent tradeoff between economic growth and inflation. We can raise the ceiling on noninflationary growth by judicious changes in policy.

INCREASING ECONOMIC GROWTH

Overhaul the tax code

The single biggest step we could take to revive economic growth in America would be to completely overhaul the tax code to make it fairer, flatter, simpler and to eliminate double, triple and quadruple taxation of income. Numerous plans are under discussion, ranging from House Majority Leader Dick Armey's Flat Tax to Ways and Means Committee Chairman Bill Archer's national sales or consumption tax. All of the plans have the great virtue of dramatically increasing the incentives to work, save and invest.

Frankly, I doubt that President Clinton and the Republican Congress will be able to make the kinds of comprehensive tax reforms required but there is no reason we cannot make progress in the right direction during the president's second term. First, Congress should vote on Congressman Joe Barton's tax limitation amendment this April 15. Second, there are a number of significant legislative changes that can be made to the tax code immediately which should garner bipartisan support. Cut the capital gains tax in half (to zero in Enterprise Zones) and index it for inflation.

Reduce the estate tax to a single, low rate and raise the threshold

Congress should pass a tax bill and send it to the President before the Fourth of July.

Overhaul the regulatory process

The second major undertaking necessary to boost long-run economic growth is a total revamping of how the federal government imposes regulations. Congress has delegated extraordinary rule-making authority to the regulatory agencies which should be reclaimed. Regulatory agencies routinely fail to provide benefit estimates for their major rules. Not only should Congress adopt stringent cost-benefit requirements before regulations are imposed, the entire regulatory process needs to be overhauled to restore Congress' full legislative role as envisioned by our Constitution.

In my opinion, Congress and the President should enact all major regulations into law—since regulations as we know them today are laws—before they are permitted to go into effect. Moreover, regulations should expire on a date certain to ensure continuous congressional monitoring and oversight.

In addition to reforming the way the federal government makes rules to implement legislation, we must do something to fix our broken civil justice system which imposes a horrendous burden on the economy. Rather than providing an efficient and effective means of resolving disputes and enforcing contracts, the civil justice system has created a litigation industry which feeds on itself to the detriment of everyone but the lawyers who benefit from it.

Restore honest money to guarantee price stability and low interest rates

It is time to restore sound and honest money to America. As a start, Congress should repeal the Full Employment and Balanced Growth Act (Humphrey-Hawkins). This legislative relic sought to improve employment and economic conditions through increased government intervention and economic fine tuning. It codified command-and-control policies throughout the federal government and specifically required the Fed to manipulate monetary policy in pursuit of three goals—full employment, maximum production and "reasonable" price stability.

In pursuit of these goals, the Fed was required by the Act to establish numerical goals for production and employment. In place of Humphrey-Hawkins, Congress should require the central bank to conduct monetary policy solely for the purpose of ensuring price stability, preferably with a price rule, and ideally, in my opinion, by reestablishing the dollar's link to gold.

The effects of this kind of monetary reform would be dramatic. Price stability would result, and real economic output would accelerate. As a direct consequence, a considerable amount of the budgetary pressure facing the nation would be relieved. Interest rates would fall—home mortgage interest rates would not likely exceed six percent and probably would settle in the four-percent to five-percent range. That is the answer to refinancing America's national debt.

Reduce the size of government

The federal budget deficit is a by-product of an undisciplined Congress and an economy that has grown too slowly. The deficit will go away only if we revive economic growth and Congress regains fiscal discipline. Unfortunately, an overemphasis on reducing the budget deficit has confused the issue of what needs to be done to enhance economic growth, and it has made it difficult to set long-range goals to bring government and the private sector into more reasonable balance.

When "balancing the budget by a date certain" is set as the goal, the public is given the impression that policy makers are intent on "slashing" government benefits. Interest groups become extremely protective of their programs, and it becomes difficult for Congress and the President to reform programs to make them sustainable and effective over the long run. Entitlement reform, for example, can only come about in an atmosphere of trust, not in the pressure-cooker environment of deficit reduction.

If immediate steps are taken to reduce the economic drag by cutting tax rates and alleviating some of the excessive regulatory burden on the private sector, the economy could be restored quickly to annual growth above 3 percent. At this point it will be possible to succeed in reducing the overall size of the government relative to the size of the economy without doing damage to the safety net for senior citizens and those struggling to get a leg up on the ladder of opportunity.

Free trade

During the past few years, the volume of international trade in goods and services has grown at a rate four times faster than total world output. Countries across the globe are beginning to put aside "beggar thy neighbor" and isolationist policies. They are embarking on a path to freer trade across borders and oceans. While this remarkable shift in thinking represents a great victory for American ideas of economic freedom and growth, the need for U.S. leadership has become even more important.

In our own hemisphere, the Free Trade Agreement of the Americas presents a tremendous opportunity to expand free trade across the thirty-four countries in our region. Similarly, the Asia Pacific Economic Conference (APEC) provides a framework through which America can topple barriers to trade with and within the dynamic markets of the East. These agreements take us another step toward a world in which goods and capital flow freely across all of the nations of the planet.

Indeed, even as we knock down obstacles to free trade with our neighbors, we must never lose sight of our ultimate goal: a world of economic freedom and opportunity. Our regional free trade agreements—as important as they are—must be stepping stones on the road to that objective, not building blocks of new walls around competing regional trading blocs.

Ensure retirement security for young and old

The 1996 Report of the Social Security Trustees concludes that Social Security is seriously out of balance in the long run. We must begin to act now to ensure that current retirees and those near retirement enjoy the full benefits promised by the current Social Security system.

First, in the tax bill it passes this year, Congress should expand Independent Retirement Accounts (IRAs) and Medical Savings Accounts (MSA's). Additionally, we must act to create a new, market-based system of retirement security for our younger generations and tomorrow's generation of workers. Not only will this action guarantee retirement security and freedom for individuals, it will vastly improve the overall economy.

This will take some time, and probably a Republican president along with a Republican Congress, to accomplish. But in the meantime, we can begin the process with a step I believe President Clinton will sign.

During the recent balanced budget amendment debate, the president and his party went on record opposing the idea of using the current Social Security payroll-tax surplus to help balance the budget. The problem is, the only thing the federal government can do with payroll-tax surplus is spend it. Everyone now has caught on to the fact that all that is left after the surplus is spent are federal government IOUs to itself which do nothing to improve the actuarial condition of Social Security.

There are two possible solutions. One is to cut the payroll tax so that each year it brings in exactly the amount required to pay Social Security benefits. Alternatively, continue to collect the surplus but then distribute it back to individual taxpayers into personal, retirement security accounts.

I favor the latter. It would lay the foundation for creating a new universal retirement security system based on private, personal accounts with real assets that people own.

Empower parents for a stronger America

Finally, we must empower parents and give them the freedom to choose the best way to educate their children just as in every other aspect of American life. President Clinton is proposing to go 180 degrees in the wrong direction—a Washington-knows-best, mandate driven approach to education reform. What we need instead is a free-to-choose, empowerment approach. Parents know best, and when families are given the freedom to act in the best educational interests of their own children, they will act in concert without need of direction from government to create the world's best educational system, for their children.

Market-based reforms in education are essential to create the best qualified work force in the world. They also can be instrumental in restoring social tranquility among families of different cultural and religious viewpoints. Freedom in education not only would raise the quality of education and improve worker productivity once they enter the workforce, it also would produce enormous beneficial spill-over effects to defuse some of our most divisive social tensions.

Will children be permitted to pray in school? Will they be required to? Will they receive sex education in the early grades and if so what will be the content? Will creationism be taught alongside evolution? Will strict codes of dress and behavior be imposed? Will schools have health clinics and if so who will run them? Phonics? Outcome-based standards? Trying to answer these sensitive questions with a one-size-fits all educational policy handed down by education experts is destined to fail and to erode the very foundations of our democracy.

Trust the people

Empower moms and dads, and let parents decide.

CONCLUSION

The end of the millennium has arrived and with it the collapse of totalitarian collectivism in all of its various guises: fascism, socialism, communism, apartheid. Democratic Capitalism remains. Now we must be about the business of deciding what kind of democratic capitalism we will have.

Whatever new threats and challenges may arise beyond the year 2000, America will always find its greatest strength in the ideas of freedom and equality before the law, concepts that are not only the essence of democratic capitalism but also its principle virtues.

Freedom encourages people to transcend limits, to innovate and explore new possibilities. In this regard, liberty is both the lifeblood of our polity and the spark of economic growth and progress. Equality instills in people a right to question dogma of all sorts, be it a tyrant's claim to legitimacy or alleged constraints on economic potential postulated by a group of experts.

The policy proposals that I have outlined are illustrative, not exhaustive. But they all share a common element: They are based upon the precept that our society is at its best when it leaves people free and empowers individuals and families to make the decisions that affect their own lives.

Habitat for Humanity project, 1998

Progress Is Not Foreordained

The Honorable Jack Kemp

The Ronald Reagan Presidential Foundation:
Eight Years That Changed the World:
The Reagan Legacy in the New Century
Simi Valley, California February 5, 1999

"[W]e must establish a comprehensive economic policy based on the ideals of the last lion of this century. I can think of no better monument to the revolution that he started."

We are living in a time of limitless possibilities. Yet, there is a pervasive feeling abroad in the land that something is wrong with America. To paraphrase Charles Dickens, it is the brightest of times, it is the gloomiest of times. Let me suggest an explanation for this apparent paradox.

In his own words, Ronald Reagan "set out to change a nation, and instead [we] changed the world." He pushed communism off a cliff into oblivion. His policies restored prosperity to America and in the process showed the rest of the world how to do the same. In the end, he gave us a majestic vision of America in the 21st Century. It was a glorious vision.

After President Reagan left office, we lost our momentum briefly-a bipartisan tax hike and credit crunch in 1990 created a recession and another tax increase in 1993 contributed to a sluggish recovery through the first half of the decade.

Then America gathered itself together and got moving again. It happened when Bill Clinton gave up notions like nationalizing our nation's health-care system and began to emulate Ronald Reagan. We gathered steam when Republicans gained control of Congress in 1994. Sound monetary policy, welfare reform, a cut in the capital gains tax along with the creation of dynamic new Roth IRAs and a high-tech productivity boom combined to overcome these earlier policy mistakes and all signals seem "go" for liftoff to the new millennium.

The hard data bear out how far we have come. Americans today are living better than ever before. We live in larger more comfortable houses, own more financial assets, have access to more labor-saving devices, consume more leisure goods while working fewer hours than ever to purchase them. Crime rates are falling. And democratic capitalism, revitalized under Ronald Reagan, has distributed prosperity more broadly among our population than ever could be achieved through governmental, tax-and-transfer redistribution programs.

Yet, as the 20th Century comes to a close, we have changed courses, and we are headed toward a much different vision than we had for America when Ronald Reagan left office. It's time to get back on course.

Limits-to-Progress 1970s Style

When I entered Congress in 1970, the Club of Rome had just published its Doomsday "Project on the Predicament of Mankind" in which it forecasted emerging natural resource scarcity and environmental disaster by the end of the century. The book that eventually resulted from the project, The Limits to Growth, was appropriately titled to reflect the pessimistic view that the only way to avoid social and ecological disaster is to suspend progress, a view that is anathema to every American instinct.

Ten years later-after a decade of ill-conceived policies had debauched our currency, disrupted commerce and labor with wage and price controls and stunted capital formation and work effort with confiscatory tax rates-it seemed that the prophecy was coming true. Consumer inflation hit 13.5 percent in 1980. The prime rate went over 15 percent that year. Gasoline prices had soared to $1.50 a gallon from 35 cents a decade before. Price controls, intended to halt the rise in fuel prices, had created pervasive fuel shortages and black markets, resulting in members of Congress calling for nationwide gasoline rationing. Unemployment had fallen below 6 percent only once in six years. Productivity growth was down. And, inflation-adjusted median family income had begun to fall.

In 1980. The Global 2100 Report to the president repeated and expanded the Club of Rome's alarmist prophecy, saying, "the world in 2000 will be more crowded, more polluted, less stable ecologically, and more vulnerable to disruption." It also presented a gloomy forecast of declining growth in per-capita income until the year 2000.

Thankfully, 1980 was also the year Ronald Reagan was elected president.

When President Reagan took office, the reigning economic orthodoxy, demand-side Keynesianism, gave an intellectual justification for the pessimism created by a decade of economic malaise, and it fueled the clamor for further government interventionism. In the Keynesian demand-side model, the economy was destined to grow more slowly in the future unless we were willing to suffer accelerating inflation in exchange for faster growth. It was called the Phillips-Curve tradeoff, where rising economic growth creates inflation, and reducing inflation increases unemployment. This meant policy makers had a choice: They could reduce unemployment or inflation but not both at once. Stagflation, rising unemployment and accelerating inflation—a phenomenon previously considered impossible by economists—had America in its grip, and the Keynesians couldn't see a way out.

Ronald Reagan saw a way out because he understood the basic fallacy on which the limits-to-growth argument rested. It rested on a false premise that Thomas Malthus was right: Resource scarcity and population growth limit our potential to advance. We had reached our limits.

Meeting with President Reagan to discuss the 1984 budget, March 22, 1983

President Reagan had a vision of boundless growth. And more growth would produce huge benefits for humanity and the environment. As Julian Simon delighted in reminding us, "higher income permits nations of the world and their citizens to pay for cleaner, more attractive and healthier living space;" and higher income will lead to "greater availability and lower prices of resources rather than greater scarcity and higher prices."

The Reagan prescription to defeat stagflation was open markets to facilitate free trade, sound monetary policy to reduce inflation and across-the-board marginal tax rate reductions and reduced government regulation to restore market incentives to the economy. Keynesians said it wouldn't work and would only make things worse.

And it wasn't just Democrats. Remember that Richard Nixon had proclaimed "we are all Keynesians now." In fact, it was Mr. Nixon who ignited the inflationary spiral when he took the world off gold, gave us wage and price controls, and slapped tariffs on Japan.

In fact, there was a rather remarkable consensus among economists. On the left, Robert Lekachman warned that "The era of growth is over and the era of limits is upon us." He went on to urge redistribution of income as the answer to our problems.

On the right, Friedrich von Hayek, whom I greatly admire, said, "You cannot stop inflation without causing a depression."

Barry Bosworth, good Keynesian economist at the Brookings Institution said, "We could return to the low levels of inflation in the early sixties by a decade of major recessions."

Kenneth Arrow, the Nobel Prize-winning Keynesian from Harvard University, confessed that, "The position of the liberal activist has been greatly injured because we are unable to reconcile full employment and price stability."

But the preeminent Keynesian James Tobin put it best when he said: "It's best to be realistic about stagflation. It can't be solved by assigning disinflation to the Fed while tax cuts and defense spending 'get the economy moving again.' The train may creep in one direction or the other, but the main result will be high interest rates, nominal and real."

Abroad, this loss of faith and confidence in free-market democratic capitalism also had profound effects. Capitalism and democracy were in retreat as the welfare states of Europe moved closer to outright socialism and the developing world flirted with Marxism. There was a widespread belief in academia and within the U.S. intelligence establishment that the Soviet economy was growing gangbusters and would surpass us soon after the turn of the century. Central planning, social engineering and income redistribution, the essence of socialist ideology, appeared to be the wave of the future, and we seemed doomed to an interminable struggle with communism.

Oh, how wrong they were.

The Keynesians were stymied because their model only permitted the manipulation of demand. Ronald Reagan operated out of a different model. He knew that the solution to the problem was to be found on the supply side of the economy in giving people greater incentives and opportunities to produce. He understood that progress is not limited by external factors, such as a scarcity of planetary resources. That is why he rejected limits to growth out of hand. He stuck by a few simple, but profound ideas, based on the big idea that with the right policies in place, progress is inevitable if men and women are left free to pursue their highest aspirations. Thus, he constantly appealed to the power of free people, free markets, free enterprise, and free trade. His vision encompassed smaller government, but went beyond it to a growing economy.

"We believe," Ronald Reagan said, "that no power of government is as formidable a force for good as the creativity and entrepreneurial drive of the American people." By the end of his presidency, the Reagan vision of democratic capitalism had become the Zeitgeist-the spirit of the times. But this was not the case when he took office, and I fear the same forces that were at work before his election are back at work trying to take us down' a third path away from the 21st Century vision of America Ronald Reagan gave us.

Today, so many people wish to honor Reagan's memory by dedicating buildings, highways or parks in his name. The desire for a tangible and permanent monument to the ideas he in which he believed so deeply, is understakable. From the Lincoln Memorial to Mount Rushmore, we have solid reminders of our country's greatest leaders. But with all due respect, does a building or highway, park or statue put more money in your pocket? Do they increase your financial freedom or give you greater opportunities to succeed? No, they do not. That is why I believe that to truly honor President Reagan, we must establish a comprehensive economic policy based on the ideals of the last lion of this century. I can think of no better monument to the revolution he started.

Ronald Reagan also understood the fundamental truth that keeping tax rates above a certain point is counterproductive. If tax rates are raised beyond a certain point, they so discourage working, inventing, investing and striving to succeed that the tax actually yields less revenue rather than more. Throughout the 1970s, inflation had combined with steeply progressive tax rates to produce a growing penalty on initiative, risk taking, saving, and investing, the very fuel of capitalism. When the Fed stoked the boiler by printing money, it created more inflation and the viscous cycle accelerated.

Reagan first became attracted to the Kemp-Roth across-the-board tax cut idea when he saw how inflation was propelling lower and middle-income workers into tax brackets that only a few years earlier had been reserved for the rich. He also understood, however, that the macroeconomic problem of high taxes rates went well beyond the immediate unpleasant reduction in workers' and investors' after-tax incomes.

Steep taxes were imposed on wholly illusory capital gains, dividends and interest earnings as well. Taxes were levied on paper profits that failed to reflect adequately the inflated cost of replacing plant, equipment and inventories. The predictable result was that rapid increases in spending, fueled by excessive money creation by the Fed, were accompanied by virtual stagnation in real production, leaving us with the ugly phenomenon of stagflation.

But something happened to get the country off course. We are no longer heading forward toward that 21st Century America that Ronald Reagan helped us envision. Neither are we heading backwards toward the New Deal/Great Society liberalism. Instead, we seem to have branched off along a Third-Way spur toward the meddling state.

Beyond Progress 1990s Style

Like its limits-to-growth precursor, the Third Way movement—represented by Clintonism in America, New Labor in Britain and Gerhard Schroeder in Germany—is built around a false premise. The Third Way movement is actually organized around an interlocking set of false premises that justifies government intervention into every crevice of private life on the grounds that government must mitigate the harmful by-products of progress and channel progress toward the common good.

New Deal liberalism offered a chicken in every pot. Third Way Clintonism offers a tax credit for everything imaginable and stubbornly resists across-the-board tax rate reductions politicians can use the federal tax code as an instrument of social engineering. And, I must say as an aside here that the Republican Party has not been immune to the temptation to use the tax code for its own favorite form of social engineering.

The vision of 21st Century America that Bill Clinton and Al Gore would like to make a reality was described almost 170 years ago by Alexis de Tocqueville as the form that despotism would take in a democracy. De Tocqueville warned that if despotism were established in America, it would be mild form of tyranny that would "degrade men without tormenting them." Americans would not "meet tyrants in their rulers, but rather their guardians." A democratic despotism, de Tocqueville warned would be "absolute, minute. regular, provident, and mild. It would be like the authority of a parent, if, like that authority, its object was to prepare men for manhood; but it seeks, on the contrary, to keep them in perpetual childhood."

De Tocqueville presciently predicted the nature of a Third-Way despotism once it become conventional wisdom that America had moved beyond progress:

> *It covers the surface of society with a network of small-complicated rules, minute and uniform, through which the most original minds and the most energetic characters cannot penetrate, to rise above the crowd. The will of man is not shattered, but softened, bent, and guided; men are seldom forced by it to act, but they are*

constantly restrained from acting: such a power does not destroy, but it prevents existence; it does not tyrannize, but it compresses, enervates, extinguishes, and stupefies a people, till each nation is reduced to be nothing better than a flock of timid and industrious animals, of which the government is the shepherd.

The Third Way movement would have us forget the great truth de Tocqueville understood about democratic capitalism in America: that while the "manufacturing aristocracy which is growing up under our eyes is one of the harshest that ever existed in the world . . . at the same time it is one of the most confined and least dangerous." Why? Because wealth in America's capitalist democracy has never been exclusive and zero-sum. It has not polarized the country into the "haves" and the "have nots," because mobility, both upwards and downwards, has always been a defining characteristic of the American system. Marxists and European socialists never seem to have grasped this fundamental truth, and between the presidencies of Franklin Roosevelt and Ronald Reagan, it seemed to allude American intellectuals as well.

"Aristocratic nations," de Tocqueville concluded, "are naturally too apt to narrow the scope of human perfectibility; democratic nations, to expand it beyond reason."

Today, I fear, our intellectual/political/media aristocracies are gaining the upper hand where our view of progress is concerned. The Third-Way aristocrats by their very nature tend to narrow the scope of human perfectibility rather than expand it.

Many of our leaders today recognize that times are good but seem to believe, this is as good as it gets, and oh boy, we better hunker down and preserve it so it doesn't get away. They are seeking to lock in today because tomorrow is unknown. They seek security at all costs, instead of pursuing growth and progress without limits.

Such thinking may be understandable—though still wrongheaded—during times of great despair, but not now when we have such inviting opportunities right before our eyes and right under our noses.

Today, we must repudiate the false premises on which the Third Way rests. We are not destined to lower productivity and slower growth. The world is not so risky and complex that citizens are helpless to solve problems, large or small, for themselves. We have not reached the limits of mankind. We don't need a nanny-daddy government today any more than we needed a sugar- daddy government in the 1960s and 1970s.

I reject an end to progress and I reject diminished possibilities and opportunities, defined and delimited by pessimistic intellectuals. Where the Third Way movement foresees the end of life as we have come to know it and a new era of diminished expectations, I see a new beginning pregnant with excitement and opportunity. Where too many intellectuals see an America stumbling toward the end of the millennium exhausted and out of shape, I see an America standing at the starting line of the 21st Century fit to compete but compelled to run the race shackled by too many government regulations and carrying a two-hundred-pound weight called the IRS Code. Getting back on course is not complicated.

We should start by:

- Cutting tax rates across the board now and completely overhauling the tax code after a new president is elected in 2000;

- Giving workers the right to devote part of their Social Security payroll-tax payments to personal retirement accounts to put Social Security on an investment basis for the 21st Century, and under no circumstances permit the federal government to invest those funds directly in private equity and bond markets;

- Pursuing free and taking NAFTA to all of Latin America, Asia and to Africa as soon as possible; and

- Leading the world to stable money by working to institute an international monetary regime linked to the price of gold.

By basing our policies on these few simple yet vital steps, we can restore America to the greatness we enjoyed under President Reagan. By seeking to change our country, we no doubt will change the world yet again. Most of all, we can rebuild that "tall proud city built on rocks stronger than oceans, wind-swept, God-blessed, and teeming with people of all kinds living in harmony and peace, a city with free ports that hummed with commerce and creativity, and if there had to be city walls, the walls had doors and the doors were open to anyone with the will and the heart to get there." Ladies and gentlemen, that is progress.

A Judeo-Christian View of Economics

The Honorable Jack Kemp

Christian Worldview Conference III
"Christians in The Marketplace" Sponsored by
The Wilberforce Forum: A Prison Fellowship Ministry
Colorado Springs, April 4, 2003

"Democratic capitalism has been history's sharpest weapon against poverty, oppression, and tyranny."

This weekend we are looking for answers to the question: what role or influence does Christianity play in the marketplace? Over the course of the weekend we will hear from some of the most prominent intellectual minds on this topic. A year ago I spoke before this same conference in Chicago. Since then, Chuck and I have talked a lot about having a forum on Christian Economics and so I was delighted when he asked me to speak at this year's conference entitled "Christians in the Marketplace."

Just what is the relationship between free-market economics and cultural values- between doing well and doing good? To some, capitalism and the prosperity it creates hold the promise of secular salvation, a utopia of affluence. To capitalism's critics, it is seen as a Darwinian struggle where only the fittest survive; where humans are driven by the basest of human drives, greed. Critics of capitalism find secular salvation in the struggle to overcome greed and ambition by altruism and human solidarity, replacing the capitalist dystopia by a socialist utopia.

Neither vision has matched reality. Democratic capitalism has not built a "New Jerusalem," nor has it returned us to the "law of the jungle." It promises, instead, three extraordinary things: liberation from abject poverty, freedom from political tyranny, and release of the individual conscience from oppression. No human system has ever kept its promises more faithfully. Democratic capitalism has been history's sharpest weapon against poverty, oppression, and tyranny.

The reason I feel so strongly about this topic is because of the close connection between economics and the family. As I have pointed out often, the word "economics" in Greek comes from "oikos" and "nomos," which mean the order and law of the family. The first understanding of "economy" was the operation of the family. One economic rule was paramount: Your family couldn't survive if you weren't enterprising.

In the introduction to the 1969 edition of Smith's Theory of Moral Sentiments, Dr. E.G. West points out that Karl Marx distorted Smith's portrait of man in The Wealth of Nations by twisting his notion of "self-love," what we would call "self-interestedness" today, into an over weaning desire for money. In fact, "self-love" in Smith's philosophy is one of the human virtues and must be understood in the context of the human responsibility to provide for himself, his family and his neighbors first.

First Timothy 5:8 reads, "but if any provide not for his own, and specifically for those of his own house, he hath denied the faith, and is worse than an infidel." This passage explains the scope of "economy" within the context of one's obligation to family and importantly, describes what Smith called "self-love" in terms of the self-interested behavior required for someone to provide for them. In the parable of the talents, Jesus also tells how we are expected to wisely invest the talents and resources granted to us so as to be productive. I can't think of a better description of entrepreneurialism.

If I can paraphrase the 11th century Talmundic scholar Moses ben Maimom, "the highest form of charity is to prevent the need for charity." The word charity is shallow when it comes to describing the Jewish idea of "tzedakah." Tzedakah does not mean charity as we think of it today; it means righteousness. The highest level of tzedakah is helping a friend who in difficult financial straits. Either a present, a loan or making him a partner in a business venture in order that he should not become poor and dependent on alms. Or finding suitable employment for someone before he slips into poverty. This is the highest level of giving - helping someone maintain himself in order that he should not fall financially and become indigent.

That's why preeminent capitalists like Bill Gates and Larry Ellison are acting charitably, not greedily, when they invest in art and build their companies. They bestow much greater benefit on their fellow human beings by investing in and growing their businesses than by giving that money instead to the United Way, or the United Nations, I might add.

Jesus said "render unto Caesar the things which be Caesar's," and I believe it follows that we are intended to render unto humans the earthly responsibility to organize the economy in such a manner as to maximize our ability to provide the greatest good for our families, our neighbors, our communities, and the world. That's why individual freedom is so fundamental. Maximum individual freedom without impinging on the freedom of others is the only social system that allows for creativity and reward which are essential for individuals to provide for those dependent on them.

Before I go any further, let me raise a cautionary note, which, I believe, should guide all of our discussions today. It's found in the Third Commandment: "Thou shalt not take the name of the Lord thy God in vain." In the Koran there is a similar command: "Make not God's name an excuse to your oaths." Discussing the role or influence of Christianity in the marketplace, it will be easy if we aren't careful, to cross the line from exploration and analysis to taking the Lord's name in vain to "justify " or "de-legitimize" various institutions and means of social, political and economic organization. I will try, and I hope we all are careful in everything we say today not to violate this fundamental commandment. In my opinion, there has been of recent, entirely too much taking the Lord's name in vain in order to justify our human earthly endeavors.

That said, let me talk for a moment about two polar opposite mistakes that intellectuals and Christian theologians alike have made in thinking about markets and capitalism.

Capitalism is not based on greed. Greed is wanting something for nothing or insisting on a reward out of proportion to one's investment. Likewise, the moral alternative to greed-based, robber-baron capitalism is not socialism based on altruism. Capitalism properly understood, as George Gilder explains, is the systematic behavior of free individuals making productive investments of their time, energy and resources in acts of faith. Specifically, he wrote in Wealth and Poverty, "It is love and faith that infuse ideas with life and fire. All creative thought is thus in a sense religious, initially a product of faith and belief."

Adam Smith, who by the way wasn't an "economist" but rather a moral philosopher, understood the driving force inside all human beings. "The desire to improve our lot in life," he wrote, "comes to us out of the womb of our mothers and never leaves to the day we die." Smith observed that if you lived on a rock in the Pacific Ocean, or, I might add a landlocked country, with no indigenous resources at your disposal, you still could create one of the most prosperous countries in the world. Hong Kong did exactly that.

And today, freed from the tyranny of the Taliban, Afghanistan has a chance and indeed, the opportunity to prove that it can work in the Muslim world as well, even without the benefit of oil. It can be done, but it will require three essential elements: respect for the inalienable rights of life, liberty and property.

But I am getting ahead of myself. How could it be that, in the United States of 1776, the year Adam Smith wrote *An Inquiry into the Nature and Causes of the Wealth of Nations*, was the same year Thomas Jefferson penned the Declaration of Independence, emphatically declaring, "We hold these truths to be self-evident"?

How could we declare the fundamental principles of free markets, the inalienable rights to life, liberty and property without having studied economics, without there being "economics"?

I think it is because our economic system is the natural offspring of our legal system. And, the origin of our common law tradition that was handed down to us from our British ancestors has at its roots, morality as handed down to them through the Bible and the Ten Commandments.

In the early history of the common law disinterested feudal lords let the commoners fend for themselves. Over time, when individuals had a dispute, friends and family would seek out a neutral third party to settle their disputes. And, not surprisingly, the most highly respected third party in most communities was usually a clergyman. The clergyman would consult moral codes, such as the Ten Commandments, and then render a decision. Eventually, these decisions became precedent for future decisions, and thus the birth of an organic legal system.

Interestingly, one of the greatest difficulties faced by common law judges in the past, are similar to the difficult disputes faced by society today, namely, disputes that arise from people from different communities and religions. Richard Maybury discusses "the two fundamental laws" in his book *Whatever Happened to Justice?* which was designed for high school level students. In that book, he argues that common law judges finally boiled down these disputes into two fundamental laws on which all major religions and philosophies agree:

1) do all you have agreed to do and
2) do not encroach on other persons or their property.

It is fascinating what Maybury observes about these two fundamental laws. They are stated and restated throughout the lore of all the great religions. Let me just mention a few passages that bear this thought out:

- The Ten Commandments are strong in support of private property devoting not one, but two commandments to this fundamental issue:

The Eighth Commandment: Thou shall not steal and
The Tenth Commandment: Thou shall not covet thy neighbor's house.

- The Bible further states, "Better it is that thou shouldest not vow, than that thou shouldest vow and not pay." Ecclesiastes, V, 1.

- The Koran says, "Woe unto the unjust who, when others measure for them, exact in full, but when they measure or weigh for others, defraud them." The Unjust, 83:1.

- And, of course, there is the golden rule in both Judaism and Christianity: Do unto others what you would want others to do unto you." The same point is made in Confucian philosophy.

So, there is a common foundation on which much of humanity and all the major religions share, it is this foundation from which free markets sprang forth and it is on this foundation which humanity and free markets must rest if we are to spread peace and prosperity to all comers of the globe.

Which bring me back to Hong Kong ... Someone once told me "Hong Kong is rich because Chinese live there." I said, "I'm sorry, aren't there any Chinese on the mainland?" As most people know, the per-capita income in Hong Kong is greater than that of the overwhelming majority of the same Chinese people on the mainland. What could account for this economic disparity? Free trade, free enterprise, private property, limited government, the rule of law and sound currency. And now that the mainland has begun to adopt these fundamental principles, it is beginning to catch up with Hong Kong.

If Hong Kong and post-World-War-II Japan economic miracle proves Smith's dictum correct, they are the exception that proves the rule outside the West.

In his book, *The Catholic Ethic and the Spirit of Capitalism*, Michael Novak writes,

> *The moral-cultural system is at once crucial to the health of democratic capitalism and easily overlooked. It is crucial because the primary form of capital is the human spirit ... It is too easily taken for granted because habits of the heart are learned in childhood, supplying reasons that reason has forgotten.*

Thus, the foundation of capitalism is firmly embedded in morality and ethics. And, just as the Bible warns in Matthew 7:24-28 of the foolish man who built his house on sand, a corporation built without morality or ethics will surely fall with a great crash, just as Enron, WorldCom and others did when the rains of recession came pouring down.

As I mentioned earlier, the study of economics is rooted in our legal tradition which is embedded in philosophy, which is encapsulated in morality.

T.S. Eliot wrote that, "It is impossible to design a system so perfect that no one needs to be good." This is simply a restatement of a very simple principle: the state of the human soul determines the shape of human society.

Every free society therefore faces an urgent question: How can it encourage the values of its people and still leave them free? Our message must be one of persuasion, not imposition.

A government conceived in liberty has none of the tools of tyranny. It cannot enforce the savage "virtue" of the French Revolution, or shape the socialist "new man." It depends, instead, on other institutions— structures between the individual and the state—that instill character, purpose and virtue. Churches and synagogues that raise a moral standard. Parents who provide a moral and spiritual example to their children. Schools that teach only the basics of citizenship and character lessons that come from an understanding of the Decalogue as well as the Declaration of Independence.

Edmund Burke called them the "little platoons" that temper our freedom with internal restraint. They enable us to achieve the ideal of the American founding: liberty constrained, not by law, but by character.

Wall of Fame induction, Rich Stadium, Buffalo New York; Fall 1984

FREEDOM, DIGNITY, OPPORTUNITY

America's Religious Heritage

The Honorable Jack Kemp

Liberty Baptist College
Lynchburg, Virginia, November 1, 1983

"Martin Luther King and Jerry Falwell would disagree on many issues of public policy. But surely on this central idea they are united, as all Americans should be: Democracy without morality, or freedom without faith, is impossible."

Reverend Falwell, President Guillermin, faculty and students, my friends: I thank you for the privilege of speaking to you tonight, and for your warm hospitality to Joanne and me. I think it's a tribute to you and to your students, Jerry, to provide such a forum in the political arena to politicians of different parties and different philosophies. A month ago, you extended your hospitality to Ted Kennedy, a bleeding heart liberal, and tonight you are turning the other cheek by inviting me, a bleeding heart conservative.

Many people ask, "How can you be a Christian and still be involved in politics?" But one can equally ask, "How can you be a Christian today and not be involved in politics?" Yet we must be clear about our motives. The doctrine of "election" means one thing to a theologian and something else to a politician.

One of my favorite Broadway plays is "A Man for All Seasons," which is about Sir Thomas More. At one point in the play, Sir Thomas is asked for advice by an ambitious and budding young politician named Richard Rich. More says, "Why not be a teacher? You'd be a fine teacher. Perhaps even a great one." Rich replies, "And if I was, who would know it?" More answers: "You, your pupils, your friends, God. Not a bad public, that." What a beautiful answer! The notion that a thought or an occupation is not important unless everyone knows about it shows a lack of interest in the inner life of the soul. It denies the reality of things which are known to ourselves and God alone.

If we are going, to combine religion and politics, it must be an expression of our faith not the lack of it. An attitude that begins badly ends badly. Richard Rich finally provides the perjured testimony which condemns Sir Thomas to death. And at the trial we suddenly see Richard wearing the great seal of Wales over purple robes. More says to him, "Why Richard, it profits a man not to give his soul for the whole world . . . But for Wales?"

What I like best, though, about "A Man for All Seasons" is its insight into the life of Sir Thomas More. Thomas More was "poor in spirit," but he was also good politician. In fact, he was respectably born and almost indecently successful—first as a scholar, then as a lawyer, then an ambassador, and finally as Lord Chancellor of England. More also had a keen sense of humor, and his guest book was a sixteenth-century Who's Who. He adored, and was adored by, his family. In short, Sir Thomas More had more to part with than most men in this life—and yet he parted with everything, for the sake of his faith and his conscience; and he became an inspiration to later generations.

The critical issue, as usual in politics, was far from clear cut. Henry VIII wanted an excuse to divorce his wife; but he also wanted an heir, to prevent another civil war which would plunge England into chaos. There must have been much force in Cardinal Wolsey's argument when he said, "All right, [it's] regrettable, but necessary, to get us an heir. Now explain how you as Chancellor of England can obstruct these measures for your own private conscience."

"Well," More replied, "I believe, when statesmen forsake their own private conscience for the sake of their public duties . . . they lead their country by a short route to chaos." It was More's Christian faith which made him take the road less traveled, and it made a difference to history.

G. K. Chesterton once described the attitude of all the great Christian heroes as "a paradox of great humility in the matter of their sins combined with great ferocity in the matter of their ideas." And I think this is the spirit we must have. We must dispel the delusion—whether it is held by ourselves or by others—that by talking about religious truth we set ourselves up as the standard for judging others. Only God can establish the standard, against which all of us fall short. But while we must strive toward it, our falling short must not prevent us from insisting on that standard in the field of politics or anywhere else.

Last month Senator Edward Kennedy addressed you on the subject of "tolerance and truth." Much of what he said is valuable, and I commend him for saying it. To defend the truth while defending the right of others to disagree is the very essence of what it means to be an American. The Founding Fathers were firmly convinced of John Locke's argument for religious tolerance: "The care of souls cannot belong to the civil magistrate," Locke wrote, "because his power consists only in outward force; but true and saving religion consists in the inward persuasion of the mind, without which nothing can be acceptable to God." This heritage transcends political divisions between liberals and conservatives.

But Senator Kennedy left the distinct impression that there is some kind of tradeoff between religious truth and religious tolerance. He said, if I read him correctly, that there are even some areas of politics where religious values do not apply. But this is far from what the Founding Fathers intended. John Locke's argument for religious tolerance does not minimize differences about religious truth; the possibility of persuasion depends on them.

Leaving aside for a moment what "separation of church and state" means, it is clear what it cannot mean. It cannot mean that there is a separation of religious truth from politics, or that there can be a political part of our life which is sealed from the spiritual part of our life. Everything in the Jewish and the Christian faiths, and the basic laws of the United States, rejects this idea. The Law of Moses covers every aspect of life. And Jesus tells his disciples to be the salt, the yeast, and the light of the world. Does salt season only part of the broth? Does yeast leaven only part of the dough? Does light penetrate only part of the darkness?

Nowhere did Jesus make this clearer than when he spoke of "rendering unto Caesar." Jesus replied, "Render therefore unto Caesar the things that are Caesar's, and unto God the things that are God's." What Jesus did not have to spell out—because it was obvious to the audience—was that while Caesar's image is stamped on each coin, God's image is stamped on each child of God. Far from dividing life into a spiritual and political realm, I think Jesus was saying that while civil government rightly claims a part of our life, God rightfully claims all of it.

When Christ was hauled below Pontius Pilate, Pilate said, "Don't you know that I have the authority to condemn you?" Jesus replied, "You have no authority except that which has been given you from above."

The laws of the United States are also based on the idea that the government has no authority except that which has been given from above and delegated by the people. "The God who gave us life gave us liberty at the same time," wrote Thomas Jefferson. This is not some temporary intellectual fashion from two-hundred years ago. Only recently, in speaking of Poland's trade union "Solidarity," the Pope said "the right to free association" is "given by the Creator who made man as a social being."

The Declaration of Independence expands this idea into a philosophy of government: We hold these truths to be self-evident, that all men are created equal, that they are endowed by their Creator with certain unalienable rights, that among these are Life, Liberty and the Pursuit of Happiness. That to secure these rights, Governments are instituted among Men, deriving their just powers from the consent of the governed.

The self-evident truths are the basis for all of our civil rights and human freedoms. If there is no Creator, or if we cannot recognize Him without violating the separation of church and state, then there is no ground on which to base the separation of church and state.

The First Amendment prohibits Congress from establishing any official religion and from interfering with freedom of worship. Thomas Jefferson once wrote that this erects a "wall of separation between church and state." In what way is there, and in what way is there not, such a separation?

The answer is clear from the very same sentence of Jefferson. He says the separation of church and state is based on the belief "that religion is a matter which lies solely between man and his God, that he owes account to none other for his faith or his worship, (and) that the legislative powers of government reach actions only, and not opinion."

In other words, we have the right to absolute freedom of belief, and absolute freedom of worship, but not always the right to absolute freedom of action if it abuses the civil rights of others. For example, murder, theft, polygamy and tax evasion are all against the Constitution and punishable by law, even if they are motivated by sincere religious belief. Why? Because the rights of others are guaranteed by the same self-evident truths which guarantee freedom of religion. In this sense, there can be an absolute separation of religion and politics only if there is also an absolute separation between faith and action.

By the same token, the laws of our land do not violate the separation of church and state, even though they presuppose a Supreme Being and coincide with most of the Ten Commandments. Self-evident truths are not always evident to everyone. But this does not stop them from being true—or from being the basis of our laws.

But if we believe that these self-evident truths are universal that they apply at all times and to all people—can we fail to apply them to ourselves? According to the Declaration of Independence, the fact that "all men are created equal" means not one but two things. All human beings have the same human rights; but all citizens also have an equal voice in government. This places an extra burden on those who think they know what is right to do, what is right in the right way.

Unfortunately, decisions made by a proper democratic majority are not invariably right. But those who insist on their equal rights do not always respect the equal rights of others to participate in the decision. This means, in a sense, that the founding of our government is never finished. Each generation must try to bring the democratic law of the land into line with the "law of Nature and the Nature's God."

This is where we face the real test of our religious and political convictions. It is easy to be tolerant when we think the other person may be right; but tolerance is called for precisely when we are convinced that he is utterly wrong; and that given the force of law his wrong opinion may be causing great injustice and suffering to the innocent. Under these circumstances, the difficult process of mobilizing public opinion on the right side seems even longer than usual. It is frustrating to change unjust laws in a lawful way. But it is hard only because it is right. There are few greater tests of loving our neighbor then the working of democratic government.

The lesson for conservatives is that to be true to our religious beliefs we become politically more inclusive. A true commitment to the principles of American government means that the party in power must be the government of all the people—including the people who voted against it. The Declaration of Independence says that, to the degree the rights of the minority are not protected, the government cannot have any "just powers." This means that the principle of the Good Shepherd is as necessary in government as in daily life: If we are all to move ahead, we can't leave anyone behind.

Where our actions affect others, religion and politics not only may but must often intersect. But we have to recognize that this is very much a two-edged sword. In government, as in our personal lives, the power to make the right choice is also the power to make the wrong choice. This does not mean we can avoid choosing. But it does mean we must be as jealous of the rights of others as of our own.

Senator Kennedy argued—and I agree with him—that there are some kinds of action, dealing with "uniquely personal parts of our lives," in which the government has no right to interfere. On such issues, he said, religion may only appeal to the individual conscience, not to the coercive power of the law. Unfortunately, he did not tell us how to draw this line; and to judge by the examples he gave, I think he has drawn the line wrongly. The examples he gave of "uniquely personal" issues were prohibition and abortion. I think he may be right about prohibition—because it involves the rights of only one person — but wrong about abortion—because the rights of two people are involved.

Only a few paragraphs later, Senator Kennedy reminded us that religion has been abused even to justify slavery. Yet he does not seem at all troubled that the argument used to justify abortion is the same argument which was used to justify slavery. The slave owners argued that the slaves were their property, guaranteed by the Constitution. Those who favor abortion say that the Constitution guarantees their liberty, which is the right to the property of their own bodies. But in both cases, the rights of another person are also involved; and those who favor abortion, like those who favored slavery, must deny that the other person is a human being.

Alexis de Tocqueville wrote that, despite the separation of church and state in America, religion is the first of all political institutions here. What he meant was that our sharing the Judeo-Christian world view was the basis for the confidence of the minority in the decisions of the majority. But many of our political debates today result from the breaking down of this Judeo-Christian consensus. Many Americans no longer recognize the self-evident nature of the truths on which our country was founded. For them, the final authority of the law is no longer, as Francis Schaeffer puts it, "the infinite-personal God who is there objectively whether we think He is there or not," and to Whom "not everything is the same."

For those who do not believe in this higher law, the only basis for our human laws is expedience or the will of the majority. When this happens, the original intent of the Constitution can be shifted by 180 degrees. As I pointed out earlier, rather than talking about "separation of church and state," it is more accurate to say that the First Amendment prohibits discrimination on the basis of religion. The Constitution establishes freedom for religion, not from it. But the First Amendment has lately been interpreted in such a way as to deny the equal protection of the laws to those who believe in God.

Many of these issues involve our schools. For example, children are permitted to form a club on school grounds to study Marxism, but not a club on school grounds to study the Bible. Students are permitted to distribute counterculture newspapers at school, but the Gideon Society is prohibited from distributing free Bibles.

A Massachusetts school board is prevented from removing a book from the school library for vulgar and offensive language, but the Supreme Court orders copies of the Ten Commandments removed from Kentucky classrooms. In that decision, the majority of the Supreme Court wrote, "If the posted copies of the Ten Commandments are to have any effect at all, it will be to induce the school children to read, meditate upon, perhaps to venerate and obey, the Commandments." Yet the same Ten Commandments hang in the U.S. Supreme Court, apparently without ill effect.

Senator Kennedy seemed to say that to oppose such court decisions means that those who believe in God are trying to "impose their will" on others. I disagree. I think these are clear cases of equal protection of law being denied on the basis of religious belief.

A court in New Jersey has ruled that children may not even observe a minute of silence at the beginning of the school day. Not just freedom of speech, but freedom of silence, is now suspect. This reminds me of the fussy parent who suddenly thinks it's too quiet and shouts: "Hey, you kids: whatever you're doing, cut it out!"

It is instructive to see how Jefferson himself dealt with the problem of religious nondiscrimination in public schools. When he founded the public University of Virginia, Jefferson established no school of theology, but he invited all religious sects who so desired to establish their own schools of religious instruction on campus, and offered free use of the campus facilities to their students. And he published regulations which said, "The students of the University will be free and expected to attend religious worship at the establishments of their respected sects, in the morning, and in time to meet their school in the University at the stated hour." Yet Jefferson's name is misappropriated to oppose exactly such non-discriminatory measures today.

What about those issues where Senator Kennedy feels religion has nothing to say? "I respectfully suggest that God has taken no position on the Department of Education," he told you, "and that a balanced budget constitutional amendment is a matter for economic analysis, not heavenly appeals. Religious values cannot be excluded from every public issue, but not every public issue involves religious values."

This is too neat, because it begs the question. Do Christians and Jews in public life face exactly the same choices as other citizens, or do they have a larger task? I think they have a larger task. We must be cautious in claiming that God is on our side; but we must never stop asking ourselves whether we are on God's side. The faithful must master their field of politics or economics or law or business or education. But in addition, they must suffuse those views with a Christian or Jewish perspective.

No field of human endeavor can be unaffected by the knowledge that God is there, and that not all is the same to Him; that there is right and wrong. Like Senator Kennedy, I oppose the balanced budget constitutional amendment on its merits, because I don't believe a useful and workable amendment can be devised. But I deny the notion that prudent fiscal policy and sound money have nothing to do with right and wrong. Honest money is above all a matter of simple justice—justice between buyers and sellers, borrowers and lenders, between the past, the present, and the future. When the government's policies cause money to fluctuate wildly against the things money can buy, it is not just a "matter for economic analysis." It is gross injustice that cries out for correction.

But of course, Senator Kennedy himself does not believe that fiscal policy has nothing to do with right and wrong. What is the "fairness issue" if not a statement about the morality of federal fiscal policy? And I think it is a legitimate topic of debate. But to President Reagan, fairness means equal opportunity to compete on the basis of merit, and equal protection of the laws; while to Senator Kennedy it means unequal treatment of individuals in an attempt to achieve equality of result.

And the argument is not whether, but how, to feed the hungry. Senator Kennedy seems to think we measure compassion by the size of the federal budget. But the medieval Jewish philosopher Maimonides said, "Anticipate charity by preventing poverty .... This is the highest step and the summit of charity's golden ladder." A central feature of any debate over fairness must be the role of economic growth in public policy. I believe economic growth must come first, not because it is inherently more important than other personal and social goals, but because without growth, our progress as a nation toward one goal can be achieved only by impoverishing something or someone else.

In fact, I find it hard to think of a political issue that does not involve the choice between right and wrong in some way—not even foreign policy, which is supposed to be the realm of realpolitik. I think few things are more dangerous to world peace and the advancement of democratic government than the kind of "moral relativism" in foreign policy which replaces the truth that "all men are created equal" with the notion that all governments are created equal. This doctrine paralyzes any purposeful action, because it renders us incapable of making objective judgments between democracy and totalitarianism, between true human rights and manufactured "rights," between the free market and Marxism's denial of the right to private property.

Let us recall, in contrast, President Reagan's May 1981 speech at Notre Dame University: "The West won't contain communism; it will transcend communism. It won't bother to denounce it; it will dismiss it as some bizarre chapter in human history whose last pages are even now being written."

In other words, Soviet Communism is a negative, a denial of self-evident truths and basic human rights. The answer to a negative is not another negative, such as "anticommunism." The only answer is a positive statement and application of the truths for which we stand.

The deterioration of American foreign policy since the Second World War, which reached its low point shortly before President Reagan was elected, is due neither to the power of Marxist ideology nor to Third World hostility nor to the realities of nuclear weapons. It is caused by the acceptance among too many American political leaders of the notion of moral relativism, which has replaced the doctrine of democracy and human rights. The same moral relativism is the philosophic ground of the historicism which underlies Marxist ideology. Adopting such a point of view is a formula for paralysis; it is quite literally disarming the American people.

There may be genuine moral fervor among those who favor unilateral disarmament or the nuclear freeze, but this is no substitute for facts. A true prophet does not cry "peace, peace," when there is no peace. It is no use to say that our intentions were good if our actions have made war more likely. We should tremble at the parallels with the 1930s, and at Winston Churchill's prophetic statement after the appeasement at Munich:

> *The people should know that we have sustained a defeat without a war . . . They should know that we have passed an awful milestone in our history. ... and that the terrible words have for the time being been pronounced against the Western democracies: "Thou art weighted in the balance and found wanting." And do not suppose this is the end; this is only the beginning of the reckoning. This is only the first sip, the first foretaste of a bitter cup which will be proffered to us year after year unless, by a supreme recovery of moral health and martial vigor, we arise again and take our stand for freedom as in olden times.*

It is rightly said that if you can choose the site of battle or establish the issues of debate, your chances of success are greatly improved. I think this is why our geopolitical position has eroded so much since the Second World War, while the Soviet Union has established hegemony over larger and larger areas of the globe: We have been fighting on territory chosen by the enemy. The lack of a coherent relation between our political principles and our global strategy makes us constantly reactive, while the Soviets initiate actions on a broad front.

President Reagan has given us a much-needed new beginning in foreign policy, one which restores our American political ideas to their rightful place at the center of American foreign policy. I would state the principles as follows:

1. The central feature of the American political tradition is the legitimacy and superiority of democratic self-government which observes the God-given rights of man.

2. The first purpose of our involvement in world affairs is the defense of our nation and its vital national interests, as the birthplace and exemplar of modern liberal democracy.

3. It is our duty to support other established democratic governments—politically, economically, or militarily, depending on their needs and our capabilities.

4. It is our duty, insofar as it is possible and prudent, to assist democratic movements and peoples struggling under tyrannical regimes in these same three respects.

5. The greatest single threat to self-government in this world comes from Soviet imperialism, and it is our obligation as believers in peace, freedom and democracy to minimize Soviet global ambitions.

Followed seriously, such an American foreign policy strikes a lethal blow at the "scientific" claims of the oligarchs in the Kremlin. It cuts away the ideological roots of Soviet authority by revealing communism for what it is—a residue of world history rather than some inexorable wave of the future.

Sadly, in the past, an effective foreign policy based on democracy and human rights has too often been emptied on the left by vacuous moralism, and on the right by small-minded provincialism. The makers of American foreign policy should pay more attention to the truths which Americans live by, and less attention to whatever the elites in power happen to want. If they did, they would find that the American people, and the people of the world, are eager to embrace a vision whose foundations rest on the truths which Americans have defended for more than 200 years with their lives, their fortunes, and their sacred honor.

The efforts of those who cherish our Judea-Christian heritage made an enormous difference in 1980.... Senator Kennedy quoted his brother, President John Kennedy, as saying, "I believe in an America where there is no (religious) bloc voting of any kind." While I admire and respect President Kennedy, and while this is a fine sentiment in the abstract, I hope that I never live to see such an America. Because when Americans stop voting on the basis of their spiritual heritage, they will have lost part of that which distinguishes them as Americans.

Tomorrow, President Reagan will sign into law a bill which passed Congress overwhelmingly, making the Reverend Martin Luther King, Jr.'s birthday a national holiday. I supported that bill, and I'll proudly be there at the signing ceremony. Dr. King did not think that personal religious beliefs have nothing to do with the public good. He was not content with the abstract statement of the truth that all men are created equal. He believed that abridgments of the civil rights of Americans which conflict with this truth must be eliminated. His life was dedicated to the idea that the reality of daily life as well as our ideals should reflect the equality and brotherhood of all people.

Martin Luther King and Jerry Falwell would disagree on many issues of public policy. But surely on this central idea they are united, as all Americans should be: Democracy without morality, or freedom without faith, is impossible. This belief is, so to speak, the tiny mustard seed out of which the great tree of democratic liberty took root and has its being.

Rose garden signing ceremony for bill establishing
Martin Luther King, Jr. holiday, November 2, 1983

Let us learn to be tolerant of sectarian differences. But let us never forget the moral truth that makes all tolerance possible. For as it is written in the book of John the Evangelist: "You shall know the truth, and the truth shall make you free." Blessed indeed is the nation whose God is the Lord. Thank you, and God bless you.

An Inquiry into the Nature & Causes of Poverty in America and How to Combat It

Secretary Jack Kemp

Heritage Foundation
Washington D.C. June 6, 1990

"America is divided into two economies: mainstream (democratic capitalism, entrepreneurial) and that created for the poor (dependency, welfare bureaucracy, social costs)."

We are living in the single most dramatic era in world history, other than perhaps at the founding of our Republic in the Revolution of 1776. Consider this quotation:

> *In an ironic sense, Karl Marx was right. We are witnessing today a great revolutionary crisis—a crisis where the demands of the economic order are colliding directly with those of the political order. But the crisis is happening not in the free, non-Marxist West, but in the home of Marxism-Leninism, the Soviet Union. What we see here is a political structure that no longer corresponds to its economic base, a society where productive forces are hampered by political ones.*

Ladies and gentlemen, that was not last month or last year, that was said in June 1982 by President Ronald Reagan in an historic speech to the English Parliament. How far we've come! And we've come a lot further than even Mikhail Gorbachev understands. Just a few days ago at Stanford University, he said that it doesn't matter who won the Cold War. With all due respect, it does matter, very much.

The real Cold War victory is not our arms over their arms, it is a victory of the American Idea of democratic capitalism over the Soviet idea of statist socialism. The truth is President Gorbachev will not be able to repair socialism, it must be replaced. All around the world, despite the resistance of the old guard, freedom and free markets, democracy and capitalism are increasingly on the march. From Eastern Europe and Latin America to Africa and Asia and even the Soviet Union, people are dreaming of freedom and democracy after decades and even centuries of oppression, poverty, despair, and debt.

Permanent Revolution

In his State of the Union address, President Bush called it the revolution of 1989, but perhaps it may be in reality just the continuation of the American Revolution of 1776. Marxist Leninists used to talk about their "permanent revolution," but as it turns out the only permanent revolution the world has ever seen is the American Revolution. Yet, in such revolutionary times, Charles Dickens's observation on the French Revolution may well still apply: it can be the best of times and the worst of times simultaneously.

Here in the U.S., we're enjoying unprecedented economic growth and opportunity, yet after nearly eight years of continuing expansion, there are some parts of our nation and all too many of our people left out and left behind, suffering from the tragedy of homelessness, poverty that stretches over generations, and a sense of hopelessness and despair about the future. As Ed Feulner said recently, the world is looking to us for advice on the free-market ideas of Adam Smith: "They don't want lectures on income redistribution and capitalist exploitation, they want income and capitalism."

Ed is right; but after one and a half years of representing the. Bush Administration at Housing and Urban Development (HUD), I know that not only is Eastern Europe looking to us for market-oriented answers, but so is East Harlem, East St. Louis, and East LA. If we are to present the example of democratic capitalism and the rule of law to the rest of the world, we've got to make it work for the low-income people and distressed neighborhoods and communities right here in our own country.

Right Morally

Helping those left behind and left out is not only a moral imperative for our nation, I am convinced it is also a winning—indeed decisive—political strategy for bringing impoverished communities and low-income people and minorities into the ranks of the Party of Lincoln. Whether it's called bleeding heart conservatism, capitalism with a social conscience, or populist conservatism, it's the right thing to do, the right time to do it, and we're the right people to help lead it.

Robert Kuttner of the New Republic, an equally-bleeding heart but liberal columnist, recently wrote that polls continue to show that the voters trust Republicans more than Democrats to conduct foreign policy, manage the economy, hold down inflation, and resist higher taxes. Democrats still score only on the question of who cares more about the common American. He goes on to conclude that if Republicans ever figure out that they can capture the issue of caring as well, the Democrats might as well go out of business. Now, I don't want to put them out of business, just out of the Congress!

Traveling across the country, I've seen thousands upon thousands of low-income people and families in public housing communities eagerly seeking change and responding positively to our ideas. They don't want more government promises and egalitarian welfare schemes, they want to live in neighborhoods free from crime and drug abuse, with good jobs and opportunities to own property and homes; they want quality education so that they and their children can live better lives. They want what we all want—a chance to develop their talent, potential, and possibilities.

Republicans Understand

Our friend Kimi Gray of Kenilworth-Parkside recently said that her residents and public housing tenants throughout the country may be registered Democrats, but they work with Republicans because Republicans are "the ones that seem to understand that we do not want to stay a poor and permanent underclass." Well, of course that's true. And that's how Mr. Lincoln built the Republican Party. As he said, "When one starts poor, as most do in the race of life, free society is such that he knows he can better his condition: he knows that there is no fixed condition for his whole life."

New HUD Secretary visits public school 1989

Cuomo's Tale

In 1984, Governor Mario Cuomo of New York electrified the Democratic Convention with his tale of America as two cities, one rich and one poor, permanently divided into two classes. He talked about the rich growing richer and the poor becoming poorer, with the conclusion that class conflict, if not warfare, was the only result, and redistribution of wealth was the solution. But with all due respect to Governor Cuomo, he got it wrong.

America is not divided immutably into two static classes. But it is separated or divided into two economies. One economy—our mainstream economy—is democratic capitalist, market-oriented, entrepreneurial, and incentivized for working families whether in labor or management. This mainstream rewards work, investment, saving, and productivity. Incentives abound for productive human, economic, and social behavior. It was this economy led by President Reagan's supply-side revolution of tax rate cuts in 1981 that generated 21.5 million new jobs, more than 4 million new business enterprises, relatively low inflation, and higher standards of living for most of our people.

This economy has created more jobs in the last decade than all Europe, Canada, and Japan combined. And according to the U.S. Treasury, federal income taxes paid by the top 1 percent of taxpayers has surged by over 80 percent—up from $51 billion in 1981 to $92 billion in 1987. Harvard and White House economist Lawrence Lindsey estimates that by 1985, economic output was between 2 and 3 percent higher than it would have been without the tax cut. But the best news of the eighties was that good policies lead to good results, confirming what deep down we always understood, that the real wealth of America comes not from our physical resources, but our human resources; not from things, but from ideas.

But there is another economy—a second economy that is similar in respects to the Eastern European or Third World "socialist" economy if you will—and it is almost totally opposite to the way people are treated in our mainstream capitalist economy, and it predominates in the pockets of poverty throughout urban and rural America. This economy has barriers to productive human and social activity and a virtual absence of economic incentive and rewards that deny entry to black, Hispanic and other minority men and women into the mainstream, almost as effectively as hiring notices 50 years ago that read "no Blacks (or Hispanics or Irish or whatever) need apply."

Noble Intentions Gone Awry

The irony is that the second economy was set up not out of malevolence, but out of a desire to help the poor, alleviate suffering, and provide a basic social safety net. But while the intentions were noble, the results led to a counterproductive economy. Instead of independence, it led to dependency. In effort to minimize economic pain, it maximized welfare bureaucracy and social costs that are near pathological.

Now, let's pause, and step away from our orthodox notions and examine this from afar. What if you wanted to create poverty? What policies and principles would you use to destroy the economy of cities and make people dependent on government? How would you do it? Let me offer some suggestions:

1) Impose steeply graduated and progressive tax rates and then inflate the currency to push people into ever higher tax brackets.
2) Reward welfare and unemployment at a higher level than working and productivity.
3) Tax the entrepreneur who succeeds in the legal capitalistic system much higher than in the illicit underground economy.
4) Reward people who stay in public housing more than those who want to move up and out into private housing and homeownership.
5) Reward the family that breaks up rather than the family that stays together.
6) Encourage debt, borrowing, and spending rather than saving, investing, and risk taking.
7) But most of all, if you really wanted to create poverty and dependency, weaken and in some cases destroy the link between effort and reward.

Examples abound of how Third World disincentives have created poverty in inner cities. I recently read a Wall Street Journal article about a woman on welfare in Milwaukee, Wisconsin who tried to put away a few pennies, nickels, dimes, and dollars so that one day she could do what every other mother wants to do: send her daughter to college. She managed to build a savings account of just over $3,000, but there was a catch. The social welfare agency said she was violating welfare rules. She was taken into court, prosecuted for fraud, and fined $15,000. But since she didn't have $15,000, they just took her $3,000, gave her a year's sentence in jail, but suspended it. Guess what? According to the same Wall Street Journal article, she now spends every cent she gets, and she must rely on government subsidies to pay for just about everything.

Incidentally, the story may have a good ending for this woman. After I talked about her in a speech, a man came forward from the audience and offered to finance a trust fund for the cost of a college education for the young girl. Eugene Lang, a wealthy businessman from New York City, also believes in the power of incentives to produce positive behavior. According to the New York Times, he went into P.S. 121 elementary school in East Harlem and told children that if they stayed in school, got good grades, stayed drug free, and qualified, he would personally pay for a college education. Talk about behavior modification! Whereas, 60 percent of those children were dropping out, today 90 percent are in their first two years of college.

Negative Pay

The startling fact in America today, however, is that the highest marginal tax rates are not being paid for by the rich, but by welfare mothers or unemployed fathers who want to take a job. In most cities, a welfare mother would have to earn $15,000-$18,000 in a private-sector job to earn the equivalent of the average tax-free welfare payment. According to a study by Christopher Jencks and Kathryn Edin in the American Prospect magazine, a working mother with two children employed at about $5.00 per hour, would actually take home pay of about minus 45 cents per hour. She'd be losing nearly $4.00 a day after taking into account the loss of government benefits, taxes, and work-related expenses such as transportation and child care.

The heavily-regulated U.S. housing market is another example of government-created scarcity. Rent controls in many major cities have crippled rental housing by making it unprofitable to be a landlord or investor in affordable housing. And make no mistake about it, rent controls do not help the poor. The foreign minister of communistic North Vietnam vividly recalls the lessons of rent control in this own country when he said recently that the war couldn't destroy housing in Hanoi, "but we have destroyed our city by very low rents. We realize it was stupid and that we must change policy." Ladies and gentlemen, if communists can learn to change, why can't bleeding heart, liberal Democrats!

Subsidies for Affluent

While affordable housing is a real-national challenge, and we in the administration are taking steps to solve it, there is no shortage of low-income housing in some so-called tight markets—it's just occupied by affluent people. Author William Tucker points out that Ed Koch maintained a $441 per month Greenwich Village apartment during his twelve years as mayor of New York and actress Shelly Winters paid a little more for a two-bedroom apartment near Central Park.

Another glaring example of counterproductive government policy is how HUD was subsidizing vacant public housing until we took over. It had been costing the taxpayer over $1,300 per unit to subsidize vacant public housing often used as crack houses for gangs and drug pushers. You'll be glad to know that we have started a policy called Operation Occupancy where only units actually occupied by low-income people will be subsidized with public housing funds.

As I said earlier, the good news is that government policies can change and that good policy can lead to good results. Productive human effort can be promoted; behavior can be modified or altered. Work effort can be unleashed. The forces that cause poverty can be reversed. President Bush said that for these seeds of productive behavior to grow, we must give people—working people, poor people, all our citizens— control over their own lives. And it means a commitment to civil rights and economic opportunity for every American." Along with planting a billion new trees in the decade of the nineties, we ought to plant the seeds of millions of new minority enterprises.

In other words, expanding the base of capitalism and access to capital can alter the conditions of poverty. In the Bush Administration, we recently set as a goal the creation of more than 1 million new home owners by 1992 through our Homeownership and Opportunity for People Everywhere (HOPE) initiative. We plan through urban homesteading, privatization of public housing, and reform of Federal Housing Administration (FHA) to make homeownership and empowerment the hallmark of this administration's housing and urban development policy. As columnist William Raspberry wrote recently "... when assets are present, people begin to think in terms of the asset. If a young mother owns her own home, she begins to pay attention to real estate values, property taxes, the cost of maintenance and so forth .... Note," he says, "that it is the assets themselves that create this effect, as opposed to just educational programs or exhortations toward better values."

Freedom and Opportunity

Stuart Butler and Bob Woodson point out that to the liberals, empowerment means giving power to government to control our lives. But empowerment really means not control over others, but freedom to control one's own affairs. The poor don't want paternalism, they want opportunity—they don't want the servitude of welfare, they want to get jobs and private property. They don't want dependency; they want a new declaration of independence.

In that spirit, let me outline some ideas for a national agenda to help low-income people and our nation find the keys that will unlock the shackles and cycles of poverty and despair.

First, cut the capital gains tax to 15 percent for the nation and eliminate it altogether in distressed inner cities and rural communities we would designate as Enterprise Zones.

President Bush correctly implored the Democratic majority in Congress to cut the capital gains tax rate and finally—after ten years—to establish what 37 states have already implemented, Enterprise Zones, as a national policy. The capital gains tax reduction isn't to help the rich or secure old wealth, but to free up or unlock old capital and old wealth to help new business, new risk takers, job creation, and economic growth.

Virtually every survey shows that the major problem for inner-city entrepreneurs is the absence of seed capital. The capital gains tax reduction, coupled with Enterprise Zones, will help "unlock" existing, status-quo capital to fund and support a whole new generation of budding entrepreneurs in America's inner cities where economic opportunity is needed most. When the top capital gains tax rate was reduced from 49 percent to 20 percent, the number of small company startups more than doubled, rising to 640,000 and creating 15 million new jobs.

By dramatically reducing the capital gains tax rates again, and greenlining inner-city neighborhoods, we can expand the economy and put that enormous job-creating potential to work w h ere it is needed most. Not only would a lower capital gains tax rate help the poor, but it would also increase tax revenues. Lower capital gains rates would greatly increase the number of capital gains transactions passing through federal, state, and local tax gates, raise the total value of assets throughout the economy, and make the economy bigger, more efficient, and more productive.

Second, an expansion of resident management and urban homesteading in public housing can empower residents to acquire private ownership and control of their homes and receive pride and dignity of ownership.

Third, housing vouchers and certificates should be significantly increased and expanded so as to give low-income families greater choice and more freedom where to live, while expanding access to affordable housing for those most in need.

Fourth, a new version of tax reform is needed to remove low-income families from the tax rolls and dramatically increase the after-tax income of welfare mothers and unemployed father s who go to work. In 1948, at the median income, a family of four paid virtually no income taxes, and only $30 a year in direct Social Security taxes (1 percent). This year, the same family's tax burden would be over $6,000. To be comparable to 1948, the personal exemption—the tax allowance for the costs of nurturing children—would have to be well over $6,000 today. Instead, it is only $2,000.

Fifth, a dramatic expansion of the earned income tax credit, the creation of up to a $6,000 exemption for children under 16, and the President's Child Care Tax Credit to roll back this tax burden on low-income families and unemployed parents.

Sixth, helping homeless people who now wander aimlessly in streets or are warehoused in shelters. Congress should pass the administration's new Shelter Plus Care program to expand community-based mental health facilities, drug abuse treatment, job training, and day care. This program will help homeless Americans get shelter, transitional housing, and support service s to help them reenter the mainstream economy.

Seventh, in order to enhance education and opportunity, we've got to expand true choice and competition through magnet schools, education vouchers, tuition tax credits, and the type of choice-enhancing policies that Wisconsin state representative Polly Williams and Detroit councilmember Reverend Keith Butler recommend.

Eighth, Congress should pass President Bush's HOPE legislation, including IRAs for first time homebuyers, the low-income housing tax credit, and Operation Bootstrap linking housing vouchers to strategies for gaining self-sufficiency.

Winning the War

Over 200 years ago Adam Smith wrote the recipe for creating wealth. It was titled *An Inquiry into the Nature and Causes of the Wealth of Nations*. Today, I'm asking for an inquiry into the nature and causes of the wealth of cities. It's a variation on Adam Smith's theme of "natural liberty." As I said in another speech to Heritage about what George Gilder called the quantum age of new technology, our greatest assets are not in the wealth we see around us but the potential which is unseen ... in the minds yet to be educated, in the businesses not yet opened, the technologies not yet discovered, the jobs waiting to be created. Wealth is not what we've done, but what we have yet to do.

This is a country of dreams. America has long dreamed of a better future for people everywhere. America's permanent revolution has brought a fresh air of freedom that's blowing around the world. Yes, it's a struggle. Yes, we need to stay strong. Yes, we need to maintain our alliances. Yes, we must maintain peace through strength. But also it's time to bring the revolution back home to America to extend the capitalist economy across our whole society, and put it to work for all of our nation's people.

In May 1981, Ronald Reagan said that "The West will not contain communism, it will transcend communism. We will not bother to denounce it; we'll dismiss it as a sad, bizarre chapter in human history whose last pages are even now being written."

Just as Ronald Reagan predicted the transience of communism, so must we commit ourselves to put poverty on a path toward elimination. Let us make the decade of the '90s the time we win the war against poverty, just as the decade of the '80s was the time we won the Cold War against communism. Let us dedicate this decade to the rebirth of human potential, freedom, and equality of opportunity for all.

Lincoln's Vision of Democracy

Secretary Jack Kemp

Lincoln Fellowship
Gettysburg, Pennsylvania November 19, 1990

"Mr. Lincoln ... envisioned an America where freedom is inseparable from economic, political and social opportunity, and upward mobility."

On this field of honor 127 years ago, Providence revealed the future of mankind.

The battle of Gettysburg confirmed that freedom is not just the God-given birthright of Americans, but the destiny of all men and women everywhere.

Here a great battle was fought to save the Union ... but the battle and the war itself were incidental to the larger principle set forth 87 years before in the Declaration of Independence.

Liberty itself hung in the balance ... a principle so vital to the nation that Mr. Lincoln had once said he "would rather be assassinated on this spot than to surrender it."

It is with special purpose that we return to this sacred site, for we cannot properly commemorate the Gettysburg Address of 1863 without celebrating what President Bush has called the "revolution of 1989."

A hymn of freedom is now resounding in an ever-rising chorus from around the globe.

On the eve of a new millennium, people all over the world bear witness to the revelation of this battlefield ... and to the wisdom of Mr. Lincoln's timeless words.

Were he here today, Lincoln would remind us that this global surge toward freedom really began in the Revolution of 1776, the revolution whose promise won't be fulfilled until all nations embrace the inalienable rights Jefferson inscribed in our Declaration.

Abraham Lincoln was not the first to link the success of American democracy to the hopes of all mankind. From our republic's earliest days, Washington, Hamilton, Jefferson, Webster, and other great statesmen believed that the American experiment in human freedom and democracy was without precedent. They knew, as did Mr. Lincoln, that if democracy failed here, it would not succeed anywhere.

But until the Civil War, the threat to American democracy had come only from foreign powers. Lincoln faced America's supreme crisis: the nation that embodied mankind's last best hope seemed hopelessly divided. He believed that "as a nation of free men, we must live through all time, or die by suicide. "

By a longstanding tradition now forgotten, Presidents rarely gave public addresses after their inauguration. Gettysburg was one of Lincoln's few exceptions. He yearned for this occasion to unfold the profound meaning of these patriot graves and implant it deep in every American heart.

On the day of dedication, the president led the procession, riding upright on horseback. Suddenly the cemetery came into view with its thousands of wooden crosses ... the temporary resting sites of the fallen. Lincoln's head bowed in reverence.

When later he rose to speak after Edward Everett's grand two-hour oration, the huge crowd, standing so long and restlessly, was hushed. Men removed their hats ... 15,000 people leaned forward to catch the president 's opening words.

Lincoln did not invoke Jefferson 's "self-evident truths." In but 268 inspired words, he spoke instead of an American "proposition" dedicated to the future of human equality and liberty.

Democracy is not a mathematical deduction proven once for all time. Democracy is a just faith ... fervently held ... a commitment to be tested again and again in the fiery furnace of history.

President Lincoln came to Gettysburg to teach us that our nation was born of an age-old dream and. charged with an eternal mission a nation impelled by its faith to perfect itself.

America was to be a "light unto the nations."

Slavery was the first great test challenging democracy's central principle of equality.

Lincoln's moral indignation over slavery was unbounded. In his Peoria speech replying to Senator Douglas, he said:

I hate ... the monstrous injustice of slavery itself. I hate it because it deprives our republican example of its just influence in the world—enables the enemies of free institutions, with plausibility, to taunt us as hypocrites—causes the real friends of freedom to doubt our sincerity, and especially because it forces so many really good men amongst ourselves into an open war with the very fundamental principles of civil liberty—criticizing the Declaration of Independence, and insisting that there is no right principle of action but self-interest.

Slavery was an abomination, a hideous stain defiling the nation's soul; it could only be cleansed by a baptism of fire in civil war.

Since the day Lincoln was taken from us by an assassin's hand, American democracy has met other challenges again and again ... the injustice of segregation ... the evil of Jim Crow laws ... the despair of the Great Depression ... the crises of two world wars ... the shameful denial of voting rights.

And our democracy is being tested today by levels of poverty, homelessness, and despair unacceptable to a compassionate and affluent nation. As the world's example of democracy we must make it work better at home.

While acknowledging the achievements of the last decade—the restoration of the spirit of entrepreneurial capitalism at home, the collapse of communist totalitarianism abroad, and the beginning of the triumph of democratic ideals throughout the world—we must recognize that our work is not yet done, that there is much left to be accomplished.

Far too many black and minority Americans have yet to share in our national prosperity and the full promise of the American Dream.

At a time when democracy is capturing the imagination of Eastern Europe, we are challenged at home in those poor communities where democratic opportunity and entrepreneurial capitalism have yet to be extended, or even tried.

We must build a new national consensus around economic growth and opportunity, greater access to property, jobs and entrepreneurship. For those left out or left behind, we must bring the great promise of democracy to every community, to every city, and to all our people.

Abraham Lincoln—the only Chief Executive to have presided over a full scale civil war—was unparalleled as a proponent of economic and political consensus. No American statesman ever championed the cause of national unity with stronger resolve.

So opposed was Lincoln to dividing the nation that after the fearsome battle in these very fields, he paid profound tribute to all the "honored dead," resisting in magnanimous silence any distinction between the slain of the South and the slain of the North.

In his pleas for unity, we hear an echo of his first inaugural address, "We are not enemies, but friends. We must not be enemies. Though passion may have strained, it must not break our bonds of affection ...' And while Lincoln's plea went unheeded, he insisted that Americans were one people, one nation "conceived in liberty," one family with a stake in each other's welfare ... and civil war itself could not shake his conviction.

Lincoln helped establish a political party to form a new national consensus around the Declaration of Independence. Yet he always put country before party and the next generation before the next election. His expansive vision of democracy elevated him above any politics of division, envy, and conflict.

Today we hear much in our politics about division ... of rich against poor, black versus white ... indeed almost of class warfare, disguised as one word—" fairness."

In today's political vocabulary, fairness seems to have become a euphemism for class warfare and redistribution of wealth. But any true concept of fairness must recognize the necessity of a link between reward and individual human effort. The advocates of egalitarianism and class warfare talk as if there are limits to growth ... only so much wealth to go around ... that life is a static condition ... and that poverty is perpetual.

Lincoln ridiculed this theory. He envisioned an America where freedom is inseparable from economic, political, and social opportunity, and upward mobility.

As he put it, the "progress by which the poor, honest, industrious, and resolute man raises himself, that he may work on his own account, and hire somebody else ... is the great principle for which this government was really formed."

We were fortunate to have Governor Cuomo of New York here last year to remind us that Lincoln needs to be shared with the world. He deserves our gratitude for organizing a group of scholars to translate Lincoln's words on democracy for the people of Poland. This was an act of enormous generosity and wisdom, and let's pray that Lincoln will soon be available to all peoples in every language.

But wouldn't it be tragic if Lincoln's teachings were misinterpreted?

At the very moment when liberal democracy, private property, and free enterprise are bringing down the Iron Curtain and tearing down the wall between East and West, we in America are being asked to choose between two opposing ideas—the politics of class warfare or Lincoln's all-embracing vision of boundless democratic opportunity.

According to the politics of division, we are told that America is divided in two ... two peoples, one rich, one poor... two classes, one upper, one under ... two cities, one glittering, the other despairing. This division, we are told, is near immutable, and redistribution of wealth is the only way to make peace.

We are even supposed to conclude that a Lincoln of our day would elevate the poor by redistributing wealth ... that he would provide for some at the expense of others.

Of course Mr. Lincoln would be deeply concerned about the extent of poverty, but rather than evoke class conflict, I believe he would move to place poverty, homelessness, and despair on the same "course of ultimate extinction" that he proposed for slavery in his own time.

Let me share Lincoln's very own words with you:

> *I don't believe in a law to prevent a man from getting rich," he said, "it would do more harm than good ... I want every man to have the chance—and I believe a black man is entitled to it—in which he can better his condition—when he may look forward and hope to be a hired laborer this year and the next, work for himself afterward, and finally to hire men to work for him! That is the true system.*

Lincoln's legacy cannot honestly be claimed by those who would diminish one person to elevate another.

Why struggle to redistribute existing wealth? Let us commit ourselves to Lincoln's vision of democracy—creating new wealth, empowering the poor, opening up access to property, expanding homeownership, creating more jobs, encouraging more entrepreneurs, reducing the need for welfare.

We all know he favored cutting up the public lands into plots for the poor. He wanted every poor family to have the opportunity to own their own home and have access to property and in return, they would build the home and improve the land.

Lincoln's Homestead Act of 1862 gave 160 acres to any poor family who wanted to carve their share of the American Dream out of the wilderness. It was one of the most popular measures in American history and today it is the source of inspiration for a new homesteading program in urban America. We in the Bush Administration will provide any resident of public housing the same kind of opportunity to control, manage, and ultimately own his or her very own home.

Yet the Homestead Act did not enhance and empower government.

It enhanced and empowered people. It not only emancipated the economy; it helped emancipate the poor from poverty and government dependency. Today, turning low-income people into property owners is the next vital step in making democracy work and combating the conditions of poverty.

Mr. Lincoln would not offer government as the first alternative for dealing with problems. He would focus government action where it could be used best—to break down barriers to freedom and opportunity ... to enable every man and woman to fulfill their potential, develop their God-given talent, and pursue their inalienable right to human happiness.

After all, isn't that what the terrible battle fought here was really about ... the noblest effort any people ever made to dismantle the cruelest barrier to human freedom?

One hundred twenty-seven years after Gettysburg, Lincoln's belief that all human beings are created equal and endowed with inalienable rights—the faith upon which liberal democracy is based—is beginning to prevail around the world.

Because of democracy's long march from Independence Hall through Gettysburg to the very streets of Moscow, the world knows the simple yet profound truth: the yearning for freedom cannot be extinguished ... the struggle for inalienable rights will never end short of victory ... nothing can deny the transcendence of democracy.

As Americans, we cannot rest until the blessings we enjoy are shared by all.

Let us fulfill our nation's destiny by making Mr. Lincoln's great proposition of democracy—set forth on this battlefield—into a self-evident truth for every man, woman, and child on this earth.

A Cultural Renaissance

The Honorable Jack Kemp

"Culture Wars: The Battle Over Family Values"
Shavano Institute for National Leadership
Hillsdale College, MI, February 22, 1994

"I've often argued that economic prosperity will help solve many of our serious social problems, but I've never argued that it is sufficient. An economy and a government have limits set at the boundaries of the human heart. And the habits of the heart are learned in families—shelters for civilized standards and ethical behavior."

Nearly a decade ago, in a speech at Hillsdale College, I talked about the inseparable connection between economics and strong families. The word economics, I observed, comes from the Greek "oikos nomos," which literally means "the law or custom of the home." Economics originally meant the study of the family and the home, not merely the production or distribution of material goods.

A decade ago, that debate was interesting. Today it is urgent, even critical, to the future of our nation.

Aleksandr Solzhenitzyn argues that from time to time in history we come across a "knot"—a moment when trends and issues are tied together; an hour when alternatives are clear; that brief period before decisions harden into fate.

I believe we now face a "knot" of our own. Ours is a fundamental choice disguised as a political argument that grows in intensity and ferocity.

There are those who say that conservatives must make a Hobson's choice between a message of economic growth and a message of cultural renewal. Take your side, we are told. Let the fight begin. It's either economics or cultural values.

Moments like this call for clarity. So today I want to argue as directly as I can: This choice is false; this conflict is destructive; and this decision, if forced on conservatives and Republicans, would come at a great cost to our coalition.

It is false in the realm of ideas—because it misunderstands the moral roots of our economic order.

It is destructive in the realm of policy—because it ignores the full range of human needs. And it is costly in the realm of politics—because it undermines our coalition of conscience that could help transform our nation, renew our culture, and, ultimately, help provide an example of freedom and democracy to the world.

I. The Realm of Ideas

Just what is the relationship between free-market economics and cultural values—between doing well and doing good?

To some, capitalism and the prosperity it creates has held the promise of secular salvation, a utopia of affluence. To critics, it is seen as a Darwinian struggle where only the strong and fittest can survive.

Neither vision has matched reality. Democratic capitalism has not built a "New Jerusalem," nor has it returned us to the "law of the jungle." It promises, instead, three extraordinary things: liberation from abject poverty, freedom from political tyranny, and release of the individual conscience from oppression.

No human system has ever kept its promises more faithfully. Democratic capitalism has been history's best weapon against poverty, oppression, and tyranny. Free markets have generated unequaled living standards for unrivaled numbers of men and women. Yet capitalism's accomplishments are much deeper. Its enduring appeal is not its toasters, televisions, and transistors, but its respect for individual innovation, creativity, and upward mobility.

Capitalism has never been a utopian vision, unlike socialism. It never promised to build the Kingdom of God on earth. But it has succeeded in allowing people to stand upright and dignified in the kingdoms of this world.

Yet for all its material success, capitalism cannot stand alone. It depends on a system of values and morality it reinforces but does not create—on moral and cultural habits that determine its appeal, its power, and, in the end, its success.

President Roche of Hillsdale College has made the case: "There is a clear moral sense to economics involving sympathy and trust .... Markets reflect our spiritual values as well as our free economic choices."

Consider the virtues of capitalism. An ethic of work, savings, and self-reliance. The integrity and honesty essential to contracts, trade, and money. A passion for excellence. The impulse given to charity and philanthropy. All these things depend on values, not on greed. A free market does not insist on perfect virtue, but it does depend on common morality.

In his book, The Catholic Ethic and the Spirit of Capitalism, Michael Novak writes, "The moral-cultural system is at once crucial to the health of democratic capitalism and easily overlooked. It is crucial because the primary form of capital is the human spirit ... It is too easily taken for granted because the habits of the heart are learned in childhood, supplying reasons that reason has forgotten."

Economic success is built on moral foundations. An economy reflects the moral image of its people.

"It is impossible," wrote T.S. Eliot, "to design a system so perfect that no one needs to be good." This is simply a restatement of the first conservative principle: the state of the human soul determines the shape of human society.

Every free society therefore faces an urgent question: How to encourage the values of its people and still leave them free? Our conservative message must be one of persuasion, not imposition.

A government conceived in liberty has none of the tools of tyranny. It depends, instead, on other institutions—structures between the individual and the state—that instill character, purpose, and virtue. Churches and synagogues that raise a moral standard. Parents who provide a moral and spiritual example to their children. Schools that teach, not only the basics of math and history, but the basics of citizenship and character that come from an understanding of the Decalogue as well as the Declaration of Independence.

II. The Realm of Policy

While to some, this is an abstract argument, the implications are as tangible as the violent headlines that fill our newspapers, the poverty that divides our cities, the moral relativism that confuses our young. We cannot isolate economic opportunity from cultural renewal because both are required to confront and conquer the problems we face.

The Wall Street Journal's Alex Kotlowitz, in his wonderful book, There Are No Children Here, recounts a conversation with a young ten-year old named Lafeyette Rivers at the Henry Horner public housing community in Chicago: "I asked Lafeyette what he wanted to be. 'If I grow up, I'd like to be a bus driver,' he told me. 'If,' not when. At the age of ten, Lafeyette wasn't sure he'd even make it to adulthood."

How do we respond when graves are filled with boys not old enough to shave? When girls not yet in their teens are taught how to use condoms, but not the responsibilities of motherhood? When poverty grows rampant among the ruins of families? When despair paralyzes responsibility and initiative? And when unemployment leaves 50-60 percent of males on the streets of some urban ghettoes and barrios?

Economic opportunity is important. There are Americans who live each day behind the barbed wire of limited opportunity. This feeds moral despair. If the future holds no hope, the present holds few reasons to be responsible.

The insightful columnist William Raspberry observed: "You and I are guided by the belief that good things will happen to us in the future if we take proper care of the present. But without hope for the future, hard work at a low-paying job makes no sense. Avoiding a police record makes no sense. Working hard in school or pleasing a boss or avoiding pregnancy makes no sense."

This is not an excuse for irresponsible behavior, it's an explanation of a phenomenon that confounds the left and frustrates the right.

I've often argued that economic prosperity will help solve many of our serious social problems, but I've never argued that it is sufficient. It will not heal a broken home. It will not provide a child with a father's discipline and love or a mother's nurture and comfort. It will not restore honesty and respect for life. An economy and a government have limits set at the boundaries of the human heart. And the habits of the heart are learned in families—shelters for civilized standards and ethical behavior.

Strong families are often stronger than the deepest poverty and the worst disadvantages. Broken families often frustrate all the help we can provide. The primary need of children is not better laws or public programs. It is better childhoods.

We have no right to conclude that most of the poor lack values. The vast majority of the poor are working long hours, obeying the law, taking care of their children, and overcoming great odds. They have the same dreams and aspirations that you and I have for our families.

These hopes are universal. They are not confined to one class, or one race, or even one hemisphere. It was Adam Smith who taught us that "The desire to improve our lot in life comes to us out of the womb of our mothers and never leaves to the day we die."

As Mother Teresa said at this year's National Prayer Breakfast, which Joanne and I were privileged to attend, "Those who are materially poor can be spiritually rich."

But we can conclude that America's most urgent question is this enduring question: How do we instill the values of our parents in the lives of our children?

The National Commission on Children concluded its 1993 report with sober words: "Today, too many young people seem adrift, without a steady moral compass to direct their daily behavior or to plot [a] responsible course for their lives."

While this remains true, there will never be enough police and prisons to end the lawlessness in our streets if it starts in our hearts. There will never be enough government policies and welfare programs to conquer the poverty of the spirit. And there will never be enough prosperity to bring the peace for which we long.

To me, this is the real meaning of the "culture war." It is not conducted between battling spokesmen from the left and right. It is not won or lost at the end of an election. It is a battle for the souls of our children, for the strength of our families, for the peace of our neighborhoods. Its victories are won in individual lives, but its outcome depends on the strength of cultural standards.

Pope John Paul II in Veritas Svlendor warns of "the risk of an alliance between democracy and ethical relativism." Too often from our culture's commanding heights—in government, the media and academia—we hear that all moral judgments are purely personal and finally equal. We are told the choice between Madonna and Mother Teresa is merely a matter of taste; that traditional values are relative to time and place.

This is something different and deeper than a crisis of crime, a crisis of the economy or a crisis of welfare. It is certainly deeper than President Clinton's pathetic use of a health-care "crisis" to win support for his plan to nationalize America's medical system.

This moral relativism indicates a crisis of confidence in our own ideals. It is the strip mining of our public spirit. It leaves men and women unable to believe in anything, even in their own courage and conscience. It leaves our children to wander without guideposts in dangerous, unfamiliar territory.

Consider a recent interview by the New York Times with a 17-year-old Lakewood, California high school student arrested for rape and sexual harassment. He told a reporter, "They pass out condoms, teach sex education and pregnancy—this and pregnancy—that ... But they don't teach us any rules."

Ending this moral ambiguity—attempting to reintroduce into our culture the ideas of right and wrong—is the first commitment of meaningful cultural renewal.

This is not a matter of self-righteous moralizing. It is a matter of compassion, for it is the vulnerable who suffer most when standards are weakened—children making choices about work, sex and violence, when the stakes can be despair or prison or even death.

A society that is indifferent to its moral and spiritual life is indifferent to its future.

Our welfare system is a case study in these ideas. It is an example of how the capital of the human spirit can be squandered in the course of a few generations. Our best intentions were transformed into an assault on human dignity because we ignored the incentives of the market, the urgency of virtue, and the desire of all people to improve their lot in life.

While previous generations of Americans have known poverty, today we are seeing something unprecedented—a kind of poverty in which children are deprived, not just of resources, but of hope and nurture, of principles and values.

We are witnessing one of the most dramatic and destructive social transformations in our history.

Just twenty-five years ago, one out of every ten children was born to a single parent. Today, that number has tripled to one in three. By the end of the century, it may reach over 40 percent.

America now has 1.2 million children being born into single-parent homes each year.

Nearly 20 years ago, George Gilder argued that single males, replaced in families by welfare, would become trapped in a culture of abject poverty and barbaric violence. He argued that civilization itself depends on the civilization of young males by stable families—first by a mother and father, then by a wife. He predicted that a society could commit "sexual suicide" by ignoring human nature and human needs. And that is precisely what we're seeing—a Hobbesian world where life is solitary, poor, brutish, and, all too often, short.

Homes headed by one parent have a poverty rate of 55 percent. Among two-parent families it is just 7 percent.

Five hundred percent more teenagers from broken homes are suspended or expelled from school than from two-parent homes.

Seventy percent of minors who wind up in reform school or prison were raised without a father in the home.

Single parents, mostly mothers, so often do heroic work against terrible odds. But broken homes too often leave broken lives. We are gathering the bitter harvest of no-fault fatherhood.

There is one lesson we must draw from this record of failure: Our welfare system must be radically overhauled.

I am not talking about marginal reforms to the current system. The type of tinkering that President Clinton proposes will simply prolong a system that prolongs dependency and produces perpetual poverty.

We need to start from scratch by changing the fundamental premise of our welfare system. Robert Rector of the Heritage Foundation — where I'm proud to serve as a Distinguished Fellow—has demonstrated that our current system sends a simple, yet profoundly destructive message. The government will provide a young woman with welfare benefits, but only on the following conditions: she must have a child, she must not work, she must not save, and she must not marry the father of her children.

Every attempt at success is met with hostility, if not outright prohibition, by the rules of the system. When a system is designed like this we must conclude that it's not so much the values of the poor that we should question, it's the values of the welfare system we must challenge and change. We must first remove the incentives to fail. But we must also create the opportunity to succeed.

Michael Sherraden, a professor at Washington University in St. Louis, has written a fascinating book called Assets and the Poor, which reveals the problems inherent in our benefits-based welfare system.

The whole theory of cash benefits, he argues, weakens personal initiative.

We provide enough benefits for day-to-day subsistence. Our goal is merely to anesthetize the poor against daily suffering. For them, the future only reaches as far as the next welfare check.

But when men and women have the opportunity for assets and ownership, all this is changed. Mothers and fathers with assets think not only of the next year, but of the next generation. Ownership leads men and women to defend not only their own property, but the property of their neighbors as well. It gives them an equity position in the American Dream.

Benefits breed dependence. Assets build hope.

What would an asset-based welfare system look like? Here are a few ideas:

First, we should eliminate the income and payroll tax up to about 170 percent of the poverty line on any man or woman who takes a job and tries to work their way out of poverty. An unemployed welfare recipient who takes a minimum or low-wage job earns less by working than by remaining dependent. It's unconscionable that a man or woman on welfare who takes a job faces a higher marginal tax rate than America's wealthiest individuals.

Second, we should privatize every government-owned piece of housing in this country. Socialism has already failed in housing, just as it would certainly fail in medicine.

Every public housing resident should have the opportunity to own their home or apartment. In 1862, President Lincoln's administration gave away 200 million acres of land through his Homestead Act, instantly transforming millions of former slaves, immigrants, and laborers into independent and productive citizens. Today, a new urban homestead act could do the same for low-income people living in America's 1.5 million units of government-owned housing.

Liberals oppose this idea because they don't believe the poor can ever escape poverty and become rich, or at least richer. But to be rich in America, Lincoln said, means to be rich in opportunity, not baubles, beads, or bracelets. It is not just material poverty to which our liberal welfare state has consigned the poor, it is a poverty of opportunity.

Third, we should end the criminalization of savings among the poor. Right now, the most basic act of faith in the future—saving for your children, or for a home, or for your education—is a crime under our Aid to Familiies with Dependent Children (AFDC) laws.

Fourth, we should turn every single poor community in America into real Enterprise Zones, where entrepreneurs and investors would face a zero capital gains tax on the businesses they build, the investments they make, and the jobs they create. Our goal is not to lure big business from the suburbs to the cities, but to unleash the creative spirit of entrepreneurs who, with access to capital and credit, can start the next generation of small businesses that provide jobs, anchor communities, and allow fathers and mothers to provide for their children free of the "welfare plantation," to use Bob Woodson's phrase.

Fifth, every parent in America should have the right to send their child to the school of their choice, whether public, private, or religious. Wealthy parents and many middle-income families already have this option; low-income families should no longer be denied the opportunity to break free of a public education monopoly that, in too many cases, is failing their children. Assets are more than just material possessions. A child's education—the development of his or her intellectual potential—can be the most important asset of all.

Bill Clinton says he wants to "end welfare as we know it," but he is trapped in the elitist thinking of the past. He has eliminated the only federal program to encourage homeownership for public housing residents. He wants experimental "empowerment" zones, with only six urban zones, to test whether capitalism will actually work in the inner city.

Ladies and gentlemen, it isn't capitalism which has failed ... it's government which has failed.

Bill Clinton wants labor, but no capital. He wants employees, without employers. You can't have capitalism without capital, so I say there should be no capital gains tax at all!

We cannot call it a failure of capitalism in our inner cities when capitalism hardly exists. Sixty percent of East Harlem is owned by the government. Almost one third of its people are totally dependent on welfare. Itis not part of America's mainstream economy. It is an island of Third World socialism amid our sea of democratic capitalism. In less than thirty years, we've spent over $4 trillion fighting poverty and poverty is still winning.

But if this is all we have to say, we have not said enough. Yes, we should reform the welfare system. But there are important limits to what government action can accomplish. Renewing our culture depends on respecting and encouraging the work of voluntary associations.

Imagine if we could design a program with these results: 47 percent fewer inner-city youths drop out of school, drug use drops by 54 percent, crime falls by half? Who would not support it?

But we don't need to design it. It already exists. Richard Freeman, an economist at Harvard, found all these results when young people have strong roots in religious faith.

This is the unique contribution of our churches and synagogues. Religious values are not important just because they are useful. They are important because they are true; but they are useful as well. Faith has always been the strongest weapon against despair. Our society needs more than chains to bind the body. It needs moral standards to bind the conscience.

Those standards must be supported by our culture. It is easy to sneer at "family values" from the comfort of success. But these commitments are a tenuous lifeline for those threatened with hopelessness. They are much easier to criticize than replace.

The voice of these values must grow to a crescendo, not echo in a void. And this is the broad responsibility of churches, schools, the media, and government. It violates no one's rights to put voices of higher authority in service of what is right, what is true, and what is lasting.

As HUD secretary, almost every day some new study crossed my desk on the "root cause" of some social crisis. The root cause of homelessness. Of juvenile delinquency. Of educational failure.

Studies like these are important work, but they are not our primary work. We need to ask why most juveniles are not delinquents. Why most poor mothers are good mothers. Why most of the disadvantaged work hard for low pay.

We should concentrate, not just on the causes of social decay, but the causes of virtue. Not just on what leads to poverty, but on what leads to wealth. And we are always led back to the alliance between family and freedom.

III. The Realm of Politics

Many of these issues are beyond politics, but they are not without political implications.

The relationship between economics and values is a matter of philosophy. Addressing both is a matter of compassion. But appealing to both is the only way a political movement is built.

A political movement that ignores our moral aspirations is not tolerant, it is irrelevant.

Conservatism, in particular, can seem cold and calculating when it ignores our moral life—the passion that can transform an election into a cause. When economic conservatism is separated from moral values, as Russell Kirk has said, both rot separately, in separate tombs.

This is a challenge to every economic conservative who believes our nation can live by bread alone. This is a challenge to every cultural conservative who believes that tax rates, jobs, or growth are somehow beside the point.

This is a moment, not just to raise our voices, but to raise our sights. To prove that a broad agenda need not be shallow. To build a consensus that can win victories without sacrificing its principles.

We have the guidance of history—at another "knot," another moment of far-reaching decision.

At its founding in the mid-nineteenth century, the Republican Party was supported by two pillars. The first was a moral assertion—that slavery was "a great moral, social and political wrong." The second was a progressive economic message—a message of "free labor" that honored social mobility, economic growth and political democracy.

Almost immediately, a struggle began. Some Republicans claimed that the moral controversy of abolition weakened the party's economic appeal. One such politician argued that principle was expendable, "provided the country is quiet and prosperous."

Radical Republicans responded: "Yielding a principle through fear, the party disgusts the moralist, and dampens the ardor of the young and heroic whose service has been determined by the nature of our boldness and constancy."

It was Abraham Lincoln who argued that abandoning either economic hope or moral commitment would cause the Republican Party to "go to pieces."

This combination of economic opportunity and moral passion proved unbeatable. It was the real explanation for decades of Republican dominance. When it was abandoned, that dominance abruptly ended. Frederick Douglass wrote, "The life of the Republican Party lay in its devotion to justice, liberty and humanity. When it abandoned or slighted those great moral ideas and devoted itself to materialistic measures, it no longer appealed to the heart of the nation ...."

That debate from the last century could have been taken from this morning's paper. The feelings are just as strong. And the response must be the same.

It should be our goal to create a coalition of conscience that will inspire both moral and economic hope, and build a culture worthy of freedom.

Can we separate economics and values? The choice is not necessary. The achievements of capitalism depend on the achievements of the human spirit, nurtured in families. I am a believer in the power and promise of free markets, free minds, and free nations. I am also a believer in fostering the values that make them possible. And I will admit no conflict between them.

We are seeing attempts to divide us and divert us. If we yield to this temptation, we will squander our substance on endless, fruitless struggles.

The culture war must not be a civil war. Its enemies are destructive ideas, not our neighbors.

But if we build on the common ground of a broad agenda, these ideals can both unite and inspire. Such an agenda can unite the conservative movement and the Republican Party and appeal to every class and race and inspire our friends in the Democratic Party who are being abandoned by the social policies and anti-capitalist mentality of the Clinton Administration.

This is the way debates are won. This is the way movements are built. This is the way nations are changed.

What Pro Football Taught Me

The Honorable Jack Kemp

Washington, D.C. August 14, 1995

"The lesson that stands out above all is that when a team walks onto the field, ... race, color, religion—all artificial differences—get left on the sidelines, and if they don't, the whole team goes down to defeat."

One of the most thrilling events of my life, other than marrying my college sweetheart Joanne in 1958, was being drafted by the Detroit Lions. As a 17th round draft choice in 1957, my first pro contract was only $6,500, but the chance to play in the NFL made me feel like my boyhood hero, the great quarterback of the L.A. Rams, Bob Waterfield.

The incredible opportunity to play pro football was my shot at the American Dream. It was also a continuation of the lessons I was learning from sports about competition and cooperation, teamwork and tenacity, and most of all, what it means to live and work in our multiracial and culturally diverse American society.

Breaking into pro football taught me that nothing great ever happens without much inspiration and lots of perspiration. For me, the inspiration came one memorable day as a freshman at Occidental College in Los Angeles. My freshman football coach, Payton Jordan, called me into his office and told me—privately and in great confidence—that if I sacrificed enough, worked hard, and never, never gave up, someday I could play in the NFL. Wow! I walked out of his office on cloud nine, and I practiced, perspired, worked, and sacrificed harder than ever. (I even studied.)

Many years later at a college reunion, I learned that Coach Jordan had the same "very confidential and personal" conversation with almost every player on our team.

All the same, he inspired me to live up to my God-given potential and never give up on my dream. In fact, he'd done the same for every football and track star he ever coached, which incidentally includes my old teammate, roommate, and good friend, Jim Mora, coach of the New Orleans Saints.

Playing quarterback in pro football taught me a lot about incentives. Everything a quarterback does on a football field involves cost-benefit decisions, risk-reward ratios, and marginal analysis. All decisions of a quarterback on the football field are quantifiable and measurable. You get about 30 seconds to call the play, 3 seconds or less to get the ball off. The play either works or fails; the team either moves forward or is stopped; and, of course, the customers (i.e., the fans) are always with you—" win or tie," at least in Buffalo.

Bills v. Denver Broncos at War Memorial Stadium, Buffalo New York, 1964

Sports taught me other lessons as well: loyalty, determination, audacity, perspicacity, and much more. But the lesson that stands out above all is that when a team walks onto the field, socioeconomic conditions and ethnic, racial and cultural diversity disappear. Race, color, religion—all artificial differences—get left on the sidelines, and if they don't, the whole team goes down to defeat. As Coach Sid Gilman of the Chargers used to say, you win or lose as a team, as one family, one unit. There can be no room for racism, bigotry, anti-Semitism, or prejudice on a successful team or on a team that hopes and plans to succeed.

When people ask me why I'm so passionate about combating poverty and empowering the poor, about helping blacks and other minorities capture the American Dream, I tell them I'm a quarterback. I tell them that having captained every team I played for, I learned that in a democratic society—whether it's your family, your business, your football team, or your nation, we must all move forward together and we can't leave anyone behind.

Personally, I could never live with myself or look at a picture of Mr. Lincoln or Dr. King or face my former teammates and friendly opponents if I were not a voice in the great arena of political debate for the poor, for the left out, a voice for racial harmony and civil rights, like my friend Bill Bradley, an advocate for empowerment and minority enterprise and ownership.

For me, the true model of leadership, whether in a family, on a football field, in a business, or in politics, is the Good Shepherd. He left "the 99" to save one stray lamb. Ultimately, that has been the most valuable lesson of all, that our precious and unique experiment in human justice and dignity, in political and economic freedom will be judged by how we treat the poor, how we treat those who have been left behind or left out. America cannot lead the world to democracy and private property, to free enterprise and equal opportunity, if we don't make those principles and ideals work for all our people here at home.

POLITICS AND THE COMPETITION OF IDEAS

A Republican Tidal Wave

The Honorable Jack Kemp

Address to the Republican National Convention
Detroit, Michigan, July 15, 1980

"The American Idea was never that everyone would be leveled to the same position in life. The American Idea was that each individual should have the same opportunity to rise as high as his effort and imitative and God-given talent could carry him."

There is a tidal wave coming in this country—a political tidal wave as powerful as the one that hit in 1932, when an era of Republican dominance gave way to the New Deal. Soon we are going to find millions of Americans of every racial, cultural and economic background surprising themselves by voting Republican.

For the past 25 years, the Republican Party has been the minority party in government. But today we represent the majority philosophy of the American people. In November, we will convert this philosophic majority into a governing majority—in the White House, in the Congress, and throughout America.

We're going to get that majority not just because people have grown tired of the Democrats, but because they see in the Republican Party a better chance to realize the American Idea.

That idea has made us the freest, most prosperous and generous society on the face of the earth. But in recent years, it has been threatened by an administration which has allowed our country to decline in every way—economically, militarily, and spiritually. But the Republican Party does not plan to make a career out of merely criticizing what the Democratic Party stands for. We are telling the American people what we stand for.

As Governor Ronald Reagan has been saying, this is not just a campaign to defeat Jimmy Carter or to replace Democrats with Republicans, although these things must happen. It's a crusade to expand opportunity for all of our people. To restore a dollar that's as good as gold.

To revive incentives in our economy for both labor and capital. And to rebuild a defense and foreign policy worthy of respect.

This is the central purpose of a political party—to offer people superior ideas, and leadership.

Our party was founded on the irresistible idea that the Declaration of Independence applies to everyone. Mr. Lincoln inspired our party with the conviction that the ultimate source of progress and prosperity is the equal freedom of all Americans to fulfill their hopes and dreams for a better future.

The America idea was never that everyone would be leveled to the same position in life. The American Idea was that each individual should have the same opportunity to rise as high as his effort and initiative and God-give talent could carry him. If you were born to be a master carpenter, or a mezzo-soprano—or even a pro-football player—here in America you could make it.

America was founded on this sense of social and economic boundlessness. For the first time in history, a government was established, not with the power to bestow happiness—or withhold it—but to create the climate in which each individual, guided by Judeo-Christian values, could pursue his or her own happiness.

This idea of government was not only revolutionary, it's the only one that has ever really worked. It has not worked flawlessly; there have always been those among us who have been unjustly deprived or opportunity. But over the years, more and more of our citizens have gotten their chance to participate in the dream, and the lesson remains unchanged: No government has ever been able to do as much for people as they can do for themselves—and for each other—if only they are given the opportunity.

But somewhere we have gotten off the track. We have strayed from this idea, and every single America n knows it. For the first time in our history, we feel our strength ebbing, our sense of national purpose waning. After a quarter-century under the Democrats, our country no longer projects a national vitality to the rest of the world. And the Soviet Union behaves as if the United States has already been eclipsed as the world's most respected power.

Even President Carter senses this. But somehow he has persuaded himself that people are to blame. One year ago tonight, in a televised address, he told us that the country is in the grip of a malaise, an economic and social crisis of confidence.

He said: "Too many of us now tend to worship self-indulgence and consumption." He told us we are demanding too much, expecting too much, and are too unwilling to give. His solution is to impose limits on us, to shrink our opportunities for personal and national growth.

Again and again, in word and deed, Jimmy Carter has clearly stated his belief that people are the problem, and that austerity is the answer.

Ladies and gentlemen, austerity is not the answer; austerity is the problem. The American people are not the problem. They are the answer.

This neo-Malthusian idea that "less is more" is nonsense. Less is less. You can't help America's poor by making America poor. But the policies of this administration are making the whole country poorer.

Mr. Carter believes that unemployment is the answer to inflation. If that were the case, then the Carter anti-inflation plan ought to be enjoying its finest hour. The notion that laying off workers will fight inflation doesn't make sense to the steel workers of Buffalo or the auto workers of Detroit. By that definition, they've been fighting inflation for the past ten years.

Detroit and Buffalo have a lot in common. They both depend heavily on the steel and auto industries. And they are both places where the pain of a contracting economy is felt first and most sharply. When the jobs disappear, you can immediately see what a tragedy it is for working men and women and their families.

But an even larger tragedy is that this forced suffering is needless. As Margaret Bush Wilson of the NAACP has told us, "Inflation is not caused by too many people working," Only the government can cause inflation. Throughout history, the single cause of persistent inflation has been the government's cheapening of its currency.

It's immoral to tell working men and women to hold their wage increases to 8 percent while the government devalues their paychecks at 12 percent.

No, ladies and gentlemen. Recession is not the cure for inflation. And inflation is not the cure for unemployment.

By restoring opportunity through economic growth, we can have full employment without inflation, a rising standard of living, and a strong defense. The American people know we can, because we have done it before.

This is the choice before Americans in 1980. We can have growth, expansion, hope and opportunity—for our nation, our cities, our neighborhoods and our children. In this kind of atmosphere, we can live our lives and settle our differences calmly and reasonably.

Or, we can have contraction, suffering and austerity with the bitter social divisiveness that these conditions bring. Which will it be? An era of limits, or an era of expansion? An era of despair, or one of hope?

Not long ago, a reporter asked President Carter's office spokesman, Jody Powell, what a second Carter term would be like. He said: "Another term probably wouldn't be markedly different from the first."

Can you imagine anything more depressing?

The next four years must be markedly different—not only for our own welfare and destiny, but for the world's. Our nation's defense is the ultimate guarantor of world peace. World peace should not be held hostage by our economic and military weakness.

But the world is ultimately ruled not by military might; it is ruled by ideas. From the founding of this nation, ideas have been our chief export to the rest of the world.

In recent decades, we have been exporting the wrong idea that government is the source of prosperity. Those who took this advice, especially the emerging nations of the Third World, have found that it did not work. The reason, of course, is that our own progress was not achieved in that way. Our country was built on individuals, through their families and communities. It was built from the people up, not from the government down.

In the 1980s, as we rediscover this formula for our success, we must remedy the past and export the true American Idea—not merely in search of allies, but because we believe in it and because it is the right thing to do.

This is the difference between a positive foreign policy and the one we have now, which merely reacts to one disaster after another.

No other nation in the world faces this opportunity or this responsibility. Two years ago at Harvard, Alexander Solzhenitsyn said, "If America does not lead the Free World, the Free World will not have a leader."

Republican Convention, Detroit, 1980

And, ladies and gentlemen, it is equally clear that if the Republican Party does not lead America, America will not have a leader.

Fellow Republicans. Fellow Americans. We will provide this leadership. Here this week, here in Detroit, here in this hall—as a party united at last—with Ronald Reagan, we will begin the American Renaissance.

Black Americans and the Republican Party

The Honorable Jack Kemp

National Urban League Conference
Cleveland, Ohio, July 30, 1984

"Our party was born out of the struggle for equality and opportunity—the two always went together ... But somewhere along the way the Republican Party blundered and strayed ... One day millions of black Americans are going to surprise themselves by voting Republican again."

I'd like to thank John Jacob for his warm introduction and for inviting me to address the 1984 conference of the National Urban League. I've considered John Jacob a friend for a long time, and it is characteristic of his habit of putting others first that when he invited me to speak, he said I would be doing him a personal favor—when of course he was doing me a great honor.

John does not seek the limelight, but as president of the National Urban League he has shown a steady capability and quiet courage in speaking candidly, both inside and outside the black community, about the challenges facing disadvantaged Americans, and what needs to be done. I've been hoping for a chance to say publicly how much I admire his leadership and dedication, as I do that of Vernon Jordan before him.

I would also like to pay tribute to the National Urban League. For 74 years, you have brought hope and an equal chance to the jobless, the homeless, the unskilled, the lost and the least. You have initiated self-help efforts, demonstrated what works, and built partnerships of trust with institutions that ought to get involved. You have earned the respect of business and labor, civic and civil rights leaders, and both political parties. Through personal experience with dedicated people like Leroy Coles in Buffalo I have learned how much the Urban League is doing on a local as well as a national level.

As you know, I don't stand before you as a candidate for anything—except for re-election to an eighth term as a congressman from Buffalo. But I would like to take this opportunity to share with you some thoughts on the condition and direction of our nation. And most of all, I would like to speak to you, from the heart, about something that has been on my mind for a long time—the relationship between black Americans and the Republican Party.

Back in February, my wife Joanne and I happened to watch a fascinating program on Tony Brown's Journal, called "the longest struggle." It was a dramatization of the lives of black Americans in the period after reconstruction, which he described as a "reign of terror" against blacks and Republicans, aimed at depriving black Americans of their First Amendment right to vote. And at one point in his narration, Tony Brown said, "during this period the best friend that blacks had was the Republican Party, led by two radical Republican congressmen," representative Thaddeus Stevens of Pennsylvania, and Senator Charles Sumner of Massachusetts.

Frankly, rather than making me feel good as a Republican, this really saddened me. Perhaps it was the thought of how long it's been since black Americans could feel that way about my party. And perhaps the feeling was deepened because many people at various times have called me a "radical" Republican—and not always meaning it kindly. But according to the dictionary, "radical" means going to the roots of things. And I remember thinking how much the Republican Party needs radical Republicans in that sense.

The Republican Party would not even exist except for black Americans. Our party was born out of the struggle for equality and opportunity—the two always went together. When you look back at the years from 1860 to 1932, when Republicans dominated American politics, it was always because of two reasons: civil rights for all, and economic opportunity for all. Once chattel slavery was abolished and all Americans had the constitutional right to vote, campaigns were fought and won on slogans like "a full dinner pail," "honest money," and later, on restoring pre-World War I prosperity and "normalcy." Back then we Republicans seemed to know in our bones that without full and expanding economic opportunity for everyone, pressing for legal equality, important as it is, was not going to be enough and as long as we pursued both, the American people, and especially black Americans, responded with loyalty.

But somewhere along the way the Republican Party blundered and strayed. Somehow we mislaid the key to prosperity and full economic opportunity for all. The policy failures of 1929-1932—when Republicans preached not economic growth but economic austerity, not internationalism but protectionism, not civil rights but "what's good for business is good for America"—paved the way for the massive electoral shift toward the New Deal and the Democratic Party.

That shift is taken for granted today. But for black Americans, it didn't occur without a struggle. In 1932 the Republicans, after all, were still the party of Lincoln and civil rights, while the Democratic Party was still mired in reconstruction mentality, still implicitly defending white Supremacy.

I've met elderly blacks who can still remember black preachers preaching furiously against the Democrats and the New Deal, threatening hellfire and damnation for those who would dare desert the party of Lincoln. A majority of black Americans still voted for Hoover in 1932. And in 1940, Dr. Ralph Bunche could still say that the black vote was "essentially Republican"—the GOP had accumulated that much loyalty. While Republicans have a negative image with blacks today, consider what Roosevelt had to contend with. When a black minister opened one session of the 1936 Democratic Convention and a black congressman seconded FDR's nomination, Senator "Cotton Ed" Smith stormed out of the convention, saying, "I cannot and will not be a party to the recognition of the 14th and 15th amendments."

But it was no use. Hoover Republicans offered a balanced budget, and Roosevelt offered buttered bread. In a book called Farewell to the Party of Lincoln: Black Politics in the Age of FDR, N.J. Weiss has written: "It was not civil rights, it was jobs that brought blacks to the Democratic Party. Blacks became Democrats," Weiss observes, "because the Democrats had a program that was going to help the underprivileged, or the poor, more than the Republican Party." In fact, in this month's Ebony magazine there's an article that quotes an 82-year-old black activist named Valores Washington, who said: "I was born when there was nothing but black Republicans. I can remember when you couldn't find a black Democrat. But the Democrats fed blacks when they needed feeding."

The Democratic Party deserves its due, and I'm not ashamed to give it. Besides the New Deal and the War On Poverty, the Democratic Party—at least a large portion of it—carried to completion the fight to get rid of legal barriers to social and political participation for minorities. I'm proud that a Republican Chief Justice, appointed by a forceful Republican president, eliminated legal segregation of schools at Little Rock and elsewhere; and that overwhelming support by the Republican minority in Congress finally made the right to vote a reality for black Americans. But that doesn't change the fact that most people today, Republicans and Democrats alike, have come to consider the Democratic Party as the "natural" political home of black Americans.

For many reasons, I'm convinced that this situation is not healthy—not for blacks, not for my party, and most of all, not for America. I don't have to tell you how strong the temptation has been for the Democrats to take the black vote for granted, and for the Republicans to write it off. But I believe the Republican tendency comes not from indifference or ill will, but from a kind of utter despair built up during 50 years of failure to reach out successfully to black Americans, and perhaps to fully understand the true basis of equal opportunity as well as we used to. I was impressed when Jesse Jackson said in San Francisco that "democracy guarantees opportunity, not success." Equal opportunity has been likened to a race where everyone starts out together and the prizes go to those who most merit them. What I think some members of my party don't fully appreciate is the degree to which past impediments are preventing many blacks from beginning at the same starting line with others who never had those impediments.

My hope for the future of my country and my party rests on the fact that the American people are forgiving. They are forgiving because they are forward-looking. They are less interested, ultimately, in what you've done for them in the past—or to them, for that matter—than in what you plan to do for them in the future. This is why I am confident that if my party puts forward a vision of the future that embraces freedom and justice for all Americans, and a way of getting there, it will not be long before the Democrats find a tidal wave of "their" supporters returning to the Republican Party.

The recent black family summit conference, co-sponsored by the National Urban League and the NAACP, put the first item on their agenda for economic security for black families very simply: "Top priority should be placed on full employment at livable wages for all persons able and willing to work." And as John Jacob told us so eloquently last night, "jobs are the single central burning issue on the black agenda in 1984." I'm proud to say that it is the Republican Party which has begun to take the lead in moving the country toward full employment with no inflation.

Believe it or not, adopting the goal of full employment four years ago was considered a risky thing to do. Remember that back then, economists and politicians were almost universally telling us that it simply couldn't be done without high inflation, or perhaps not at all. The Carter administration was telling us that we were in the grip of a malaise, and Federal Reserve Chairman Paul Volcker said we had to lower our standard of living.

Prof. Alfred Kahn, the chief "inflation-fighter," actually said that the solution to the energy crisis was to ride bicycles. And Robert Lekachman, one of the most prominent liberal-democratic economists in the country, summed up this mentality when he said: "The era of growth is over and the era of limits is upon us. It means the whole politics of the country has changed. All problems have become distributional. We already see it," he said, "in a whole set of divisive tendencies: black versus Jew, men versus women, and the whole debate over energy policy." How can you be fair to anyone in a country suffering from 13 percent inflation, 21 percent interest rates, closed factories and lost jobs?

If this country was not in fact going to tear itself apart in a struggle over pieces of a shrinking economic pie, we had to ignore the "experts," get this economy expanding again without inflation, and above all create jobs. I think it's fair to say that by 1980 the Democrats, like the Republicans in 1932, had lost the key to expanding economic opportunity, but frankly, we "radical" Republicans simply turned to the ideas of the last president who actually achieved full employment without inflation: John F. Kennedy, a Democrat. In fact, that's where we got the idea of cutting tax rates across the board.

Just after the 1980 elections, I saw an interview with Walter Mondale on what it was like to be a Democrat during President Kennedy's growth policies. It seemed like such a good description of what I hoped we could accomplish in the next four years that I saved it. Here's what he said about the early 1960s:

At that time, we were able to cut tax rates, increase revenues, add jobs, fund new programs, and keep a stable dollar. That was a good time for a Democrat to be alive ... We did a lot of good things. One of the reasons was that you could get our nation in a more compassionate frame of mind when you were sharing additional resources from growth. Nobody was losing anything ... You could say: 'how about feeding the hungry? How about educating those poor kids? How about having some decent housing for these families that are living in desperate conditions?' People would say, 'that's right, let's do some of that.'"

Ladies and gentlemen, at that time, Walter Mondale got it right. That's what we have tried to do by cutting tax rates across the board. The tax rate cuts were not designed to be an attack on government or its revenues. They were an effort to get the country moving again. We need a safety net, but we also need a ladder of opportunity. And opportunities on the public payroll are no substitute for jobs in the private sector. But people naturally choose public jobs over private jobs when private employment isn't there.

True, mistakes have been made. The across-the-board tax cuts were delayed. The Federal Reserve took us into a deep recession and kept us there too long with a misguided policy of high-interest-rate monetarism. And I've caught flak for saying so, but I still believe you can't make big cuts in social spending when the economy is flat on its back.

Despite these flaws, under this administration the 1981 tax cuts have powered a noninflationary economic expansion that began at the end of 1982. With inflation at its lowest level in 20 years, 6.7 million Americans have found work in the last 19 months. That's more jobs than the entire continent of Europe has created in a decade.

But it's not enough. It's not nearly enough. As Vernon Jordan says, putting America back to work means putting black Americans back to work.

I think we need to do more, much more. And I would like to outline some ideas that I believe can be effective in reaching the poor, the minorities and the inner cities.

But first I would like to say a word about keeping the recovery going. If we want to marshal the social resources we need to reach out to the poor and to assist the decayed inner cities it is imperative that we keep this economic expansion going, and going strongly. Strong economic expansion is the foundation for social justice: you can't help the poor by making America poor. An economic slowdown would stop or even reverse the progress on job creation, and the ones hurt most would be the last hired and first fired. It would also be an incalculable social and political blow—because it would intensify all the tensions and zero-sum wrangling in our country that Robert Lekachman talked about.

As I see it, there are two major threats to this economic expansion. One is monetary policy. Incredibly enough, the Federal Reserve Board believes that it must slow down economic growth and keep unemployment from falling too fast so as to keep inflation under control. That's not just insensitive; it's irrational. Inflation is not caused by too many people working. When commodity prices are falling sharply as they have in the past few months, and the dollar is hitting record highs, this means high interest rates are signaling that money is too tight, not too loose; we have deflation, not inflation. If the Fed doesn't change course and allow interest rates to come down, we could see a slowdown, a rise in unemployment, defaults in the Third World, further despair in our cities—and higher, not lower deficits.

The other major threat to expansion would be the enactment of a major tax increase. And if you will forgive me for a moment for being partisan, the bigger threat comes from the Democratic, not the Republican candidate for president. Mr. Mondale has promised a big tax increase across the board to reduce the deficit. The president says it would be counterproductive. I wish that Mr. Mondale would read a speech that President Roosevelt gave during the campaign of 1936, when the Republicans were saying all the same things about the deficit that the Democrats are saying today. The speech was titled, "The Only Way to Keep the Government Out of the Red Is to Keep the People Out of the Red." In that speech, Mr. Roosevelt explained:

> *The money to run the government comes from taxes; and the tax revenue depends for its size on the size of the national income. When the incomes and the values and transactions of the country are on the downgrade, then tax receipts go on the downgrade too. If the national income continues to decline, then the government cannot run without going into the red. The only way to keep the government out of the red is to keep the people out of the red. And so we [have] to balance the budget of the American people before we [can] balance the budget of the national government.*

"That makes sense doesn't it?" FDR asked. "To pile on vast new taxes would get us nowhere because values [would go] down, and that makes sense too."

In that same speech, Mr. Roosevelt addressed another of Mr. Mondale's recent worries. He said,

> *And now a word about this foolish fear about the crushing load the debt will impose on your children and mine. This debt is not going to be paid by oppressive taxation on future generations. It is not going to be paid by taking away the hard-won savings of the present generation. It is going to be paid out of an increased national income and increased individual incomes produced by increasing national prosperity. The deficit of the national government has been steadily declining for three years running.*

And the deficit is declining right now as we put people back to work. Over the past year, revenues have risen at a rate of 12 percent while spending has risen only 4 percent. Despite all the talk you've heard, the deficit has never reached $200 billion, and it never will—if we can keep the economy expanding and continue to move America toward full employment and price stability, the stated goal of the Humphrey-Hawkins legislation.

President Roosevelt used to say that we have nothing to fear but fear itself. I hope it never comes to be said of his heirs to the leadership of the Democratic Party, that they have nothing to offer but fear itself. Democrats who cherish the future of their party had better hope that the "new realism" does not turn out to be the "old Hooverism." We Republicans will wish them as much luck as we had with it.

As I said, while keeping the economic recovery going, we still must do more for the poor and the unemployed, especially in our inner cities. As far as I'm concerned, we have barely begun to address the problem of expanding economic opportunity to everyone. But Bobby Kennedy was right when he said, "to ignore the potential of private enterprise is to fight the war on poverty with a single platoon, while great armies are left to stand aside."

I am proposing a three-part urban initiative, and I want to make it a plank in the Republican platform. First, a complete overhaul of our tax system, designed especially to break the poverty cycle that is holding back so many low-income Americans. Second, a new Urban Homesteading Act designed to bring us closer to the national goal stated in the 1949 Housing Act, of "a decent home and a decent living environment for every American family." And third, an inner-cities, private-sector jobs creation bill to expand opportunities for inner-city residents.

First. Senator Bob Kasten and I, along with many colleagues, have proposed legislation to replace our current complicated, unfair and unintelligible income tax system with a fair and simple tax that closes loopholes and lowers tax rates. There is much said today in both parties about tax reform. And that is a good sign that reform may be possible. Some think tax reform means taking more taxes from some people and giving it to others; but true reform is aimed at expanding the income of everyone—permitting wealth to be created, not just shifted around.

One of the most glaring injustices today is that there are people below the poverty level who are paying, in effect, the highest marginal tax rates in the country. For example, what happens when a poor black woman drawing welfare payments, food stamps, and other benefits tries to increase her income by finding full-time work? She discovers that between paying income taxes and losing benefits, she, loses between 80 cents and $1.50 for every additional dollar of income. Her effective marginal tax rate is between 80 and 150 percent. That's one key reason for the poverty cycle.

The Kemp-Kasten tax bill helps poor people by doubling the personal exemption for each family member to two thousand dollars, increasing the standard deductions, and excluding one-fifth of the first $40,000 of wages from taxation. This means that almost a million and a half working poor would be completely taken off the federal income tax rolls. A family of four would not pay income tax on the first $14,375 of income, compared with less than $9,000 under current law. And because we index the tax

Code against inflation, no American below the poverty level will ever again pay federal income taxes under this plan.

Second. Owning your own home is nearly synonymous with the American Dream. Yet today homeownership for the urban poor is nearly impossible, when decent homes in any city can't be bought for much below forty or fifty thousand dollars, at double digit mortgage rates.

This week I'm introducing legislation addressed to those thwarted hopes. Under the Urban Homesteading Act, the poor living in public housing will have the chance to buy their homes from the government at a large discount, or to manage their own projects. Under my bill a tenant or tenant association could purchase their dwelling at only 25 percent of market value and the public housing authority could "take back" a mortgage at reasonable rates. Tenants could also build equity toward their down payment by maintaining the housing project.

This program has important tenant protections. First, ownership is completely voluntary. Second, there can't be any evictions of current tenants. Third, housing must be brought up to minimum standards before they are sold. And fourth, homeownership would be transferred to tenants only after it is certified that they can afford the cost.

This program would benefit both the urban poor and taxpayers as a whole. Taxpayers would gain from reduced operating subsidies as public housing is turned over to tenant owners. But the effort is really concerned with more than buildings or budgets. It deals with the overall problem of community and neighborhood development. There are some tenant managed projects operating today, and they have relieved some very difficult social problems by reducing crime, drug abuse, and even teenage pregnancies. Homeownership also encourages stable and intact family life. Considering the tremendous gain in pride, dignity, and sense of community; the longer outlook on life and the future; the new reasons to work and save—this kind of home ownership initiative would help more Americans realize the American Dream.

Third, and linking the first two initiatives, we must have Enterprise Zones. Ghetto and barrio residents know only too well the phenomenon known as "redlining," which has pushed the deterioration in some areas even further down the slope of despair. The idea of urban Enterprise Zones is to turn those red lines into green lines, by providing incentives for people to work, hire, invest, and start up new business ventures in cities with officially defined "pockets of poverty" where unemployment is particularly high. It only takes common sense to realize that we can't have more employees without more employers. "Enterprise zones," to quote journalist Carl Rowan, "will make jobs available to many and thus give hope to almost all. And hope may be the most precious item at this time."

On no other issue has a wider, more devoted and broadly based consensus emerged than on Kemp-Garcia Urban Enterprise Zone legislation. Members of the Congressional Black Caucus have endorsed it. The Urban League, I'm happy to say, has supported the idea. My friend and colleague from Philadelphia, Bill Gray, has called it one of the most important pieces of urban legislation in years. Hispanics, liberals, conservatives, Democrats, Republicans, big city mayors, suburban and rural areas, all support it as a constructive and progressive effort to help put our people to work in productive, real jobs in our inner cities and other depressed areas.

This measure has passed the Republican-controlled Senate twice this session. Yet Speaker Tip O'Neill of Boston and Ways and Means Committee Chairman Dan Rostenkowski of Chicago are preventing Congress from voting on this jobs-creating bill. I hope you'll forgive me another partisan comment if I say that we heard a lot in San Francisco about the Democratic Party's compassion for the poor. Let's just hope they don't love the poor so much that they're trying to keep them poor by bottling up enterprise zone legislation.

What I've just outlined is the nucleus of a plan that I think can help restore the hopes and dreams of inner-city residents. I agree with the Urban League that such proposals should be considered an adjunct, not a substitute, for current programs. And we must do still more. I joined recently with Bill Gray in introducing the "Pre-Vocational and Community-Based Organization Act." This bill will bring the Urban

League and other community-based organizations like Rev. Leon Sullivan's Opportunities Industrialization Centers (OIC), into the different boards and councils that administer vocational education programs, and make possible grants and set-asides. This is another important way to expand invaluable self-help efforts for our urban minorities and rural poor who need a helping hand.

Ladies and gentlemen, we can't allow fighting poverty to become passé. The civil rights revolution opened doors that had been closed by law. But as Martin Luther King Jr. reminded us, it will not be complete until America's doors of economic opportunity are fully opened and our minorities are integrated into the mainstream of the American economy. When black Americans have struggled for decades for the right to buy a ticket on the train of opportunity, we can't allow that train to be stopped in its tracks. We can't stop thinking creatively about fighting poverty, and renewing our cities.

The American people are compassionate. They aren't against helping people. They aren't against welfare. But we must measure our compassion not by how many people are on welfare, but by how few need welfare. We've learned that equal opportunity doesn't mean making the rich poor; it means making everyone better off, from the bottom up. It is true, as some say, that that government is best which governs least; but it is equally true that that government is best which does most for people. Leadership requires understanding the proper role for government.

I agree with Walter Mondale, that we don't need a referendum on the past. We need a vision for the future. But I would remind him that this means more than saying you want to get to the land of milk and honey. It means showing us exactly how we can get to the promised land. And black Americans this year should seriously ask the Democratic Party—as well as the Republican Party—exactly what they have in mind for the United States of America in 1985 and beyond. It's my firm belief that whichever party can show the poor, minorities, and all Americans that it has both the necessary vision and the means to achieve that vision, will command the loyalty of the American people.

As a Republican, I am going to work to make sure that my party is the majority party in coming years. To do that, we have to get back to our roots—become radical again. We must be the party of all the people—

even the ones that haven't voted for us lately. If we do our job—and I think, we can—then one day millions of black Americans are going to surprise themselves by voting Republican again.

And do you know what? When that happens, it will restore something to my party that's been missing for almost half a century. Because the Republican Party won't be whole again, until black Americans consider it their natural home again.

My Friends, We Have a Revolution to Finish

The Honorable Jack Kemp

Remarks Prepared for Delivery to Republicans at Federal Hall
New York, NY, March 27, 1987

"The American Revolution is the only revolution in history which did not disappoint its architects. But that productive tension between principles and action must continue to challenge and motivate, to move an energize us today. Ours is an unfinished revolution..."

My friends, my colleagues. We assemble here today with two agendas: to look back at the Constitution and to move our country forward. But first, I want to preface my remarks with a personal reflection.

I can 't help looking back on 16 years with you—with our House Republican Conference. As I start my ninth term, I realize how much I've learned from all of you. And even during those times when I was talking—and talking, and talking—believe it or not I was listening too, and learning. I was learning what it means to transform ideas into policy, what it means to support and be supported by one 's colleagues and friends, what it means to represent a district while at the same time serving the interests of our nation in the peoples' House: The House of Representatives. My time in the House may be coming to an end now, but from the bottom of my heart, I want to thank you for the privilege of serving with you, and fighting side by side with you. Whatever may happen, wherever I may go, I want you to know that I will always be a man of the House.

And now together we look back with awe at the genius of those who framed our Constitution. In 1787, in a world struggling under a multitude of tyrannies, with no existing model of freedom and democracy to guide them, the Founders were able to fashion a document which has guided us through two centuries, and will help steer us through many more. We all know the American Constitution is the oldest charter of free people in the world—yet it is also the youngest, because it was written to be renewed and rejuvenated. As Goethe observed: "That which our fathers have bequeathed us must be earned anew by each succeeding generation."

When the Founders set out to "establish justice, insure domestic tranquility, provide for the common defense, promote the general welfare, and secure the Blessings of Liberty," they could not have known two-hundred years later the world would still be struggling under tyrannies—some far more dangerous and despotic than those of the Eighteenth century. But they did not need to see the future, for they understood the frailty of human nature—but they were sustained by the ultimate Judeo-Christian belief that, as Jefferson said, "the God who gave us life gave us liberty at the same time."

At President Reagan's first State of the Union address

No nation, no people, no elected representatives in the world have a prouder legacy. The American Revolution is the only revolution in history which did not disappoint its architects. But that productive tension: the tension between principles and action must continue to challenge and motivate, to move and energize us today.

Ours is an unfinished revolution—and I'm not referring now only to the eighteenth century, but to the 1980s. The Reagan Revolution remains unfinished. And it falls to us to move it into the 1990s.

As a member of the House of Representatives, and as a member of our conference, I truly feel blessed that I have seen and taken part, with you, in a great "sea change" in American politics. During the past six years, we, though a minority in the House, have achieved unprecedented victories. Together with President Reagan, we have changed the debate. We changed it on the economy. We changed it culturally. And we changed it internationally. Just as Ronald Reagan has been to our era what Jefferson was to his—the visionary, the realignment figure—I believe that the modern Madisons, Hamiltons, Jays, and Adams are in this room today.

We have made a beginning, but only a beginning. While we have changed the terms of the debate, we have yet to win the debate.

Two-hundred years ago, freedom was only a brave theory and a moral imperative. It had never been tried. Today we see the stunning success it has brought to every part of the world it has touched. What began in cities like Philadelphia and New York has helped to transform the hopes of the globe. We were the first.

But the same ideals are having similar, if younger, anniversaries from Europe to Asia, and from Latin America to Africa. And despite the false claims and illusions of socialism and Marxism, we know—and are proving—that the best answer to poverty and despair is freedom. For freedom leads to democracy and free enterprise, which lead to growth and opportunity for everyone—and the poor most of all. You and I know freedom works, but the debate and the struggle are far from over.

Some think that to talk about the poor is the same as helping them. I believe the truly compassionate course is to create opportunities for the poor to become the formerly poor: to create jobs for those on welfare and ladders of hope and dignity for our youth and our minorities. Shouldn't the family in public housing who works hard and saves, get the chance to buy that housing and become homeowners? Shouldn't inner-city and rural poor have the same opportunity to become employers and employees through Enterprise Zones as the rest of the country? Shouldn't working men and women be able to count on government policies which will guarantee. the purchasing power of the dollar for today and tomorrow?

Two-hundred years ago, after the collapse of the Continental dollar, the Framers recognized that the burden of bad money falls on the people themselves: when there's inflation, the breadwinner loses his savings; and when there's inflation, he loses his job. The value of money sounds like an academic debate, but it translates into hard political reality. Americans deserve to know that their future security, savings, and potential for world trade, are not at the mercy of fluctuating currencies and volatile exchange rates.

Let's give the American people a choice. Let's allow them to choose between the politics of taxes and spending and envy and the politics of full employment, honest money, and equal opportunity. The revolution is unfinished.

My friends, I believe that as we move forward into our third century, we need to look even more closely at how we define compassion. From the day that we first affirmed our commitment to "Life, Liberty, and the Pursuit of Happiness," we have struggled as a society with the question of just who would be included under the protection of those inalienable rights. In Lincoln's day, black men and women were decreed to be non-persons by the Dred Scott decision of 1857. Today, the question of who is a person and therefore protected by our laws and basic human dignity divides us again.

The debate now, like the debate over slavery, is a human rights issue. It goes to the heart of our Judeo-Christian reverence for life. The 1973 Roe v. Wade decision tried to take personhood away from the unborn. And when you take personhood, you take human rights.

There is no escaping the fact that this issue stirs strong emotions. We must therefore proceed, like Lincoln, in a spirit of national union and reconciliation—offering help and forgiveness, not judgment nor self-righteousness. To be consistent and compassionate, we must also, as a society, show as much concern for a child and its family after it is born as before. But for the sake of our future, and our children's, I don't see how we can avoid the issue any longer, and still hope to become the nation we started out to be. Therefore, we must continue to push for the appointment of judges who believe in judicial restraint and who respect innocent human life. We must continue to press for constitutional protections for the unborn. And further, as legislators, we must try another route as well: passing legislation which would define "person" explicitly to include the unborn. The revolution remains unfinished.

No public policy decision we make in the next ten years, not on taxes or spending, not on agriculture nor on defense, will be as important as the decisions we make about strengthening and protecting the very bedrock of Western democratic values: the family. There is no better engine of economic growth, job training, savings, and investment than the traditional family.

There is no greater moral teacher, disciplinarian, help for the weak, protector of the young, or builder of character than the family. Our Democratic friends urge us to look to Washington as father and mother. But they have it exactly backwards. The family is the first and best Department of Health and Human Services, and Labor, and Education. The revolution is still unfinished.

I said at the beginning that the Framers of the Constitution understood human nature. But I doubt whether even they, with their suspicion of unchecked power, could have anticipated the organized, comprehensive assault on human dignity which the twentieth century's Nazis and Communists have introduced into the world. The Framers gave us the tools to form a "more perfect Union" but we must search within ourselves to find the tools to confront the central challenge of our century: the struggle between democracy and totalitarianism.

This morning we reflected on the constitutional mandate to "provide for the common defense." Yet today, in the Senate of the United States, the Democratic Chairman of the Armed Services Committee threatens a constitutional crisis unless the Anti-Ballistic Missile (ABM) Treaty is interpreted so narrowly as to prevent us from doing exactly that. My friends, there is no constitutional crisis—but there is a political and strategic challenge to our security. Let those who would prevent American technology from protecting American lives say so.

I say the United States of America has stood unprotected before Soviet nuclear weapons too long. The world has relied on Mutual Assured Destruction long enough. We have the knowledge and the skill to defend ourselves, and it should be obvious to all—especially when we are celebrating the birth of our Constitution—that we have no more urgent duty. No treaty interpretation, no arms control deal, is more important than defending America. The decision to move to early deployment of Strategic Defense Initiative (SDI) is not legal or technological: it is political—and it is overdue. Until we begin deployment, the revolution is unfinished.

The debate over Central America is the East/West struggle brought to our very doorstep. It is the basic challenge for those of us who do not view freedom and democracy as just another political preference—but as the fundamental rights of man. Resistance to communist expansion and support for those who are trying to escape communism's iron grip is a crucial aspect of U.S. national interest. But it is larger and deeper as well. It defines not just what we are against, but what we are for. The Reagan Doctrine is not framed in the negative. It doesn't seek to contain communism or achieve detente or mere coexistence. The Reagan Doctrine is hopeful, optimistic, and resolute. Simply put, it asks: "Why not victory?"

My friends, the Constitution of United States was written for the citizens of the United States. The Declaration of Independence was written for all mankind. Alexander Hamilton said, "The sacred rights of man are not to be rummaged for among old parchments or musty records. They are written, as with a sunbeam, in the whole volume of human nature, by the hand of Divinity itself, and can never be erased or obscured by mortal power." Those sacred rights belong as much to the refuseniks in the Soviet Union as to the campesinos in Central America; as much to the steelworkers in Gdansk as to the poor in Africa and the freedom fighters in Angola or Afghanistan, in Kampuchea, Mozambique, and Nicaragua. In foreign policy especially, the revolution for democracy is unfinished.

Finally, I do not view America's future responsibilities as a great power and the Leader of the Free World with dread. I think we are fortunate—I think it's exciting—to be living in a time when freedom is on the march and when it is within our power to change the great question of our day from: "Can we resist communist expansion?" to "Can they resist democracy?"

We have the opportunity to be more than just the custodians of a noble tradition. We can be the missionaries. It is our duty to take the magnificent legacy of America and hand it down to our children intact. But we have a chance to do more. We can broaden and extend and export that legacy, for Americans and for the world. We can fulfill the promise of the past six years—and the past two hundred.

My friends, we have a revolution to finish.

The Politics of the Impossible

The Honorable Jack Kemp

The Heritage Foundation's President's Club
Washington, D.C., November 15, 1994

"Let me share a vision of the American Idea, deeply rooted in the conservative vision of the Founders. Return to people their resources, and they will accept their responsibilities. Return to people power, and they will rebuild the institutions of a free society. Return to people authority, and they will create the moral capital to help renew our nation."

To be a realist in America today, you must believe in miracles. Think of the things that until last Tuesday seemed a conservative pipe dream.

Who could have imagined Mario Cuomo giving a concession speech? Or Speaker Gingrich looking over the president's shoulder during the State of the Union? Or a new House committee on deregulation and privatization? Or The Heritage Foundation replacing the Kennedy School of Government at Harvard as the dominant intellectual force in the United States Congress?

Of course, the White House and the media are in deep denial.

President Clinton says the people voted for a quicker pace of "reinventing" government. We at Heritage reply that big-government programs cannot be reinvented that should never have existed in the first place.

Liberals say the election was not a rejection of Bill Clinton. We reply it is even more than that—it is the beginning of Ronald Reagan's third term.

Liberals say this election was a triumph of negativism. And we reply it was Democrats who tried to scare the elderly on Social Security, played the cards of race and class warfare, and practice bigotry against religious conservatives.

It is interesting, isn't it, that Franklin Roosevelt said in 1932, "the only thing we have to fear is fear itself," and today the only thing the Democrats have to offer is fear.

Democrats tried to make this an election about anger. But thanks to Newt Gingrich and Dick Armey, and with the help of organizations like

The Heritage Foundation and Empower America, we made this into an election about ideas—about opportunity, ownership, entrepreneurship, responsibility, education, safe streets, and jobs for all.

The Republican "Contract with America" turned an electoral victory into a national man-date. Now our challenge is to implement that mandate and truly build the city on a hill, plank by plank, brick by brick, and export it to a waiting world.

The election of 1994 was not just a rejection of the party in power. It was the rejection of the party with an elite view of power: power exercised by benevolent bureaucrats, power wielded by arrogant experts, power centralized in the hands of what Margaret Thatcher called the "nanny state."

It is not an exaggeration to say that 50 years of American history have found their resolu-tion in this moment. In that half century, Americans saw the power and potential of government devoted to the accomplishment of great goals. People trusted a federal government that had humbled the Kaiser, stormed Normandy, liberated Europe, split the atom, and helped win the long twilight struggle against communism. People gave of their taxes, gave of their freedom, and even gave their lives to show they were equal to the challenge of their times.

But that same federal power was soon applied—and, in most cases, misapplied—at home.

The organized, centrally directed prosecution of a war became the dominant metaphor of American politics: a liberal war on poverty, a war on crime.

That metaphor became the liberal theory of power top-down and organized by an aristocracy of experts. This became the official ideology of the Democratic Party—the only real banner it carried into battle.

Government, it was promised, could defeat poverty, could replace families, could create wealth and redistribute it, and almost wipe the tears from every eye. The inalienable right to pursue happiness enshrined in our Declaration became an "entitlement" program.

But confidence in government has been broken against the simple, solid fact of human suffering and government failure. After $5 trillion in well-intentioned but misguided spending, the sleep of children in our cities is disturbed by gunfire. They enter their school through a metal detector.

They sit in a classroom where no learning takes place. They are children without childhoods, and their experience is the final, conclusive testimony in the trial against imperial liberalism.

The rest of America is left wondering why we still bear the burdens of domestic wars that consist almost entirely of retreats and surrenders.

Why is the average family forced to pay nearly 40 percent of its income in taxes?

Why must parents be forced to take two or three jobs to support, feed, and educate their children?

Why are more Americans today employed producing government red tape than making cars, computers, or other manufactured goods?

Americans see no connection between this sacrifice and the performance of their government. They have lost faith in a liberalism which promised to save the world but could not save the peace in our streets.

For years, Democrats belittled anyone who questioned their methods as somehow selfish and hard-beaned or even bigoted and cruel. But Americans are not cold. They are not stingy. They are the most compassionate people in the world. But they cannot deny the evidence of their senses—clear evidence that the Great Society has done more harm than good, that welfare has created more dependence than opportunity.

We are not talking about money alone. We are wasting more than our national treasure.

We are undermining the essential elements of American character and of the American Idea—the things that make freedom work in our nation.

Centralized, bureaucratic power is undermining both community and responsibility. It attacks community because the power to replace an institution like a family or a neighborhood is the power to destroy it. And it destroys individual responsibility when government creates incentives to fail, when government penalizes marriage, family, work, and savings, all of which are stepping stones toward self-reliance.

The vacuum left by the collapse of liberalism has given Republicans and conservatives an opportunity few Americans have ever been given—a chance to remake America. Our goal now is not the containment of liberalism; it is to roll back its boundaries everywhere in our lives and expand the frontiers of freedom and opportunity for all.

The Bible says, "To whom much is given, much is required." Ladies and gentlemen, much has been given to conservatives in this election, and much is expected.

Our unfinished business is more difficult than any we have undertaken. Without a compelling vision, a new generation of reformers becomes a new establishment, to be rejected in turn. But the conservative movement has prepared for this moment for decades—since the founding of National Review, since the nomination of Barry Goldwater, since the election of Ronald Reagan, since The Heritage Foundation was just Ed Feulner's dream. Our revolution was interrupted, but never abandoned and now we are poised to complete it.

Let me share a vision of the American Idea, deeply rooted in the conservative vision of the Founders: Return to people their resources, and they will accept their responsibility. Return to people power, and they will rebuild the institutions of a free society. Return to people authority, and they will create the moral capital to help renew our nation.

This begins with some form of bureaucratic birth control. In 1937, a presidential commission concluded that government programs need "a coroner to pronounce them dead and an undertaker to dispose of the remains." Too many endless, useless public programs remain unburied. If a new Republican Congress can't privatize the National Education Association (NEA), then our mandate will be meaningless. And the National Endowment for the Humanities (NEH) and the SBA and the REA and PBS and agricultural subsidies. And while we're at it, we should privatize HUD, the IMF, the World Bank, and on and on.

But that is just the beginning. Our concern is not only for government's cost, but for its role and reach. Einstein said "a problem can never be solved by thinking on the same level that produced it." We must think on a deeper level—finding ways to reverse the tide of 50 years of impersonal centralization.

First, this means relocating government control from the federal level to states and localities close to their own problems.

Problem solving at the federal level means 500 experts, meeting in secret, producing 1,400-page "solutions." When problems are solved by states, you get a Tommy Thompson promoting school choice for inner-city children, a John Engler moving welfare recipients into work and education, a Christie Todd Whitman slashing income tax rates by 25 percent, a Fife Symington eliminating state income and capital gains taxes, and a George Allen empowering residents of public housing to manage their own communities and ultimately own their own homes.

This was the meaning of this election: wisdom lies outside Washington, and we should locate power there as well.

Second, a new conservative philosophy of government should disseminate power beyond government, directly to families and churches and community groups—institutions with spiritual and moral authority denied to federal power.

We should give families control over education and health care.

We should reduce their taxes so they can care for their own needs, be generous to others, and save for the future.

We should provide help to those in need, whenever possible, through private and religious groups experienced at both reform and reformation.

We should provide a safety net below which people should not be allowed to fall but, more important, a ladder of opportunity upon which all people can climb.

This would be a radical change, but it would also be a return to normalcy—to life as lived before American government was centralized by the struggles of our century.

It would mean the return to lower taxes, economic growth, stronger communities and families, and a limited federal government—to a stronger era of American life.

An America where the goals of education are set by the PTA, not the NEA

An America where the debate in Congress is over which taxes to cut, not which taxes to raise, about which government programs to privatize, not which ones to nationalize.

An America where prosperity begins on Main Street and extends to Wall Street, not the other way around.

An America where the character of children is shaped by their parents and grandparents, not by Donna Shalala and Joycelyn Elders.

But conservatives must offer more than a lament for a lost America. We must offer the vision of a new one. We have a responsibility, not just to diagnose what has failed, but to propose what will replace it.

With the Ryan brothers Tobin and future Speaker Paul Ryan, 1998

We need a tax code that is flat, fair, and simple—one that rewards work and entrepreneurial risk taking, that sets economic growth for all as its highest goal, not the redistribution of wealth or soaking the rich.

We need an education system where parents have influence and values have a voice- with school choice for parents in every community.

An antipoverty agenda based on democratic capitalism not socialism; on private ownership, not government control. Our definition of compassion is not how many people live on the government welfare plantation, but how many of our people are liberated from government dependence.

Our approach must empower people, not government. It helps men and women without robbing them of their birthright-control over their own lives.

The goal of government is not to secure happiness. It is to secure the God-given inalienable right to pursue happiness, to live our lives in obedience to conscience, not to government.

Conservatives must communicate a simple principle: that government governs best that allows us to govern ourselves.

We have stood together since a time when we met in the catacombs, not in conventions. Since a time when conservatism was known as "the forbidden faith" and "the thankless per- suasion." We have lived to see conservatism pronounced dead. We have lived to see it survive all of its would-be conquerors. And not just to survive, but to come to this threshold, when dreams become objectives and hopes become plans. It is an historical process that should be familiar: "the stone which the builders rejected has become the chief and corner stone."

Ladies and gentlemen, it is liberalism that now defends an old, crumbling order—an order maintained by threats and propped up by fear. Now it is conservatism that is the creed of intellectual liberty, of free markets, of faith in people.

We can be proud but not prideful, confident but not content, because our work is not done. It is time to become missionaries for our message in every forgotten corner of the American community. It is time for a new governing conservatism captured by a passion for the possible with a commitment to moving our nation ahead but, like the Good Shepherd, leaving no one behind.

One of the most dramatic moments in post-war history took place on New Year's day, 1990, in Prague. After four terms in prison, and over four decades of national repression, Vaclav Havel climbed a podium to be inaugurated as president of his county. "Let us teach ourselves and others," he told the crowd, "that politics can not only be the art of the possible, but the art of the impossible." And he ended his address with these words: "My people, your government has been returned to you."

On a cold January day, just over two years from now, a new president will mount a platform and take an oath and give a speech that should end, "My fellow Americans, your government has been returned to you." That is the politics of the impossible, suddenly made possible in our times.

Acceptance Speech – Nomination for Vice President

The Honorable Jack Kemp

Republican National Convention
San Diego, California, August 15, 1996

"Every generation faces a choice: hope or despair—to plan for scarcity or to embrace possibilities. Societies throughout history believed they had reached the frontiers of human accomplishment. But in every age, those who trusted the divine spark of imagination discovered that vastly greater horizons lay ahead."

Abraham Lincoln believed, you serve your party best by serving your country first. Ladies and Gentlemen, my fellow Americans, I can't think of a better way of serving our country than by electing Bob Dole president of the United States here on the eve of the 21st Century.

By the way, this time let's reelect a Republican Congress to help Bob Dole restore the American Dream.

Tonight, here in San Diego, Bob Dole and I begin this campaign to take our message of growth, hope, leadership and cultural renewal to all Americans.

As I said in Russell, Kansas, Bob Dole's hometown, we're taking our cause from the boroughs of New York to the barrios of Los Angeles. We will carry the word to every man, woman and child of every color and background that today, on the eve of the new American Century, it is time to renew the American promise, to recapture the American Dream and to give our nation a new birth of freedom ... with liberty, equality and justice for all.

I am putting our opponents on notice. We are asking for the support of every single American. Our appeal of boundless opportunity crosses every barrier of geography, race and belief. We may not get every vote, but we will speak to every heart. In word and action, we will represent our entire American family.

And so, in the spirit of Mr. Lincoln, who believed that the purpose of a great party is not to defeat the other party but to provide superior ideas, principled leadership and a compelling cause, I accept your nomination for Vice President of the United States.

Our convention is not just the meeting of a party, but a celebration of ideas. Our goal is not just to win, but to be worthy of winning.

The 1996 Republican Presidential ticket

This is a great nation with a great mission, and last night we nominated a leader whose stature is equal to that calling. A man whose words convey a quiet strength, who knows what it means to sacrifice for others, to sacrifice for his country, to demonstrate courage under fire. And who brings together women and men of all parties and backgrounds in common cause.

In recent years, it has been presidential practice, when delivering a State of the Union address, to introduce heroes in the balcony. Next year, when Bob Dole delivers the State of the Union address, there will be a hero at the podium.

There is another hero with us tonight—in our hearts and in our minds. He brought America back and restored America's spirit. He gave us a decade of prosperity and expanding horizons. Communism came down, not because it fell. He pushed it.

Our campaign is dedicated to completing that revolution that he began. I am sure he is watching us tonight. So let me just say to him, on behalf of all of us who love him. Thanks, Gipper.

And so tonight, as the party of Lincoln, Reagan and Dole, we begin our campaign to restore the adventure of the American Dream. With the end of the Cold War, all the "isms" of the 20th century—Fascism, Nazism, communism, Socialism, and the evil of Apartheidism—have failed. Except one. Only democracy has shown itself true to the hopes of humanity.

Democratic capitalism is not just the hope of wealth, but the hope of justice. When we look into the face of poverty, we see pain, despair and need. But, above all, in every face, we must see the image of God. The Creator of All has planted the seed of creativity in us all, the desire within every child of God to work and build and improve our lot in life, and that of our families and those we love.

And in our work, in the act of creating that is part of all labor, we discover that part within ourselves that is divine. I believe the ultimate imperative for growth and opportunity is to advance human dignity.

Dr. Martin Luther King believed that we must see a sleeping hero in every soul. America must establish policies that summon those heroes and call forth the boundless potential of the human spirit. But our full potential will never be achieved by following leaders who call us to timid tasks and diminished dreams.

Every generation faces a choice: hope or despair—to plan for scarcity or to embrace possibilities. Societies throughout history believed they had reached the frontiers of human accomplishment. But in every age, those who trusted the divine spark of imagination discovered that vastly greater horizons lay ahead.

Americans do not accept limits; we transcend them. We do not settle; we succeed. I learned this lesson as a child growing up in Los Angeles. My dad was a truck driver. He and my uncle bought the truck, started a trucking company, and he put four kids through college. From him and my mother, a teacher, I learned to never give up. To me, faith, family and freedom are the greatest gifts of God to humanity.

I believe that today America is on the threshold of the greatest period of economic opportunity, technological development and entrepreneurial adventure in our history. We have before us tomorrows that are even more thrilling than our most glorious yesterdays.

And yet the genius of the American people is being stifled. Our economy is growing at the slowest pace of any recovery in this century. The income of working men and women is actually dropping. And there is a gnawing feeling throughout our nation that—in some way, for some reason—there is something wrong.

Our friends in the other party say the economy is moving forward, and it is. But it is moving like a ship dragging an anchor, the anchor of high taxes, excessive regulation and big government.

They say that is the best we can hope for. But that is because they have put their entire trust in government rather than people—a government that runs our lives, our businesses, our schools. You see, they don't believe in the unlimited possibilities that freedom brings.

The Democratic Party today is not democratic. They're elitists—they don't have faith in the people. They have faith in government. That is why they raised taxes on the middle class. That is why they tried to nationalize our health-care system. That is why today they say they are 'unalterably opposed' to cutting taxes on American families. That is the problem with all elitists, they think they know better than the people—but the truth is, there is a wisdom and intelligence in ordinary women and men far superior to the greatest so-called experts.

That is why they are the party of the status quo. And as of tonight, with Bob Dole as our leader, we are the party of change.

Our first step will be to balance the budget with a strategy that combines economy in government with tax cuts designed to liberate the productive genius of the American people.

Now, of course, naysayers in Mr. Clinton's White House say it can't be done. They don't know Bob Dole. They don't know Jack Kemp.

As he and I have said before and we will continue to say throughout this campaign: with a pro-growth Republican Congress, balancing the budget while cutting taxes is just a matter of presidential will. If you have it, you can do it. Bob Dole has it. Bob Dole will do it. And I'll be with him—at his side—every step of the way.

But this is just the beginning— the first step. We are going to scrap the whole, fatally flawed Internal Revenue Code and replace it with a fairer, simpler, flatter system. We will end the IRS as we know it.

We will start with a 15 percent across-the-board tax cut, a $500 per child tax credit and cutting the capital gains tax by half. We're going to take the side of the worker, the saver, the family and the entrepreneur. The American people can use their money more wisely than can government. It's time they had more of a chance, and we will give them that chance.

On the eve of the 21st century, in the middle of a technological revolution that is transforming the world in which we live—how can it be that so many families find themselves struggling just to keep even, just to get by? As long as it takes two earners to do what one earner used to do, how can we say this economy is good enough?

Our tax cut means that parents will have more time to spend with their children—and with each other. It means that a working parent can afford to take a job that lets them be home when the kids get back from school. It means that the struggling, single mother in the inner city will find it easier to work her way off welfare.

And we cannot forget that single mother and her children. American society as a whole can never achieve the outer-reaches of potential, so long as it tolerates the inner cities of despair.

Recently I read the account by a reporter of his conversation with a ten-year-old child at Henry Homer public housing in Chicago. As the reporter told it in his book "I asked (the boy) what he wanted to be. 'If I grow up, I'd like to be a bus driver,' he told me. If, not when. At the age of ten, (he) wasn't sure he'd even make it to adulthood."

Think how much poorer our nation is, deprived of that child's future and those like him. Think how much richer our nation will be when every child is able to grow up to reach his or her God-given potential.

Including those who come to America from other countries. My friends, we are a nation of immigrants. The former president of Notre Dame University, Father Ted Hesburgh, said the reason we must close the backdoor of illegal immigration is so that we can keep open the front door of legal immigration and keep the light of opportunity lifted beside the golden door.

Our goal is not just a more prosperous America but a better America. An America that recognizes the infinite worth of every individual and, like the Good Shepherd, leaves the ninety-nine to find the one lost lamb.

An America that honors—in all its institutions—the values that mothers and fathers want to pass on to her children. An America that makes the ideal of equality a daily reality—equality of opportunity, equality in human dignity, equality before the laws of man as well as in the eyes of God.

An America that transcends the boundaries between races with the revolutionary power of a simple, yet profound idea—love thy neighbor as thyself.

We must remember all that is at stake in America's cultural renewal—not just the wealth of our nation but its meaning.

Today, more than ever before, American ideals and ideas grip the imaginations of women and men in every corner of the globe. Isn't it exciting to think, it's 1776 all over the world.

President Reagan spoke of America as a shining city on a hill, a light unto the nations. In decades past, so many of those who looked for our light did so from behind the walls and barbed wire of tyrannical regimes. Now, because the American people stood strong, those people are free.

But freedom is never guaranteed - and our nation and its president must be strong enough to stand up for freedom against all who would challenge it. A world of peace. A world of hope. This is what America's economic and cultural renewal means at home and around the globe.

This is what our cause is all about. ... Thank you and God bless America.

PART II
REFLECTIONS ON THE FUTURE OF THE AMERICAN IDEA

In the short essays that follow, six distinguished modern commentators offer their thoughts on the meaning of the American Idea today.

Former U.N. Ambassador John Bolton
"We care more about our own national character than what others may think of us. And that is exceptional."

Author Peter Wehner
"What is required, then, for free individuals to live as part of successful human societies is that they develop good character; that they be instructed not only about their rights but also their duties, and that their "morals" and "faculties" are cultivated."

Professor Brian Domitrovic
"… left to their own prodigious abilities, the American people can generate a marvelous society, a profound culture, and absolutely storied economic success."

Economist Douglas Holtz-Eakin
"The heart of the American Idea is the opportunity for personal reinvention."

Reagan (and Kemp) speechwriter Ben Elliott
"The power of the American Idea rescued our nation. It can do so again."

Economist/Journalist Stephen Moore
"All that is missing is a 21st century Kennedy, or Reagan or a new Kemp to restore America's confidence in itself. What is certain is that he or she is out there."

THE IDEA OF AMERICA
By John Bolton

Internationally, even though America is frequently viewed with admiration, there is often also a tinge of irritation, even among our allies, which shades into outright disdain and hatred among our enemies. The strong emotions evoked even by the idea of America—let alone "the American Idea"—testify to the reality that our experience has in many ways truly differed profoundly from that of other peoples and nations.

Foreign observers understood this point as early and as clearly as Americans themselves. Lord North, British Prime Minister during our War of Independence, said in 1778, "For if America should grow into a separate empire it must of course cause . . . a revolution in the political system of the world." And the astute French observer Alexis de Tocqueville first characterized us as "exceptional" in his masterful Democracy in America, saying, "the position of the Americans is therefore quite exceptional, and it may be believed that no democratic people will ever be placed in a similar one."

Since 2014 marks the 100th anniversary of World War I's outbreak, it is worth recalling historically exactly how America has actually understood its place in the world. Many believe U.S. entry into the first World War reversed a consistent, longstanding policy of isolationism, albeit laying the foundation for the "American Century" that followed. The reality, however, is far more complex. Both before and after the American Expeditionary Force began embarking for France in 1917, we well understood that unique factors and circumstances provided us a truly different historical role and perspective.

Our geographical remoteness, the lack of pre-existing social structures, and our ancestors' intentions to find here freedom and opportunity—religious, economic, or political—all formed a historical confluence entirely different than what Europe had faced before. To be sure, Africans were brought here in bondage, and Native Americans were far too often denied elemental fairness, but these were most emphatically violations of the emerging American Idea, not elements of it. Acknowledging our errors should not lead us to denigrate or discard the idea itself, but to cherish it all the more.

Our geographical remoteness, the lack of pre-existing social structures, and our ancestors' intentions to find here freedom and opportunity—religious, economic, or political—all formed a historical confluence entirely different than what Europe had faced before. To be sure, Africans were brought here in bondage, and Native Americans were far too often denied elemental fairness, but these were most emphatically violations of the emerging American Idea, not elements of it. Acknowledging our errors should not lead us to denigrate or discard the idea itself, but to cherish it all the more.

Americans in our earliest years were never isolationist as some mistakenly contend. Instead, they were spreading across a continent and beyond, in ways fully comparable to empire builders worldwide. We were hardly stay-at-homes, uninterested or uninvolved in the wider world. We were, however, most emphatically forging and following our own path. Our experience was unique because, unlike the others, we created, in Jefferson's phrase, "an empire of liberty." While other empires have disappeared all around us, our accomplishments bear names like Florida, Texas, California, Hawaii and Alaska. We succeeded where others failed by extending our principles and forging one nation, vindicating those principles in 1861-65 in one of the Nineteenth Century's bloodiest wars.

Even as we forged Jefferson's empire of liberty, our instincts were not imperialist. While there was inspiring rhetoric about our "manifest destiny," America's expansion, politically and commercially, was entirely consistent with Edmund Burke's conservative philosophy. It was organic, resting on the accretion of reasoning from our empirical reality, and far removed from metaphysical abstractions. The American Idea emerged from our own experience, starting with the Revolution. The Declaration of Independence was not speculative or mystical but reflected what had already happened on the ground. We had already become something different from our mother countries.

In many respects, it is our penchant for looking to America's own experience for history's most important lessons that frustrates or even enrages many foreigners. We stubbornly cling to our Constitution rather than "international norms"; we remain deeply skeptical of abstract and distant multinational treaties and organizations; and we alone have mastered the art of the melting pot, despite many contemporary intellectual fashions to the contrary. We care more about our own national character than what others may think of us. And that is exceptional.

Just as a Frenchman first identified us as exceptional, it is fitting that another most fully recognized the uniqueness of today's American superpower. In 1962, visiting New York, the great French writer Andre Malraux, then Charles de Gaulle's cultural affairs minister, made this profound observation:

> *I offer a toast to the only nation that has waged war but not worshiped it; that has won the greatest power in the world but not sought it; that has wrought the greatest weapon of death but not wished to wield it. And may it inspire men with dreams worthy of its actions.*

No nation before, or likely in the future, has ever borne burdens such as ours, and for as long as we have. But as we look ahead to the American Idea's future in a tumultuous world, we should be reminded again of the exceptional people who brought us to this point. And their descendants live among us today.

Ambassador Bolton, a diplomat and a lawyer, has spent many years in public service. From August 2005 to December 2006, he served as the U.S. permanent representative to the United Nations. From 2001 to 2005, he was undersecretary of state for arms control and international security. He is now a Senior Fellow at American Enterprise Institute (AEI).

AMERICAN PROSPERITY AND THE AMERICAN IDEA
By Brian Domitrovic

Of all the major accomplishments of the American people, one stands out as perhaps more surpassing than all the others.

Our constitutional tradition, striving in form if not in function to limit government so that the nation's inhabitants might pursue their life's pilgrimage in the context of family and society, is to be sure a noble one.

Likewise, is ultimately, the nation's wrenching experience with African Americans, who so many having endured the lash of slavery, gave the gift to this nation of their own culture, "from jazz to cocktails," as Billy Strayhorn once put it, proving that the best response to being treated poorly is to dig deep and give of one's talents in charity and generosity.

The most noticeable thing about America, however, remains its prosperity, its abundance. How many millions of people—tens upon tens of millions—across our two-hundred some years have lived supremely well, not only in comfort, but in the context of doing impressive and important work. The industrial revolution found its proving ground in the United States. It is hard to imagine America being America without its tradition of mass prosperity. This is perhaps the country's greatest legacy, the characteristic that must endure if we Americans are to continue to be ourselves.

There is no political figure, arguably in the whole of the twentieth century, who grasped this as well as Jack Kemp. Kemp's interests ran the gamut, from sports to books, which is perhaps the reason he did not lose focus in politics. He knew too much to think that politics should be anything but modest. Government in this country is to do one thing above all: get out of the way of an economy full of potential.

The greatest piece of federal legislation at least since the 1960s remains the great tax cut of 1981, which began life several years before as the "Kemp-Roth" bill care of Kemp and his colleague in the Senate, William V. Roth. The big cut in tax rates that came in 1981 was a wonderful example of the government getting out of the way.

Before 1981, the economy had been bedeviled by two big problems, unemployment and inflation. Both were caused by the government. High taxes and loose monetary policy stifled the pooling of capital into productive enterprises, killing jobs and opportunity. The consequent collapse in production engendered inflation, as ever-scarcer real goods became valuable against the greenback dollar.

The 1981 tax cut eliminated the basis of the government's support of "stagflation," as the terrible economic condition was called. Tax cuts at every marginal rate, as the law stipulated at Kemp's insistence, made investments and further work effort more remunerative. These marginal tax cuts also made it easier for the Federal Reserve to supply the dollar in the absence of inflation, in that dollars were now needed to finance real economic activity. The tax cut reduced the government's impress not only in tax policy, but by extension in monetary policy as well. One of the greatest sustained booms in the nation's economic history of necessity ensued, lasting all the way to the end of the century.

It was fitting, therefore, that Kemp also pushed for a restoration of the gold standard, an effort that has been taken up by further torchbearers in the Kemp tradition today. Tax cuts put it into law that the United States would not strive to interpose itself in private economic decision-making, by means of fiscal policy. A restoration of the gold standard would have similar weight in the realm of monetary policy.

It is in the government's very narrow interest to see American society fail of its own accord. If society fails, government finds it has a justification for being big and activist. This is one of the reasons that government may try to cultivate the illusion that American society does fail—for example that "capitalism" caused the Great Depression, the stagflation era, or our own Great Recession, not to mention various social maladies.

The truth is that left to their own prodigious abilities, the American people can generate a marvelous society, a profound culture, and absolutely storied economic success.

Jack Kemp was that rare breed of officeholder who had no fear of America being America. Not only would America do great things unbound from the governmental wet-blanket, it would be very fine if virtually all work and life in America proceeded in the realm of the private sphere and the non-politically organized community. There are shades of Alexis de Tocqueville in this great man's career. We Americans owe it to the future full of immense potential, which we hold in our hands, to adopt and act on the belief that we do best when we summon our own talents, in concert with those of our family and friends in the great chain of social existence, to solve problems and greet opportunities.

Dr. Domitrovic is Chairman of the Department of History at Sam Houston State University. He has written for numerous scholarly and popular publications, including a weekly column at Forbes.com under the byline Past & Present. His book Econoclasts: The Rebels Who Sparked the Supply-Side Revolution and Restored American Prosperity *was published in September 2009.*

THE AMERICAN IDEA
By Ben Elliott

50 years ago, on October 27, 1964, Ronald Reagan strode onto the national stage to deliver his epic speech, "A Time for Choosing." When Reagan set forth his conservative vision, he also spoke prophetically to America today. "The issue before us," he said, "is whether we still believe in our capacity for self- government, or whether we will abandon the American Revolution and confess that a tiny intellectual elite in a far distant capitol can plan our lives better than we can plan them ourselves."

In 1964, at the dawn of Lyndon Johnson's Great Society, the choice Ronald Reagan articulated s was relevant. 50 years later, with government seizing control of health care, the IRS targeting American citizens, the EPA attacking the coal industry, President Obama being rebuked by the Supreme Court for abuse of power, our border being overwhelmed, and public debt soaring into the stratosphere—in short, the ongoing transformation of America—Ronald Reagan's question becomes imperative.

Republicans will be strongly tempted in 2014 to focus on failures at home and weakness abroad. However, as Ronald Reagan and Jack Kemp showed us, the way we beat a thesis is not with an antithesis, but with a better thesis—with an appeal so powerful it can reach every citizen, speak to their minds and hearts, and enlist all our energies toward a higher purpose. The one appeal that carries that power and resonance is the American Idea.

The American Idea found its genesis in Thomas Jefferson's stirring affirmation in the Declaration of Independence: our rights to life, liberty and the pursuit of happiness are inalienable—not gifts from government, but our birthright from God. That is why Jack Kemp loved to say, "Whether you were born to be a carpenter, an entrepreneur, a mezzo-soprano or an NFL quarterback, nothing in America must stand in your way to climb as high as your God-given talents will take you." Notice Jack did not say, "If your goal in life is", but, "If you were born to be.…" Jack's Kemp's words echoed our deep faith that God watches over us and has a plan for our lives and for the life of our nation.

George Washington said he eluded death from British gunfire and went on to lead America, thanks solely to his protection by God—" beyond all human probability." The brilliant James Madison, father of the Constitution, declared, "We have staked the whole future of American civilization not upon the power of government ... but upon our capacity to govern ourselves, to control ourselves, to sustain ourselves according to the Ten Commandments of God." Ronald Reagan professed his belief that a divine plan placed this great continent between the oceans to be found by people with a special love for freedom. In coming here, our ancestors created something new in all of human history—a land where man is not beholden to government, but government is beholden to man.

We are not on our journey alone. There is a plan and a purpose that faith and freedom bring alive. As President, Ronald Reagan sought to make bold policy the servant of high purpose. He embraced the Kemp-Roth plan to reduce tax rates for all, ultimately dropping the top rate from 70 to 28 percent. He threw open the gates of commerce and trade for free people to compete in free markets, at home and across the world. And, he stood resolute against expanding government. President Reagan understood that divine sparks cannot burst into creative flames if those in a distant capital insist on controlling our lives, robbing our freedoms and smothering our dreams.

What did such bold leadership produce? A tsunami of investment, innovation, jobs, growth—4.6 percent, over twice the rate today—and upward mobility; a huge rising tide that saw women entering the workforce and starting up new businesses; minority unemployment declining; a renaissance in manufacturing and, the birth of new industries, especially in high technology. Reagan said we are putting America's future back into your hands. The American people said, "Thank you Mr. President," by unleashing the most powerful recovery in anyone's memory, benefiting every income group and lifting up the entire global economy.

New opportunities to do something special—big or small—also led to what Peggy Noonan called a thousand points of light: an unprecedented outpouring of generosity and love expressed through people's gifts of time, talent and treasure to colleges and universities, and to the countless charities, non-profits and voluntary groups that define our communities— our churches, synagogues and libraries, the Boy Scouts, Girl Scouts, and fire fighters, and our symphony orchestras, the arts, Little League and Pop Warner.

In a word, America.

The power of the American Idea rescued our nation. It can do so again. We still have the capacity for self-government. Our principles have not changed. Our potential is just as great. Our purpose must remain every bit as high.

Education

The lifelong quest to learn, grow and discover our path begins in our schools. Our challenge is to identify and expand excellence—find the schools doing the best job teaching, where students work hard and learn a lot—and make them models for all. If this means rewarding better teachers, creating more charter schools, approving more vouchers, stimulating greater competition, then in Reagan's words, "Let's get started!" And, if students are to develop what Jefferson's described as "an honest heart and a knowing mind," they must also receive a balanced view of our country—not just America's blots and blemishes, but also what is honorable, uplifting and worthy of pride and praise.

The Economy

In the 1980s, The American people proved there are no limits to what we can do when we are free to follow our dreams. In 2014, we can aim high to become, once again, the global leader for jobs, growth and prosperity. Optimism can replace pessimism. But, for the American Idea to work its magic, changes must be made:

The federal spending curve must, finally and definitively, be bent downward.

The U.S. corporate tax rate, highest in the world, must become one of the lowest or, preferably, be abolished.

The personal income tax code—72,000 pages of hopeless complexity—must be replaced by the lowest, flattest, simplest and, therefore, fairest tax rate possible.

Regulatory agencies must be reined in and submit to strict congressional oversight and supervision. U.S. regulatory agencies work for the American people; we do not work for the regulatory agencies.

If President Reagan and Jack Kemp were alive today, would their rallying cry be, "We can manage the bureaucracy better?" Or, would they not remind us the American Idea is about living with less bureaucracy?

Would they be content with trying to make the IRS more user friendly? Or, would they not suggest it is time to work and plan for the day when we can eliminate the IRS?

Monetary Policy

As we strive for renewed boldness, for full employment without inflation, we must also commit to protecting the value of every citizen's earnings, savings, investment and nest egg through a strong and stable dollar that is as good as gold.

Health Care

The United States has the finest doctors, the best surgeons and the premier hospitals and treatments in the world. Rather than let heavy-handed government destroy this crown jewel, let us preserve what works well for so many. Concurrently, we can boost competition, utilize best practices, and draw upon the compassion of our people to care for the few not covered.

Foreign Policy

Finally, we know that aspirations for freedom and prosperity are not confined to one time, people or place. They are universal and eternal. We are the only nation in history that has linked the success of our democracy with the hopes and dreams of people everywhere. To lead well, we must be strong—rejecting isolationism, protectionism and weakness—but also be shrewd—keeping our powder dry, unless America's interests are truly threatened.

Conclusion

Great challenges present big opportunities. The Republican Party can transcend today's cynical and negative dialogue with a superior vision for the future ... the best of our minds, hearts and souls. We can hold up the American Idea—and victories—of progress and prosperity through freedom and faith in God. We can adapt the timeless vision of Jefferson, Lincoln, Reagan and Kemp to the challenges before us. When we do, we will recapture the high ground on the battlefield of ideas for America's future. We will be the party that champions boundless opportunity, and that encourages all of our citizens to lift our country higher—a rising America that flies like an eagle and shines like the sun.

Ben Elliott was chief speechwriter for President Ronald Reagan, and later for Congressman (and presidential candidate) Jack Kemp. He now works at Bank of America Merrill Lynch in communications and wealth management.

PERSONAL REINVENTION
By Douglas Holtz-Eakin

The heart of the American Idea is the opportunity for personal reinvention. Our mothers, grandfathers, and millions of others have streamed into America for nearly four centuries. They left behind a life of urban squalor and became a frontiersman; transformed from a menial serf to a skilled middle-class craftsman; put behind a life of crime for a future as the pillar of a growing community; and, of course, exceeded the American Dream to leave poverty behind and achieve wealth in America. A shallow reading of the American Dream focuses on the acquisition of wealth. A deeper understanding of the powerful global allure of America is rooted in the freedom for social, cultural, and religious reinvention.

Undoubtedly, however, the culture of freedom to reinvent is woven deeply into the U.S. economic success. Historically, the U.S. offered an unparalleled access to raw materials and open land, the ability to start new enterprises and retain the material returns to one's work and effort, and easy access to expanding markets. The American economy grew and transformed itself at a remarkable pace, and permitted its population to follow suit.

An important aspect of the culture of American reinvention is its forgiveness of failure. From lovable losers (e.g., the Chicago Cubs) to scandal-plagued politicians, America has a remarkable capacity to forgive and forget. In the realm of American entrepreneurship, the list of business greats that have traveling through bankruptcy to ultimate success is stunning and instructive. Walt Disney, Henry Ford, William Durant (founder of General Motors), P. T. Barnum, H.J. Heinz, and William Fox (started 20th Century Fox Film Corporation) all filed for bankruptcy at one point in their careers. More recently, news television celebrity Larry King and real estate mogul—TV star—politician Donald Trump have taken a tour in bankruptcy.

The core tenet of bankruptcy protection is the notion that a firm be re-organized to use its capital, employees, and management in a new and profitable venture. It is a system built on economic reinvention.

Economic reinvention has been at the heart of business cycle recovery and economic dynamism as well. In the depths of an economic downturn, entrepreneurs take advantage of cheap, used capital facilities and idle workers to launch them in new uses. The productive supply-side reinvention leaves behind the broken economic model and unveils a creative venture of greater social value.

A failure to appreciate this core economic dynamic lies behind the failures of big-government attempts to micromanage the economy. Keynesian stimulus is built on the notion of propping up the existing firms, labor market relationships, and purchase patterns. In the aftermath of the Great Recession and Obama Administration stimulus efforts, new-firm creation dropped dramatically in the U.S. and the recovery proved modest at best. This is not a coincidence. Interfering with the core mechanisms for reinvention harms the capacity of the economy to transform itself for the future.

A commitment to smaller, non-intrusive government is a central corollary to the desire for reinvention. As a general proposition, government does not enable reinvention. Government tags, categorizes, and labels individuals. Census forms have boxes for ethnicity, occupation, and religion. Driver's licenses show age, hair color, eye color, height, and weight. Nondiscrimination laws specify male, female, white, African-American, heterosexual, homosexual, transgender, and the list goes on.

The American Idea was that redress of one's undesirable circumstances took the form of personal reinvention and economic mobility. Government redress takes the form of ossifying an individual as a category of characteristics and circumstances, propping up those categories, or—worse—dragging others down to match them. It is the antithesis of the American commitment to reinvention.

Flexible markets, a ceaseless commitment to innovation, the capacity to organize and reorganize skills, risk capital, and technologies are the mechanisms of economic reinvention. Personal freedoms, religious freedoms, and the small non-intrusive government are the mechanisms of social, cultural, and personal reinvention. These quintessentially American characteristics are a reflection of the deep commitment to the idea that in America one can be wholly different in the future than was bequeathed by the past.

America in 2014 is not the America of 2004, 1984, 1914, 1814, or 1714. And that is the American Idea. But so is the commitment to the opportunity to be better yet again in 2024.

Douglas Holtz-Eakin is President of the American Action Forum and most recently was a Commissioner on the congressionally-chartered Financial Crisis Inquiry Commission. His past positions include Director of the non-partisan Congressional Budget Office and as Chief Economist of the President's Council of Economic Advisers.

REDISCOVERING GROWTH
By Stephen Moore

The last 100 years have ushered in more material progress for mankind than in all of the previous centuries combined. Nowhere has this spectacular improvement in health, wealth, nutrition, housing, leisure time labor-saving inventions and education been more pronounced than in the USA.

The hyper-wealth improvement didn't happen on these shores by accident. The American ideal of political freedom and free enterprise - along with an ability to attract the best and brightest and most ambitious from around the globe and turn them into Americans—created a fertile soil for the expansion of output, ideas, technology and productivity unparalleled in human history.

The average American today has a higher living standard than even the princes and kings who lived a century ago. Even many poor Americans have a living standard that would be the envy of the world today and at all times previously. Most poor families today have access to items like computers, air conditioning, cars, TVs, drugs and vaccines and other medical treatments, that most middle-class families never could afford in 1960. We have exported prosperity at a remarkable pace. Today even many of the poorest citizens of Africa have a cell phone. Soon they will all have iPads connecting every citizen of the world to the digital age.

Almost every invention of consequence over the past century— from the microprocessor to the jet engine to the polio vaccine—came from America. If we are going to continue to lead the world as the economic and military superpower of the planet, we need to keep innovating, inventing and imaging.

What makes all this possible is a set of economic principles that great leaders like Ronald Reagan and Margaret Thatcher and Jack Kemp and others understood almost instinctively. That if we cleared away regulatory, tax, tariff and other regulatory burdens imposed by government, the natural forces of growth would be untethered.

The 1980s and 1990s produced a two-decade period of progress almost unrivaled in history. The net wealth of America grew from $16 trillion to more than $40 trillion. Some 40 million jobs were created by private businessmen and women.

So why is growth interrupted? Why the slump and the shrunk shoulders and loss of confidence? Is the American Dream suspended? Can only the rich succeed?

No we've been through this before—in the 1930s and 1970s when the political class and the intellectuals argued that free-market capitalism had hit a dead end. These intellectuals rejected the free-market paradigm of Reagan and Kemp and with the election Barack Obama substituted a new economic playbook that runs contrary to all of what we know creates wealth and progress.

So we have seen Under Barack Obama a model based on government spending, crony capitalism, easy money, debt, a regulatory machete, higher tax rates, and an obsession with wealth redistribution, not wealth creation. As economist Arthur Laffer says, if you play the record in reverse, you get the opposite results." And that is why the two-decade burst of growth has turned into a new Jimmy Carter-like malaise.

The case for optimism is that Americans have (hopefully) relearned the lesson that socialism, Keynesianism, progressivism, or whatever you call it, has failed. All these fad isms, Jack Kemp would say, are far inferior to the power of capitalism. Mr. Kemp was fond of repeating the John F. Kennedy truism that "a rising tide lifts all boats." That will happen again and soon.

All that is missing is a 21st century Kennedy, or Reagan or a new Kemp to restore America's confidence in itself. What is certain is that he or she is out there.

Stephen Moore is Distinguished Visiting Fellow, Project for Economic Growth, at The Heritage Foundation. Previously he wrote on the economy and public policy for The Wall Street Journal where he was a member of the editorial board. He was also founder and President of the Club for Growth, dedicated to helping elect free market, tax cutting candidates to Congress. Mr. Moore is the author of six books, including most recently Who's the Fairest of Them All? The Truth About Taxes, Income and Wealth in America *published in 2012.*

REFLECTIONS ON THE AMERICAN IDEA
By Peter Wehner

There is no single American Idea. There are several ones, including our constitutional system of government, based on checks and balanced, delegated and enumerated powers, representation and the rule of law. What was produced in Philadelphia on that hot summer in 1787 was extraordinary; the world had never seen anything quite like it before. The Constitution was, in the words of the British Prime Minister William Gladstone, "the greatest work ever struck off at a given time by the brain and purpose of man."

But there is also something like an American anthropology, by which I mean an understanding of the human person as free, equal and created in the image of God— "endowed," in the words of Thomas Jefferson, "with certain unalienable rights."

From these propositions flow several corollary beliefs.

We Americans believe in the right to life, liberty and the pursuit of happiness; in freedom of religion, speech, assembly, and the press; and that the main purpose of government is to "ensure domestic tranquility" and protect the unalienable rights of its citizens.

We Americans believe in representative government and political equality, in liberty and self-government. Because human beings have inherent dignity, they are meant to live freely, not in chains. The greatest interpreter of the founding generation, Abraham Lincoln, put it vividly: "Nothing stamped with the divine image and likeness was sent into the world to be trodden on, and degraded, and imbruted by its fellows."

But there's more to it than that. The Founders (and Lincoln) believed, and our constitutional system presupposes, that human nature is decidedly mixed. After canvassing history and echoing the views of the writers of the Hebrew Bible and the New Testament, the authors of the Constitution believed human beings are a combination of good and bad, virtue and vice, noble sentiments and degraded ones.

The assumption of the Federalist Founders was that within every human heart, let alone among different individuals, were competing and sometimes contradictory moral impulses and currents. "The passions of men will not conform to the dictates of reason and justice without constraint," Alexander Hamilton said.

"If men were angels," James Madison wrote in Federalist Paper No. 51, "no government would be necessary." But we aren't, so it is.

What is required, then, for free individuals to live as part of successful human societies is that they develop good character; that they be instructed not only about their rights but also their duties, and that their "morals" and "faculties" are cultivated. As former Secretary of Education William Bennett put it:

> [T]eaching character is a difficult task. But it is a crucial task because we want our children to be only healthy, happy, and successful but decent, strong, and good. None of this happens automatically; there is no genetic transmission of virtue. It takes conscious, committed effort. It takes attention.

It surely does. And the institutions that are central in this effort are families, schools, houses of worship and communities. They inculcate values; they teach honesty, compassion, loyalty, responsibility, persistence and the importance of hard work. They help us to correctly prioritize the order of our loves.

Families and schools, faith and civic communities, then, are vital not just to the formation of human character, but also to the success and endurance of the American Idea.

The way people's character and moral sentiments are formed is a highly complicated matter, involving the wiring of the brain and early childhood experiences, genetics and surroundings, the influence not just of parents but friends, and the ethos of a society. Yet national character is a real thing, too, George Will once wrote, molded in part by law and politics, and is not made of marble. "Using government discriminatingly but energetically to strengthen these institutions is part of the natural program of conservatives," he said.

That seems quite right to me. Take schools as an example. The vast majority of young people in America—nearly 90 percent—attend public schools. What those schools impart, both intellectually and morally, makes a significant difference. What schools teach and how they teach and who they hire (and fire) to teach are public matters, not private ones.

As a general matter, government should first do no harm when it comes to character-forming institutions. Government should respect those institutions and not, under any circumstances, systematically undermine them.

When possible, however, government should also support them—for example, by making it somewhat less costly and difficult for parents to raise children (by supporting child tax credits), by eliminating marriage penalties where they exist in law, by making it harder rather than easier for young people to use drugs, by rewarding rather than discouraging work, and by promoting accountability, high standards and transparency in our schools.

Self-government, which is at the heart of the American Idea, isn't simply a matter of the system of government we have. It depends on the kind of people we produce—whether they are men and women of good character, whether they love truth, goodness and beauty, and whether they aspire to excellence. That is the challenge for every parent and every generation. If these types of human beings do emerge, they will be worthy and grateful inheritors of what the America Founders created.

Pete Wehner is a Senior Fellow at the Ethics and Public Policy Center. He writes widely on political, cultural, religious, and national security issues. He has written for numerous publications—including the New York Times, Wall Street Journal, Washington Post, Financial Times, The Weekly Standard, Commentary, National Affairs *and* Time *magazine Mr. Wehner is co-author of* City of Man: Religion and Politics in a New Era *and* Wealth and Justice: The Morality of Democratic Capitalism.

PART III
KEMP FORUM ON THE FUTURE OF THE AMERICAN IDEA

Friday, May 16, 2014
President Lincoln's Cottage
Washington, D.C.

OPENING REMARKS

Mr. Lincoln and the American Idea

Rich Lowry

What was Abraham Lincoln's perception of the American Idea? To get to its essence, we might turn to a wonderful talk he gave in the White House in 1864 to the 166th regiment of Ohio troops, which had been mustered for 100 days to provide guard duty here in Washington. He told them that whenever he was with soldiers, he wanted to talk with them about what the struggle is for, and what is it about:

> *It is not merely for today, but for all time to come that we should perpetuate for our children's children this great and free government, which we have enjoyed all our lives. I beg you to remember this, not merely for my sake, but for yours. I happen temporarily to occupy this big White House. I am a living witness that any one of your children may look to come here as my father's child has,*

which is a very strange way of putting it but also characteristically Lincoln because it's so modest. It's a way to avoid saying, "the way I do." Then he went on to describe the purpose of the war:

> *It is in order that each of you may have through this free government which we have enjoyed, an open field and a fair chance for your industry, enterprise and intelligence; that you may all have equal privileges in the race of life, with all its desirable human aspirations. It is for this the struggle should be maintained, that we may not lose our birthright—not only for one, but for two*

or three years. The nation is worth fighting for, to secure such an inestimable jewel.

Lincoln lived those wonderful sentences through all his policies, which were designed to give expression to them, and his free labor ideology gave those sentence a philosophical bedrock.

If you want to understand Lincoln, you really have to go back to his childhood. He was raised in the middle of nowhere, first in Kentucky and then in Indiana. When his family moved to Indiana, there was another family in the neighborhood that recounted when they had the fire going in their log cabin they would see through the chinks in the logs the eyes of bears reflected in the fire looking in. There is a story about a young girl getting killed by a panther in this area because her brother didn't kill it quickly enough with a hatchet to the skull. So this is not suburban bliss, this is an extremely unforgiving environment.

His mother and his mother's aunt and uncle all died in short order from something called "milk sick." When Lincoln was a young boy, a cow would wander out into the forest, eat a poison weed, and no one would know its milk would be poisoned. You would drink the milk and you would die a horrifying death within a week. Lincoln had to fashion with his father a wooden coffin, and they buried his mother in the back yard.

Lincoln said there was nothing to excite an ambition for education in this environment. His mother signed her name with an "X." His stepmother, who was a great blessing to him and a wonderful woman, signed her name with an "X." He told his campaign biographer in 1860 that his father could barely bunglingly sign his own name. The biographer left it out because he thought it was so harsh but it was true.

With every fiber of his being, Lincoln wanted to escape this backwoods existence. One of the great ironies of his image down through the ages is that we think of him as the rail splitter or the rail-splitter president. When he was nominated as Illinois' favorite son for president in 1860, they hauled out some rails and claimed that these were rails split by Lincoln. It was a great act of branding. Forevermore, he was known as the rail splitter. The thing about Lincoln is, he never wanted to split another damn rail in his life.

A much better prism through which to understand Lincoln is a story he himself told in the White House. The story goes that one day, when he was a young man, he had his row boat on the side of the river when a carriage drove up. There were two gentlemen in this carriage who wanted to meet a steam boat coming down the river, but there was no wharf at this part of the river; someone had to row you there. So they said, "Hey kid, can you row us out to the steamboat?" Lincoln said, "Sure" rowed them out, helped them get on the boat, and got their luggage on the boat. Then Lincoln said, "Hey wait a minute, you forgot to pay me."

Decades later, President Lincoln remembered this moment. He said, to his shock and surprise, each of these guys threw a silver half dollar down on the bottom of his boat. "At that moment, I realized I had earned my first dollar; and I was a more hopeful and optimistic being from that time on."

Lincoln wanted an America where you could earn a dollar, and where you had to earn a dollar. In a nutshell, that is why he didn't become a Democrat. Now he was surrounded by Democrats growing up; and Democrats, you know, worshiped Andrew Jackson and the great farmers of the American backwoods. They had a very romantic view of the back woods and Yeomen farmers.

Lincoln wanted none of that. He'd had that in his childhood up to his neck. So he became a Whig and he was attracted to the Whig economic program, which, very briefly, was that we're not going to have a barter economy anymore. We're going to have a cash economy, which means that we need to have banks. We're going to defend banks, financiers, and the economic elite. We are going to have an industry in this country. We're not going to be agricultural forevermore, so, we're going to have a tariff to encourage industry. We want to have an actual functioning market in this country and to do that you actually need to connect the country together. So, we're going to have railroads, steam ships, and canals, all of which Lincoln loved.

Lincoln did everything he could his entire adult life to promote these objectives. He was also very attracted to the cultural element of the Whig program, which said, "Okay, we can do all these things economically, but we need people who are prepared to take advantage of them. For that, we need people who are self-disciplined and hardworking."

Lincoln himself was an evangelist for this ethic his whole life. He exemplified this sort of Whig view of the world when he became a lawyer. Young aspiring law students would ask him, "How do I become a lawyer?" and Lincoln would write back letters saying, "Work, work, work." His step-brother stayed back in the backwoods and was short on cash his whole life. He would constantly ask Lincoln for loans. Lincoln would write back letters (which I assume were well meaning), extremely excoriating things which would have made very awkward Thanksgiving dinners. In one of these letters, Lincoln wrote to his step-brother, "You are destitute because you idle away all your time. Go to work. That is the only cure for your case."

Lincoln himself, at a time when America was soaked in alcohol and tobacco and when coarse language was the norm, didn't drink, didn't smoke, and didn't swear. He told the occasional off color story, but he didn't swear. This was a time when casual cruelty to animals was the norm, and Lincoln was embarrassingly tenderhearted toward animals. In fact, in front of this cottage where we are meeting today, there is a statue of Lincoln communing with his horse.

There's a story a dinner guest at the White House told about the Lincolns' cat. Lincoln was sitting in one chair, and apparently the cat was sitting in the chair right next to him. Lincoln was using the official flatware of the White House to feed the cat, which as any married man would expect, outraged Mary Todd. She said to the visitor, "Don't you think this is crazy? The President of the United States is feeding a cat with the official flatware." Lincoln said, "No, no, no. If this gold fork is good enough for Buchannan, it's good enough for Tabby."

So what did Lincoln do with his ethic of self-improvement? He made himself a lawyer.

Now this may be something of an anachronism, but Lincoln arguably was the foremost corporate lawyer in the State of Illinois. He was on retainer from the biggest corporation in Illinois, the Illinois Central Railroad. That doesn't really accord with the popular image of Lincoln but for Lincoln it wouldn't have been a contradiction at all. This goes to his fundamental economic views where he worshiped property rights and the rule of law. He thought if you have a properly functioning economy there should be no such thing as class conflict.

He opposed what we call "redistributionist economics." A delegation of working men came to see Lincoln in the White House during the war. He said, "let not him who is houseless pull down the house of another, but labor diligently to build one of his own."

Undergirding all this was Lincoln's profound belief in the dignity of labor and the right to the proceeds of one's own labor. He loved the line from Genesis, "in the sweat of thy brow thou shalt earn thy bread," or as he put it more informally, "He who makes the corn shall eat the corn." He felt this very, very deeply.

As his father was failing and getting physically weaker when Lincoln was a teenager, he would hire Lincoln out to do hard labor—all the kind of work you'd expect on the farm. Lincoln would get paid and his father would take all the money, which was his father's right until Lincoln was age twenty-one. Years later, Lincoln gave a speech in which he actually said, "I used to be a slave," which is obviously an incredibly self-pitying exaggeration; but it speaks to how deeply he felt this principle. It also speaks to his opposition of real slavery.

The famous phrase in his second inaugural address was "unrequited toil." It means having other people work while you wrongly take the proceeds of their labor. Lincoln thought that this principle was so basic that there is really no misunderstanding it.

You can see this principle at work by observing an ant with a crumb. If the ant finds the crumb, and is dragging the crumb to its nest, and you stop the ant and try to take the crumb, the ant will fight you. This is because the ant knows the crumb is now its own crumb because the ant worked to bring that crumb to its nest.

If you read the things Lincoln wrote and said, they are fused with a profound sense of loss. He thought the Founders had the question of slavery right. They offered no affirmative defense of it. They tolerated it because there was no good way to get rid of it, but they thought eventually it would have go away. But, in the South, in the 1840s and 50s, an affirmative defense of slavery was taking hold. For Lincoln, this was just shameful national back sliding.

Lincoln's fundamental project, therefore, was forging a renewal through a return. At any time throughout American culture and American life, we tend to celebrate what's new; it's a natural fit with our national character. But Lincoln was unabashed in celebrating what was old.

He would refer to the Founders as "those iron men of the past, the old time men, our Founders." He would refer to the old Declaration of Independence. In his famous Peoria speech, he says, "We need to readopt the Declaration of Independence." Or as he said in a wonderful phrase, "Our republican robe is soiled and trailed in the dust. Let us re-purify it and wash it white in the spirit if not the blood of the American Revolution."

Today, obviously, circumstances are different. We don't have to be as depressed as Lincoln, but I think there is cause to be dismayed or at least concerned about the state of the American Dream. I think in broad brush our project should be forging progress and forging new opportunity through the prism of those old ideas.

There's a wonderful passage often quoted in Lincoln's Lyceum address, when he was a young man of Springfield before anyone had heard him. He spoke about how even then, when America was a very immature country in the early mid-nineteenth century, we were invulnerable to military assault.

> *All the armies of Europe, Asia and Africa combined, with all the treasure of the earth (our own excepted) in their military chest; with a Buonaparte for a commander, could not by force, take a drink from the Ohio, or make a track on the Blue Ridge, in a trial of a thousand years.*
>
> *At what point then is the approach of danger to be expected? I answer, if it ever reaches us, it must spring up amongst us. It cannot come from abroad. If destruction be our lot, we must ourselves be its author and finisher. As a nation of freemen, we must live through all time, or die by suicide.*

This is what today is all about. The beliefs of figures like Lincoln and Jack Kemp. It's through the American Idea that we live.

LEADERSHIP FOR THE AMERICAN IDEA Rapporteur's Report

William Kristol, Garry Kasparov, Peggy Noonan, Bob Schoultz

"It is impossible to talk about the ideas behind American foreign policy without beginning with the American Idea, what it means to us at home." — Jack Kemp, 1983"

Session I, "Leadership for the American Idea," began with a discussion of the inherently American cause to advance and secure human rights and liberty and democracy—not just in select places where it is easier to achieve, but everywhere. Jack Kemp, the panel noted, championed this cause throughout his career. He had the utmost faith in the American people, and in free people everywhere. Just get out of their way, he believed, and they will produce wonders.

There are two images that may help illustrate and evoke these qualities.

First, an armada. The great war photographer Robert Capa is best known for his coverage of D-Day. When he arrived at the English port town from where the invasion would be launched, he was stunned by the panorama before him. Not only were there destroyers and carriers and landing crafts, but also to his astonishment—as far as the eye could see—there were fishing boats and skiffs and tugboats of every shape and size, manned by all the able-bodied seafaring citizens who could contribute to the effort. The image of that armada is much how Jack Kemp described all the ships, large and small, of the American economy going in the same direction together.

Second, a path in the woods. Abraham Lincoln, as a child, daily had to make his way through the backwoods, which were riddled with rocks and ruts and fallen branches. The woods were lonely and deep, and he learned two things: that the only way to pass was to have a very sure step, placing his whole foot down solid and measured each step of the way, and that he did not want to spend his whole life in the backwoods. What Lincoln understood instinctively in those woods carried forward to his vision for America, which endured even through the devastating Civil War. He believed in building a physical infrastructure that would enable

Americans to navigate the hills and ravines of North and South. Canals. Roads. Bridges. And a banking infrastructure that would support travel, trade, and commerce, and reunite the country.

This imagery reminds us that history is made by human beings who draw from the qualities and lessons of their personal experiences to make their mark on the greater ledger of human achievement. Clearly this was true for Jack Kemp, who brought to national leadership the goal-oriented, we-can-do-this team mindset of the professional quarterback he was. Kemp was innately optimistic; it was part of his personality. His was not the optimism of the fool who only sees the world through rose-colored glasses, but the optimism of a man who had reason and life-experience giving him a well-grounded hope and belief in America's future.

The great armada, all pulling together; the resilient infrastructure that binds the nation together and enriches its daily life; the essential optimism that looks forward with hope and vision—these are the qualities of great leaders, and of America's needed leadership in the world.

The American Idea is also grounded in the motto E Pluribus Unum: out of many different people, from different backgrounds, are forged one nation. America has been inspired and formed by the immigrant experience, which is still alive and still happening every day. Like the early settlers who formed this country, many of today's immigrants leave behind everything they knew, taking enormous risks and with great courage leave their homeland to come to America.

Recall the example of Olympic long distance runner Meb Keflezighi, who won the Boston Marathon in 2014—the first American in three decades to win that competition, and the first running of that race since the terrible bombings the year before. Meb grew up in a refugee camp in Eritrea with nine brothers and sisters. The story of how his father was able to come to America and bring his family with him is remarkable—and at the same time typical of so much of the immigrant experience. Meb lives in San Diego now, where he is a local hero as well as an American hero; when he arrived here at age 12, he did not even speak the language, yet he went on to achieve great things.

One panelist described a recent gathering of the Eritrean community to celebrate Meb's accomplishments. It was a tribute to human endurance and the human spirit and the dignity of the individual embodied in

America's founding ideals. In that room full of former refugees and full of black faces (with very few white faces in the crowd), the celebration opened with everyone rising, hand over heart, to pledge allegiance to the United States of America.

We are a country of immigrants that recognizes the precious value of human capital. People like Meb are our greatest resource. They fulfill the American Dream by seizing the opportunity that living here gives them to reach for the best they can be. The American Idea is not that opportunity should be limited to our shores, but that that same equality of opportunity should be enjoyed by all people, everywhere.

American leadership in the world also brings to mind the challenges of an expedition—how to chart a purposeful journey in the face of the unknown, that others might follow. In order to make the expedition work, everyone has to do their own share and then some—beginning with taking care of yourself and your own needs so that you can contribute to the success of the expedition and not become a burden on others. Expeditionary behavior also means a tolerance for uncertainty and adversity, and a facility for rising above them.

This expeditionary sense of America's leading is in decline. Throughout the world, people have regarded America as a moral authority and as the one country that could offer hope for liberation. It is quite painful to see how that faith in America's leadership is eroding. It is also a dangerous trend.

Much of America's fall from global leadership comes down to credibility. It's not enough that America is the strongest military power in the world and still the largest economy. The danger comes from the fact that the words of the U.S. president are no longer some sort of ultimate red line, as they were at the time of Ronald Reagan or Harry Truman or John Kennedy

One panelist recounted heading a recent delegation to meet with Prime Minister Abe of Japan. He expected that the prime minister would want to discuss China, the so-called pivot to Asia, and other matters of U.S.-Japanese relations. Instead, the prime minister's first question was, what happened in Syria? Warnings issued by U.S. presidents have to be credible. When they are not, allies are alarmed and adversaries emboldened.

In the view of another panelist, the problem is not just President Obama's infamous red line debacle in Syria; rather the last two administrations both contributed to the destruction of America's credibility, albeit from opposite ends of the spectrum. As this panelist explained, you don't want to use force all the time as was done by the previous administration and you don't want to depart from force as is being done by the current administration. The president must be able to make a credible threat.

The objective is to make sure that when a U.S. president makes a statement—draws a red line, if you will—he will not be forced to use military power; the threat will be sufficient. For example, for eleven months at the start of the Cold War, American and British planes had been supplying West Berliners with all they needed—water, food, supplies. And Stalin did not give an order to shoot down a single plane, because as a great dictator he had great animal instinct. He could smell when there would be a powerful response, and that was enough to stop him.

Putin, like other great dictators of the past, is very good at detecting when someone is bluffing because he can smell weakness. Dictators always grow stronger in the face of weakness and indecisiveness. The cost of preventing Hitler from becoming a monster in 1933 was less than in 1934, in 1935 less than 1936. It's like treating a cancer. Every day of delay makes it more challenging and more difficult and eventually it could be almost impossible to control. So in Syria, Putin bluffed while holding a very weak hand. Putin probably had a pair of tens but he acted as if he had a royal flush. By contrast, Obama had a very strong hand but he flushed it down the toilet.

By now, the bluffing and superficial red lines have gotten so ridiculous that we are on the verge of a dangerous situation. To say you're going to do something and then not do it is a sure sign of weakness, and weakness is provocative. In the face of weakness, it is the dictator who eventually overreaches. And then the United States is left with no other choice but to respond. It is the classic recipe for war.

There are both principles as well as responsibilities that the United States must uphold as Leader of the Free World. Carrying the torch of freedom is more than rhetoric; it's why and how America earned its place in the history of the human race. That is the true American leadership that good people across the world want to see restored.

International coalitions are important, but to be effective they cannot be a coalition of equals. Everybody knows that a coalition without the United States is not going to work. Leading from behind out of the White House is a recipe for disaster. Leadership means being in front, which carries responsibilities that sometimes come at a high price, but again that is a burden of leadership.

Leadership also requires a willingness to challenge conventional wisdom. Jack Kemp is notable for many things, to include how much he was willing to take on not only the liberal establishment, but also the establishment in his own party. Most people are familiar with his work on tax policy, but his influence was equally significant in foreign policy.

Kemp was able to combine a concern for democracy and human rights with a more classically hawkish foreign policy, which drove a profound change in the Republican Party's outlook between 1976 and 1980. President Gerald Ford and his Secretary of State had shunned any notion of helping or encouraging dissidents in the Soviet Union or in the Eastern Bloc. By contrast, after 1980, the Republicans would stand for the principled position of advancing liberty throughout the world.

President Reagan's assault on the Evil Empire and his landmark tax policy are probably the two greatest achievements of the Reagan administration. Both are closely identified with Jack Kemp. In the words of one panelist, "I don't think these things would have happened without Jack."

Questions and Answers

Q. The Sochi games were a huge showcase for Putin—a $50 billion extravaganza to unveil a new Russia. Then just a few weeks later he invaded Ukraine and Crimea. Do you think he knew at Sochi what was coming? Did he know what he was about to do?

A. Of course Putin's plans of taking over Crimea pre-dated the Olympic Games; indeed, Putin himself said as much. If you want to learn more about Putin's plans, just read his speeches, they are very revealing. For example, he warned President George W. Bush about a potential attack on Georgia in April 2008, and his generals also were talking about it. [The attack occurred in August that year.]

At the same time, hosting the Olympic Games is something of an intoxicating drug for dictators because suddenly they are in the epicenter of world public attention. It took Hitler twenty months from the Olympics to the Anschluss into Austria. It took Putin only twenty days from the Olympics to the Anschluss into Crimea. Putin was on the very top of the world, somebody challenged his authority and he reacted.

Also, Putin had little if any respect for his Western counterparts. He didn't expect any opposition when he moved into Crimea and unfortunately he was right. Let's not forget, six years ago he invaded Georgia. And what has NATO done in the intervening six years? Nothing. So Putin concludes, "OK, what's the difference, let's take over Crimea."

Putin has made it very clear that he will stay in power as long as he is able. Think of what that means. For the rest of his life, he will need a new mythology or legend to make up for the fact that he does not have democratic legitimacy. What is the compelling higher purpose to justify a Russian leader who doesn't have legitimate elections behind him? "Collector of Russian lands." To warrant this title, Putin cannot and will not stop, not in Crimea and not in eastern Ukraine.

The real danger that is that eventually he will challenge NATO in Latvia and Estonia. And then what? Will NATO send troops to defend those countries, as the Charter requires? Or will NATO come apart? The question should not come down to boots on the ground. It's about NATO's full commitment to protect the victims of Putin's aggression. Starting now.

Q. I was struck in working for Jack Kemp and also for Ronald Reagan that everything they said was taken seriously because most everything had a moral and ethical basis. Their advocacy of human rights was grounded in the belief that God had given each person a soul and rights because each individual human being mattered. That's an ethical/moral judgment. When it came to arms control, the logic was the same. The ethics of arms control were that agreements were to be honored, which meant that you don't just trust, you verify; and cheating had consequences. They were idealists because they had moral reasoning behind their policies which transcended mere politics. And they were realists because they knew having that internal passion and drive and faith could help shape reality through leadership. Could the panel comment on the significance of the ethical, moral or even religious basis of what people like Jack Kemp and Ronald Reagan were able to accomplish?

A. Andrei Sakharov once said that the decisions based on morality and principles eventually prove to be the most pragmatic ones. Vaclav Havel was visiting Moscow in 2007 and the Czech embassy hosted a reception for Russian opposition and activists. The Czech ambassador was trying to be very polite and cautious, explaining that the European Union must recognize Russian interests and Putin's strengths, which were separate from the issues of human rights. In the face of this diplomatic nonsense, Havel got very agitated. He threw his menu down on the table and said "While negotiating with Soviet Union about nuclear disarmament, Ronald Reagan always had a list of political prisoners on the table."

[From another panelist] Both Ronald Reagan and Jack Kemp were very confident of the values they asserted; but they were also very confident that those values would resonate with the American people. In a way they were speaking the American lingo because they thought in those terms and they were speaking to people who also spoke and thought in those terms. One wonders whether leaders now are as confident.

Q. Looking forward to the next presidential election, this morning's session suggests a good start for a foreign policy plank: "Say what you mean and mean what you say. Build your strength, don't be intimidated and don't let anyone mess with you." What else should voters be looking for in a candidate?

A. Something that has been lost in America, over the past decade or so, is the sense that we are all in this together. We need a national political figure who can talk to the American people as if we are all equal and we are all equal together, we will rise or fall together. There are plenty of leaders who can talk to their base, who are constantly talking to their base, ranging from the president to those who are challenging the president. But there is a big country out there, and the country is more than the base.

Q. Jack Kemp used to say that exporting the American Idea is America's unfinished revolution. This exhortation is not without controversy, especially at a time when the nation is suffering from war fatigue, and the question comes down to whether we should be involved in nation building abroad given the resources and risks that implies. Do you agree with Kemp's view? And if so, how does or should it find expression in U.S. foreign policy?

A. I don't like the expression "exporting" because it reminds me of exporting communism or forcing some other ideology onto people and countries against their will. I would rephrase it. I would say America's unfinished revolution is supporting those who share American ideas, who would like to join the world of democracy and free markets. I believe that America is in the position to offer this support everywhere around the globe.

[From another panelist] I would like America to be a better example to itself and the world, more economically strong, culturally strong, educationally strong. These are the things that I think make an impression on the world. When my ancestors came from Ireland to America it was not because America was trying to export the American Idea. It was because they heard, 'in America, the streets are paved with gold; you can make a living there; in America, you can rise'.

[From another panelist] First things first. America has to be strong enough not to have to use force, to have peace through strength. Smart power, soft power, diplomacy are all great provided we have the ability to follow though. I am worried that we've cut defense too much and probably foolishly as well because of the sequester, and that as a consequence we are on the precipice of not being able to do things that every American president has been called upon to do. For the first time since 1945, one can imagine a situation where the president of the United States calls in the Joint Chiefs in a time of crisis and says, "We need to do X," and the chairman would say, "Mr. President, we cannot really do X" or "we can only do X if we totally strip ourselves down in some other extremely important part of the world where our departure would invite unacceptable risks."

Defense spending is now at a historically low percentage of GDP. We are still a very wealthy country. Despite the deficit, we could actually afford to have a defense adequate to our needs. And as they see what is happening in the world, most conservatives and most Republicans are becoming more serious about defense policy.

Diplomacy is another thing Jack Kemp was very concerned about. He used to criticize the State Department not because he didn't like the State Department; he just thought they were doing a bad job at being the State Department. It's basically a system that was set up sixty years ago which is not responsive to current cultural or political developments. Our soft power is no more effective today than it was sixty years ago.

[Another panelist] People in the military still do believe and hope that the reasons why our leaders send us forward ultimately make sense, though in the last decade, there has been some doubt. I just talked to a young man who is thinking about getting out of the Navy. Rhodes scholar, Navy seal, fabulous young man. He told me that when he was in Afghanistan he was seeing things and was asked to do things that just made no sense to him. When he talked to his fellow leaders, they said it made no sense to them either. So he went to his battalion commander, who said "it doesn't make any sense to me either but that's what we have to do." So being a bold young man, he went to the battalion commander's commanding officer and said, "Sir, this doesn't make any sense," and the colonel said "it doesn't make any sense to me either but we follow orders." So he did what he was ordered to do. My point is that in my experience in the military, we have faith in the system and we don't want to lose that faith; but it has been shaken a bit in the last decade.

Q. Let's say that President Obama wakes up tomorrow morning and thinks, "I don't want to do this anymore; I want to try to actually address the situation in Russia in a productive way." What concretely can he do, if anything, at this point?

A. That is a tough question. For this president, now, making a credible threat is nearly impossible because Putin will not listen. So he would have to do something quite meaningful. For example: immediately supply Ukraine with an army of anti-air and anti-tank missiles. Those are defensive weapons only, but American military support would be a strong signal. Ukraine's army is weak today but it its big enough to cause great damage to Russia now, which is much weaker than its Soviet predecessor. He should also unilaterally impose meaningful sanctions against at least a few key people in the Putin immediate entourage including their families, because that is the way to get at their business interests and their attention.

[From another panelist] The scenario the question suggests is not without precedent. President Carter actually began to reverse things in 1980 after the Soviet invasion of Afghanistan and the Iranian hostage crisis. He acknowledged in effect that he was wrong, "mugged by reality" so to speak, and did increase defense spending and did actually toughen measures against the Soviets in 1980, over the objections of the left wing of his own party. The debate that ensued help set the stage for what President Reagan later accomplished. Similarly, today there is a need to lay a predicate for a new direction. No candidate can just show up in 2016 proclaiming new policies that appear out of thin air. It will be very important for serious officials and leaders and thinkers to spend the next few years developing the points we have discussed today, as well as others.

Q. A question about the strategic leadership of the future. We are seeing a new axis forming with Russia, China and Iran, which means that the United States has to think very differently about who our strategic partners and alliances are going to be. The cyber tax coming from China—China's theft of intellectual property—is very serious for U.S. security. Iran and

Russia are beginning to forge a new relationship, and we need a strategy to deal with that. U.S. relations with India will be important, obviously, but also think about how we bring in Latin America including in particular countries like Brazil, which are major players in the global economy. All of this is exasperated by what is happening in Russia. I think we could use some disruptive thinking to change adverse trends. Your thoughts?

A. Since 2008 and the economic crash, America has suffered a status shift. Now many of the world's leaders don't think America is such a big deal. That status shift has to do with money and the perception of American wealth and debt. It also has to do with American leadership that was unclear or incorrect or hopeless, muddled, ambivalent and weak. We need a creative way of admitting and turning around the status shift. That will require a leader or leaders who are more certain in advancing American interests in the world but also more capable at igniting the American economy.

Strategic leadership also requires understanding that the world has become one big, interlocking picture. Actions taken in Iran, for example, have an effect in China. China may see Russia as a senior partner today but tomorrow as prey because China has territorial claims over at least half of Russian territory. These complex relationships and interdependent variables have to be seen as a whole. Dividing U.S. foreign policy into compartments, which may have worked in the past, now can work against America's strategic interest.

Finally, strategic leadership requires a real strategy and its execution. Strategy doesn't mean anything if there isn't any actual substance to it. The pivot to Asia, for example, came down to the redeployment of fifteen hundred Marines to Darwin Australia, which is not a serious pivot. Rather, what was announced as a new strategy appeared to be little more than a reaction to the fact that the Middle East is messy and unpleasant, the wars there haven't gone well, and the countries of the region don't seem all that grateful to us in any case; so might as well go to Asia, which all the big thinkers think is really important, where the United States can deal with major countries like Japan, India and China. These points might make a good article on foreign affairs, but in the real world they were a pseudo-strategy at best.

Bob Schoultz, Peggy Noonan, and Garry Kasparov at Lincoln Cottage

It is time for the United States to pivot to grand strategy, starting with the election to choose the future U.S. president. It may be more difficult for America to assert its influence in today's world because the United States can no longer make the kinds of unilateral decisions it once could. But there are allies and friends in many places of the world who will follow America's lead, if the United States will show strength and commitment and credibility.

GROWTH, GROWTH, GROWTH! Rapporteur's Report

Fred Barnes, George Gilder, Amity Shlaes, Deborah Wince-Smith

"Every generation faces choices: hope or despair, the plan for scarcity or to embrace the possibilities. Societies throughout history believed they had reached the frontiers of human accomplishment, but in every age those who trusted that divine spark of imagination discovered that vastly greater horizons still lay ahead." —Jack Kemp, 1996

Jack Kemp talked about growth incessantly. And that is what this panel is about. But what is growth? Can growth be dangerous? What is it about growth that we don't understand?

In the 1920s, under Calvin Coolidge, there was a lot of trouble in the United States. Inflation (although the government was not acknowledging it). Unemployment. Labor unrest. An anti-Wall Street mood. Successive governments, including the Wilson administration as well as some Republicans (Harding and Coolidge) took steps, including cutting the government in half and raising interest rates three hundred basis points, which is effective doubling. Those steps resulted in a very good era. They had a short depression, the "Forgotten Depression" and then they had strong growth (4 percent real growth under Coolidge). They had a few recessions, but no one noticed them.

In short, the 1920s was a fabulous decade for growth. People didn't talk about GDP back then. They talked about the market and numbers, which illustrated what was good about growth.

What was bad about focusing on growth alone is that it makes people forget that it is policies that enable growth. As Coolidge said "he who builds a factory, builds a temple." After the 1920s, people just said growth is there, as though it were a mood thing like animal spirits of the market. The country, having enjoyed that growth, forgot about the rough and free-market policies that made it possible, and instead endorsed other policies. When the Depression came along, there had to be a crash, there had to be a downturn, but the country need not have suffered a ten-year, anti-growth depression.

Growth may be the answer but growth is in fact the result of policy choices. Jack Kemp understood this, Barry Goldwater, Ronald Reagan, Jack Kennedy all understood this. The right policies made growth possible, not the other way around.

Growth is a rallying cry politically, and it does reduce trouble. In the 1920s, bad things were less bad because of growth. Farmers were miserable, but they could move into a town and get a car and maybe a radio, so what had changed? Sometimes what they dreamed of didn't happen but another window opened because of growth and they forgot to ask how that happened. As a society, we cannot afford not to ask.

Our history of growth begins with the power of ideas, which was Jack Kemp's tremendous contribution among others, and combines with two other words that also begin with "I"—imagination and innovation. Think of the imagination that got people to discover the "new world," the innovation that took them to get here, and the ideas of what to do when they got here. Our future growth depends again on this intersection of ideas, innovation and imagination, plus insight and inspiration.

From the time of our Founding Fathers, the idea that led to our inclusive revolution was a reaction to policies that stifled growth. We all know that history. The British were taxing us to death, an early example of bad policy undercutting the ability to create our own indigenous industries. We had a revolution that was very inclusive. Poor farmers, wealthy ship captains, and craftsmen all came together to create this new intellectual framework of ideas and ideals of individual rights and responsibilities. Then came the innovation of new forms of government, as colonies turned into states and built an infrastructure to make of many states one nation. It is that infrastructure that enables industry and commerce, and links us from sea to shining sea.

Today, we have a tremendous infrastructure deficit, driven by the lack of domestic investment in infrastructure, and the inability to determine where foreign high value investments are coming into this country. What to do about that infrastructure deficit is at the heart of America's growth agenda right now.

When one thinks of America and our great strengths, we think of knowledge, such as Ben Franklin inventing electricity and Thomas Edison turning that invention into technology. We think of everything from the computer and the integrated circuit to the IPhone and the Internet. We think of our transportation going from the automobile that created the middle class all the way up to the airplane and space.

Most exciting, we are on the cusp of tremendous opportunities that are driven by innovation. The world is being rewritten in digital, genetic, atomic and neuron code and it's going to unleash innovation, industries, jobs, products, and services in ways that are unimaginable for global prosperity. Consider what it will mean to move from a world that many see as a world of scarcity to a world of abundance. Couple that with what is happening to the infrastructure of energy, where for the first time our country is ready to move from being energy weak to being energy strong. We're revitalizing manufacturing. It's a very, very exciting time.

But in order for all this growth to be possible, we will need an innovation friendly capital cost structure, tax system, and regulatory environment. We need a policy agenda that will unleash this innovation and imagination capacity for growth and prosperity.

We also need to understand that wealth is knowledge. The Neanderthal in his cave had all the material resources we have today. All the difference between the Stone Age and our era is the growth of knowledge.

How does knowledge grow? It grows through learning. Anyone who has studied our economy—like the Boston Consulting Group, Bain and Company, other similar consultancies—has drilled in on what's called the learning curve. They've shown that learning curves are pervasive in capitalism. With every doubling of total volume accumulated or units produced, costs drop between twenty and thirty percent. This radical effect is called the learning curve, and it applies to every kind of industry and every kind of business.

Learning is growth. It's the accumulation of knowledge. Jack Kemp above all other politicians grasped these dynamics. He absolutely understood and was deeply committed to propagating the essential knowledge that enables capitalist growth and learning.

The rule of learning, which comes from Carl Popper, says that scientific propositions have to be falsifiable. Any proposition that can't be disproven can't yield knowledge and thus can't promote growth. The government tries to guarantee everything, but any corporation that is guaranteed cannot produce knowledge and thus can't yield growth. So all the efforts by government to assure the future instead stifle growth by stultifying the entrepreneur and stultifying the economy.

Here's the first paragraph in a story on the front page of the Wall Street Journal this morning: "Five years after the financial crisis ended, soft growth in Europe, a stop-and-start U.S. recovery and waning momentum in China have policymakers groping for what to do next." A question for the panel: Why are they groping?"

One answer may be that these policymakers fail to understand a key fact that Jack Kemp championed throughout his career: a dynamic, creative economy depends on a stable currency. Imagine a politician who is actually willing to say that Milton Friedman was wrong; but Milton Friedman was completely wrong about money and Jack Kemp was completely right.

The essence of Friedman's monetarism was a belief that velocity—the turnover of money—was a constant. It didn't change. It was an expression of human psychology. But the last decades have demonstrated that the velocity of money is tremendously volatile. It rises and falls massively. What does this mean? This means that central banks don't control money—you do. People control money because it's people who decide how often they're going to turn it over.

One of the real problems of the economy today is that Milton Friedman won. As a result, we have wildly gyrating currencies all around the world. When the currency which is kind of a carrier for economic activity becomes volatile, the horizons of the economy shrink and economic activity focuses on short term trading. Now we almost have a parody of short term trading in multi-megahertz computer trading, which is a ludicrous parody of capitalism. Capitalism is based on knowledge, not on manipulating markets through trading faster than humans can actually research and develop investment ideas.

What we are seeing is a great vindication of Kemp today. We need to establish a stable money. There are two ways of doing that. George Gilder's newest book, Bitcoins and Gold: The Information Theory of Money, suggests that bitcoins may transform money on the Internet, while gold is the perpetual eternal money that can lend stability to economies around the world.

One of the problems we have with growth is the number we use for growth. When commentators on television talk about growth, they say it's GDP, right? Well, that may be problematic. For example, if GDP is very low and then grows nine percent relative to itself in a year but doesn't get back to where it was in an earlier year, the conclusion is still that the GDP is up nine percent. That's like a snapshot of the economy's recovery. But what if the economy doesn't get back to the level of GDP where it was before the crash? Then that nine percent is fun and we're glad we're getting better, but it's measured from a tiny base. That essential fallacy is a problem. If GDP is up nine percent but we're not back to where we were before, we're not recovered yet. But that's how people play with GDP.

The second way in which GDP is a vulnerable item is that it counts government activity pretty strongly. So if the government builds a good bridge in the way we were just describing, that's nice GDP. But what if the government builds a bridge to nowhere? That can be quantified as government GDP as well. So the scoring tends to favor government, only government is not very good at innovating.

And then there is the role of central banks, which are also parts of government. What they do still matters and not necessarily in a productive way. In China we see this clearly where they don't tell the truth about growth.

The way we measure growth favors government too much and neglects the private sector and therefore fails to capture the anemic quality of certain sectors now. Our GDP isn't very good but maybe we should look at some other numbers; maybe we should quantify productivity gains more prominently?

Productivity really has to be the ultimate measure, not economic growth. China has tremendous productivity problems and over time, that will have a huge negative impact as they try to have a higher standard of living. The US ability to thrive, to increase our productivity and increase our prosperity for our citizens is something that the private sector has to lead. The private sector is determining where to invest.

U.S. companies produce outside of the United States more than three times the value of all U.S. exports. In other words, U.S. companies are investing and producing three times more of their wealth outside the United States in this growing, global dynamic economy. The United States needs to have more of that investment back here in our infrastructure, in our entrepreneurship, in all of these next generation technologies. About one point four trillion dollars in U.S. companies' overseas product doesn't come back because of the double taxation on repatriation. That is something that overnight we could address if we had the political consensus, which would have a huge impact of bringing capital back to the U.S.

We are also seeing a huge drop in the number of small business formations and entrepreneurship. Job creation in this country has really come from a dynamic small business economy, but they can't come in and access capital. Venture capital isn't investing in these firms because they want to have an internalized rate of return. As a result, there is a double whammy of these macro tax policies plus what's going on in individuals' access to capital.

On top of that is the overhang of our federal deficit. We continue to get into debt. Government is spending more. When you project out the numbers, pretty soon our health-care expenditures will increase so that almost everything in our federal budget will go to healthcare and entitlements, leaving nothing for research and development and national security. It's really a perfect storm.

Questions and Answers

Q. Not a question, but I have to correct one thing. In the early renditions of monetarism, Milton Friedman did have the constant change in the velocity of money that completely broke down in the early 1980s. Later, Friedman basically admitted that Jack Kemp was right and quickly came around to a gold or other hard money standard.

Q. It seems to me that the idea of economic growth has lost its allure. In the Obama years, we've had terrible growth—2 percent at best and yet Obama was reelected easily. I don't see many stories about how horrible the growth rate is, or the repercussions of that with millions of people dropping out of the economy. You could, as Jack Kemp did, talk about growth and show the joys and the benefits of greater growth; yet Republicans in particular are the offenders because they use the word growth almost as much as Jack Kemp did and then do nothing. What about the idea of growth as a popular or significant intellectual idea?

A. Maybe the Republicans or the Democrats need something more precise such as opportunity. The idea of growth has been abused to such an extent that people aren't always sure what it means, much less the policies to get it. I would add that the U.S. has had some growth lately—not very substantial growth but some growth—and so people sort of think the economy might be okay. But the only reason it feels somewhat okay is because of the innovation in energy and because other currencies don't still regard us as the currency of last resort.

We get a kind of free ride out of this terrible paradox: When we pursue negative policy, we get rewarded because all the other money comes here because the world is in trouble because of our subpar policy. Well, that won't happen forever. There will be a challenge to the U.S. dollar. Interest rates will go up and Americans will become interested in reducing them. Government austerity can be good because we'll have to save our currency as if we were England. That can happen, and it may have a good outcome because at that point we may have a better policy mix that causes strong, real growth in the United States.

We have a kind of complacency now because we think we're the only ones that matter. Well, we're not. It's not like the seventies. China is there, Europe is there, all of Asia and India are there to compete with us and produce a currency that could bring the dollar into stress. That could be good for the dollar in the long run, but it's complacency for now until the dollar is truly challenged, which will happen in our lifetime

[another panelist] But with respect to this government manipulation of currencies, remember it was just a few years ago when Brazil for example was screaming bloody murder that the U.S. was manipulating our currency to drive it down so that U.S. exports of industrial products would be cheaper than Brazilian products. The Chinese keep their currency low to fuel their exports ....

[another panelist] Well in other words they keep the dollar high. The Chinese are supporting the dollar. We're eroding the dollar. The threat to the dollar isn't in Beijing; it's in Washington. The Chinese government is 17 percent of GDP today. They're more pro-enterprise than we are and that's the challenge we face. We now have a socialist government and its effects are debauching America. China is more capitalist today I believe than the United States is in many ways....

[first panelist] The Chinese export machine and everything they do to encourage that is state sponsored. You will not find a private-sector Council on Competitiveness in China because behind every Chinese enterprise and their boards of directors are government officials—but that's another discussion.

Back to defining growth. How do you drive prosperity for the people and ensure that they are going to have jobs and a bright future of opportunity? I think what this administration is doing is pernicious. We hear a lot of talk about inequality and non-exclusive growth, as opposed to what needs to be done to generate wealth—which brings us back to the energy and manufacturing revolution and the challenges we have going forward.

Who would give career advice to a teenager to go into manufacturing or go work in a factory? We have some of the most advanced industrial enterprises in the world, totally automated and highly skilled, but nobody wants to go into manufacturing. Yet the way things are going to be made with additive manufacturing and modeling is a revolution that will have huge value. But guess what? We don't have the skilled workforce now to participate in that revolution. People create knowledge but people have to be educated. That requires a K-12 educational system. These are huge issues for future growth capabilities in this country.

[Another panelist] Look at the world from the point of view of that eighteen-year-old and ask, what does he or she see? Are we saying to the eighteen-year-old, "where can you cynically get a job that's created by someone else that might be at a company that might produce something not very good? Or which credential can you acquire and how can you so structure your college application or job application or tax form to max out and are you clever enough to do that?" Or are we saying, "what is your idea and here are the ways we can help you with your individual idea?" At eighteen or twenty-two, do you really feel that your future is set by you? As long as we have a culture where it's a game getting into university, getting the right job, getting the earned income credit rebate so you can buy the vehicle—in essence asking who is the cleverer rat—we won't have a growth economy. A growth economy is one where the young people see lots of opportunity and are supported in leading the rest of us in creating things, not just acquiring certain things that are already available. As things stand now, they're not getting a very good signal from us. They're learning to game the system, not build the world.

Young people are part of this circular game where higher education steadily increases tuition and the government expands its educational grants, leaving young people holding the bag. They all come out of college with large debts that cripple their entrepreneurial spirit at the beginning. I believe that this was fraud that was imposed by the higher education system; it managed to get the kids to bear the burden of increasing professorial salaries for corrupting and indoctrinating a generation in some green religion. For example, 80 percent of Harvard students voted to withdraw all investments from fossil fuels; nearly 80 percent voted to withdraw all investments from Israel. These are the two great foundations of the American economy believe it or not. It's amazing what proportion of our technologies originate in Israel. These Ivy League universities are corrupting, debouching, and indoctrinating students so they can't think anymore. Imagine 80 percent of Harvard students are effectively anti-Semites. What do you make of that? This is a crisis and it's all financed by taxpayers, by the federal government. I believe there should be an amnesty on these student loans and that higher education should be taxed.

[another panelist] Actually, there are some innovative university presidents who are working on reforming higher education. But returning to that productivity metric, the two sectors of our economy that have no productivity growth are education and healthcare. It's not accidental that their costs are off the charts.

Why do you think in most parts of the world if anybody gets sick, they want U.S. branded pharmaceuticals and medical devises? Wherever you are, if you're sick and go to the drug store, you try to find a U.S. product (and you hope it is in fact U.S. made as opposed to a counterfeit) because we have set the highest standard in the world for safety and efficacy of medicines. We have an extremely competitive pharmaceutical medical device industry being strangled here a little bit by domestic policies; but in terms of what's happening globally, we lead the world still in innovation in that space, such as in genomics. The pharmaceutical industry invests huge amounts in R&D—about 3 percent of their profit. Virtually none of the profit in financial services goes into R and D.

The U.S. used to have substantial public investment in basic research. Jack Kemp was a big supporter of our basic research agenda. We used to be the largest producer in the world of research and development; now we're number three. That's not necessarily bad because it means the rest of the world is investing, but we're seeing R&D's percentage of U.S. GDP decline and decline. The Koreans are planning to invest 6 percent of GDP on research and development, while we're at about 2.6 percent (nearly half government and a little more private sector). What will happen to innovation and learning and knowledge if we don't invest in the frontier areas of the future such as nanotechnologies and advanced materials? I've seen some of these additive materials now that have energetic properties built into them—it's unbelievable—some of that work is being done at our national labs and universities. I think that's something we have to keep investing in as a nation to have growth

[another panelist] Right now the government is corrupting a whole generation of scientists. It's corrupting a whole generation of venture capitalists. It's a negative force. For example, the U.S. government has just ruled that carbon nanotubes—the greatest breakthrough in nanotechnology—will be subject to regulation controls that resemble those for asbestos. This oppressive regulation is undermining our sources of innovation in the United States. Moreover, government science is increasingly dominated by a climate change mania that is deeply destructive. We have to focus as on retrieving the culture as well as on the economy

Q. This morning, Gary Kasparov made a fairly strong suggestion that we revive our space program. He talked about the benefits deriving from the race to the moon (and I would say probably also the 1980s defense expenditures had spill-over effects). Would you support government investments in space?

A. Historically, that actually had a positive effect; but right now the space program is being led by private ventures, while the existing space bureaucracy has lost its edge and really no longer makes such contributions. There are things government can do, certainly. The tragedy today is that government is failing to do the things it should and can do. The galvanic policies that put a man on the moon and defending the country are policies the current government has abandoned. Instead, it's trying to guarantee every student loan and every beach front property and trying to eliminate risk in the economy. The result is they prohibit learning and thus prohibit growth.

[another panelist] On the subject of R&D, shale gas, which is a tremendous bonanza for this country, is enabled by horizontal drilling, which has been traced back to research at one of our Department of Defense (DOD) national labs thirty years ago. That technology, which took private-sector capital to perfect and entrepreneurship and individual property rights to exploit, is an example of how tremendous innovation in the private sector is often based on fundamental research from universities and labs over a period of thirty or forty years.

Here is something I find very concerning. Two years ago, I was in China with a team from Lawrence Livermore National Laboratory, one of our weapons labs, and we visited all twelve of the Chinese supercomputing facilities. They were all built through military investment but are run and operated by so-called private-sector companies. Virtually everyone working in these facilities are Chinese students who have studied in the U.S. at Stanford, Harvard or wherever, or have worked at IBM, Intel, EMC, Microsoft—the list goes on. I asked the leader at one facility, "Do you have any Americans working in these labs?" (of course we have Chinese working in ours); and he said, "You know, Americans are too stupid to come here. We would never let an American in one of our facilities."

[another panelist] We've been debating which federal program is a good one. Maybe space is better, or infrastructure programs, or other ambitious programs, or defense. But today all these things are squeezed by the entitlements. That's the distinction between now and the past. There would be more money for some of these projects (if we wanted them) if there weren't so many entitlements.

Entitlements dull the country and wreck the budget. The defense debate last fall was intense because national defense is in that share of the budget that is not untouchable. It isn't that defense costs that much (and in the United States it costs a lot but not really a lot), but that defense is what could be edited; whereas we're not allowed to ever say that we might cut entitlements because that's how they're structured and that's also our political belief. So all these opportunities are less because of entitlements.

I'd like to give an example of how even a good regulation can dull innovation. Who are the smartest people in the world? They are often innovators and business leaders wherever they're from. What motivates them? Capitalism. They want to make money. What else motivates them? Well, just like anyone else they care about their family. What happens when the child of a super successful venture capitalist gets a weird form of cancer, what does he want to do? He wants to save the child. He will dump millions maybe billions into whatever medical innovation might save his child. We've seen this over and over again. Some of those things that millionaire and billionaires do to save their family member end up being quackery but sometimes they end up investing in something good. What do those people want more than anything? They want to give their sick loved one a chance to try the drug. Sometimes there are new drugs that have passed Food and Drug Administration (FDA) phase one but not phase two or three. Now there's a new legal proposal in the states called "the right to try" that would give people with a terminal illness the right to try a drug that's passed some safety tests but not all the tests of the FDA. From the point of view of the sad story of the relative who wants to try a drug and can't, it's a good interesting idea and it's passing in the states. Why else is it good? Because when all those innovators focus on something and are passionate about something, sometimes they have a great innovation that could help the health of people who are not rich. But the way the FDA is structured now, that's not possible, so they go off in great frustration.

[another panelist] The whole issue of regulation is like the golden mean of classical times. It is a balance issue. Sometimes we'll go too far this way or that. We saw that with Sarbanes-Oxley and some of the other legislation.

Q. A comment. The precautionary principal is ruling now. We're spending way too much money trying to prevent bad things from happening. You can't have innovation without risk taking. Columbus wouldn't have gotten on the boat if today's regulatory agencies were around then. The big financial firms have been turned into public utilities. They can't innovate, they can't do anything now; instead, they are wards of the government, which sets the prices and all the procedures. Jack Kemp always talked about taking risks. He was a risk taker when he played football and he was a risk taker in terms of policy. He was willing to go against the conventional wisdom, and he took enormous personal intellectual risk to move the ball down the field. We've got to get back to that.

Q. We've seen anemic growth, we've seen the slowest recovery from a recession in a long, long time. Yet at the same time the stock market is hitting an all-time high. Companies are flush with cash. Corporate earnings growth is rapid. What is the main disconnect between the rapid corporate earnings growth and the slow economic growth? What are some things that could be done to help connect those things?

A. The key issue is that big companies are buying up their competitors and buying their own shares, so you have a steady shrinkage of the total amount of equity out there. When there's less equity coupled with a lot of quantitative easing, that leads to a rise in the value of the residual equity. IPOs (initial public offerings) are at an extremely low level. In Jack Kemp's day, there were seven IPOs of new companies for every merger and acquisition. Today there are twenty mergers and acquisitions for every IPO, which means the big companies can gobble up their competitors.

Big companies also can move their operations overseas. They function across the global economy and thus can't be stifled so effectively by the administration. Our economy has been seriously crippled by mazes of regulatory overreach that only big companies can address. Carbon nanotubes are illegal, but if you have a big enough company with big enough lawyers you can get waivers so you can experiment with carbon nanotubes; but if you're a small company you're out of luck and you go out of business unless you can get bought by the less creative large companies. So our whole economy is being changed and those measures are deceptive.

Q. Where is the Republican candidate who will stand up against this?

A. I think they all will. I think it will be popular to run against the current corporate state that is stifling our future. These big financial leviathans are extensions of the government, state owned enterprises that are destructive to the economy and capturing more and more of the profits and contributing massively to the inequalities that many Democrats in particular are constantly bemoaning.

[another panelist] The multinational really doesn't exist anymore. These are global enterprises, and they are optimizing where they invest and do their work and generate their talent all over the world. For us as Americans, what we need to be worried about is that we can't compete on commodities. What can we do to optimize our capital regulatory investment climate so these enterprises want to stay here and do high value work here? That's what we really want. We don't want to do work where we're competing on labor costs as opposed to the higher value.

Nobody has mentioned yet product liability. Every single study that has been done—in universities, at national academies—shows that product liability laws are having a huge chilling effect on innovation. For example, there's a whole class of advanced materials that DuPont won't make in this country because of our triple damages for product liability. Companies are domiciling outside of the United States because of product liability. Our hypothetical big company doing work on carbon nanotubes might be smart to locate outside the U.S. because if something goes wrong the investors would be destroyed.

We need to define the optimal public policies that can unleash this tremendous innovation capacity, which cut across capital, finance and regulatory issues....

[another panelist] I would suggest three, coming out of this conversation. First, product liability reform. Philip Howard's book Common Ground describes what litigation does to growth and the national spirit.

Second, Social Security reform is not hard. We could reform Social Security in one afternoon, maybe by changing the eligibility age, maybe by giving visas to high-end workers or professionals who could pay Social Security taxes, and maybe by adjusting the pension so that it rises only with inflation and not with the average real wage. A bunch of high school seniors could do it if they knew how to use a spreadsheet. Do that as a down payment in political trust; once the U.S. reforms Social Security it can grapple with much, much harder issues.

Third, corporate taxes are out of whack with the rest of the world. They might be lower, but what would also be important would be any tax that affects an entrepreneur. If the capital gains tax were lower, more money would come to the U.S. to invest in their ideas. If there were certainty about the income tax rate, that too would be very good for growth in the economy. So if three or four things like that were done, we would have the real kind of growth to which Kemp aspired.

[another panelist] High-tech immigration reform is also important as Jack Kemp understood. The auto business, like all the great new industries in America, have been heavily supported by immigration. For example, there was a company in Los Angeles called Otoy that wanted to bring sixteen New Zealand engineers who wanted to come to L.A. to contribute to American innovation, but they couldn't get visas, so instead they now have a company in New Zealand. America's immigration policies are destructive. The idea that Mark Zuckerberg just wants to have cheap programmers is just ludicrous. If you live in Silicon Valley, you know that every major technology where the hard core research and development happens is dominated by people from overseas.

Q. We've heard that the higher education system is bankrupting our students, it's not teaching them the right skills that are needed in this economy, and it's indoctrinating them. We all know the reason for this is because the institutions of higher education have been colonized by the progressive left. How do we overcome that? what do we do?

A. One of the things that I like very much as an educational tool is high school debate. In high school debate, students have to get the information and argue both sides, and they do. And they learn things much faster because competition is involved; they're not being forced-fed information from a teacher. There are many ways in which people get around a stultifying class or a monologue lesson that has only one point of view. Human nature resists indoctrination. Kids don't like it, nobody likes it. So what I see is a lot of curious minds looking for a lot of ways to learn including ideas their teachers don't mention. So I'm seeing less darkness than you see because they learn pretty fast. The Internet and online education, their faith, the travel that they do relative to what people did fifty years ago is also offsetting. So it's not as if our country is stultified in a sleep entirely; it's just a shame that the education system is so monotone.

[another panelist] I don't think that higher education in the sciences, the Science, Technology, Engineering and Math (STEM) disciplines, has been "colonized." I think that's more in the arts and humanities social sciences. But if we have K through 12 teachers teaching science who really should be teaching gym, that is a problem. We have to deal with the whole teacher union issue which is stagnating our schools.

We have a huge deficit in Americans going into math, science and engineering; and if they don't go into those fields in undergraduate school they're not going in graduate school. Almost 70 percent of all graduating engineering students in this country are not American. I agree about changes needed in immigration policy. We should staple a green card to every STEM major. But we have to train our own citizens to participate in an economy that's going to be highly quantitative, driven by all these technologies and the demographics. If people do not have jobs and cannot contribute to the economy, they'll be on welfare, they won't be paying taxes, and overtime we'll see a huge decline not only of our prosperity, but our democracy as well.

Jimmy Kemp, Amity Shlaes, George Gilder

FREEDOM, DIGNITY, OPPORTUNITY Rapporteur's Report

Juan Williams, Arthur Brooks, Ron Christie, Wayne Frederick

"The American Idea was never that everyone would be leveled to the same position in life. The American Idea was that each individual should have the same opportunity to rise as high as his effort and initiative and God-given talent could carry him. If you were born to be a master carpenter, or a mezzo-soprano—or even a pro-football player— here in America you could make it." — Jack Kemp, 1980

Jack Kemp had a strong belief, which is at the heart of "Lincoln Republican" ideals, that in order for democratic capitalism to work in America, it has to work for everyone. Today, there is a large political question about income inequality and persistent poverty, especially since the 2008 recession. Arguments about taxes, stimulus, minimum wage pervade our political discourse.

This weekend (May, 2014), we're going to celebrate the 60th anniversary of Brown v. Board of Education, which was the start of the modern Civil Rights Movement. Education, as the Brown decision highlighted, is the key to economic mobility. That mobility is especially critical in this difficult economic environment, and critical for the Republican Party as it tries to form its identity in this moment.

Recently, we've seen a number of prominent Republicans who may run for president try to establish their beachhead on this issue. Paul Ryan has looked at Jack Kemp's thinking on empowerment zones. Marco Rubio has talked about replacing the earned income tax credit with direct grants to individuals who may decide that they want job training or that they want further education. Rand Paul has been talking about how you can lower taxes effectively to allow people more opportunity for economic advancement. We've seen Rick Santorum, Mitt Romney, former Governor Pawlenty, all come out recently and say they are in favor of raising the minimum wage because they think that the Republican Party has somehow become divorced from blue collar workers. Speaker Boehner says that he'll commit suicide before he allows any such thing to happen, so there is a split within the party.

In response, some Democrats say, "Oh, all these prominent Republicans are talking about poverty now, but in reality what they're saying is they want to cut spending on antipoverty programs in order to lower taxes on the rich; and they complain about entitlement societies and therefore are insincere when they address poverty issues." So the question is, how do you deal with that, and what are the real issues at stake?

Let's start with higher education. One of the things that institutions of higher learning need to espouse for their students is that whatever their family's socio-economic level may be, education is what they're coming to get, not a degree. Education is what matters for opportunity and upward mobility. If you go back to the 1940s, 50s, 60s, when the states in the South were actually paying their African-American citizens to go to school—if they had the aptitude—because the schools were segregated. You can palpably see that upward mobility in the African-American community and the middle class of Africa America when you look at the prominent folks that came out of that time and into the 1970s too—Thurgood Marshall, Vernon Jordan and others. Their education gave them that opportunity.

Today, circumstances are different but students still face similar issues. At Howard University, for example, which is a private institution, 56 percent of undergrad students are now Pell Grant eligible. They are still coming from circumstances in which some of them are the first generation in college and their parents don't necessarily have the means to pay for them. The maximum Pell Grant award is just about $1,500, which means for a private school tuition of $24,000 there is still a significant gap. Even if universities like Howard match the Pell grants dollar for dollar, students are still facing a big gap.

Without a doubt, opportunity is one of America's greatest promises. Education is the ink with which that contract was written. Institutions of higher learning need to provide the inkwell by making sure that the students recognize that it's not just about getting a degree; they have to use their education in a way that changes the world around them so they are giving back. That service component is very important to weave into the educational process as well, because part of what enables mobility is that motivation to reach back and afford others that opportunity.

We have to keep creating the opportunities, but we have to underline those opportunities with excellence; on that, there must be no compromise. We make a lot of noise today about affirmative action in relation to opportunity and tying it to economics; but in reality, schools like the University of Michigan had four African-American graduates from their medical school back in the 40s without anybody enacting a law to afford that opportunity; rather excellence in terms of performance dictated that.

It makes little sense to push education as an opportunity in America if we don't have the economic circumstances that create jobs where that education is relevant. Today, there are a lot of students with doctorate degrees who are unemployed or who can't find employment in their fields of study. So we need to look at what we're putting into the pipeline and make sure there's an outlet for them to go out and express all of the talents that we give them in our higher education system.

We're pushing the opportunity created by higher education to have the distinct outcome of contributing to a productive society. If we strengthen our higher education system in terms of talent acquisition and the ability to apply those talents, America can become more competitive; but we have to make our education system itself more competitive to make sure our graduates can compete.

Turning to politics, some quarters of the black communities complain that President Obama is not doing enough on this poverty/unemployment issue with specific attention to people who have been left behind, people who have been hurt most. There are persistent high levels of poverty and unemployment. But what is the Republican party saying to that population as compared to what the Democrat in the White House is doing?

At a speech before Conservative Political Action Committee (CPAC) on Feb 25, 1985, Jack Kemp said: "There is only one explanation why the party of Lincoln, Theodore Roosevelt, and Coolidge—the party that Lincoln himself called eminently conservative— lost the support of black Americans. We Republicans mislaid the key to prosperity and full economic opportunity for all." Kemp continued on this very important point:

> *Issue after issue, minority Americans share the goal of conservatives. It is high time that conservatives put forth an inclusive agenda that articulates the vision we stand for. Our task is to carry that vision to every district, to every group of Americans. What minorities are wanting to hear from conservatives is not that we have 15 new spending programs to replaces failed liberal ones; instead they are waiting for conservatives to share our dream of freedom, equality and opportunity.*

Republicans today need to do a better job of articulating that vision. It's about freedom, it's about opportunity and it's about dignity. It's about the liberating thoughts of economic opportunity, recognizing the power of the individual, recognizing that we should all have the ability to engage in discourse with dignity and agree to disagree. It's recognizing that education really is the civil rights issue of the 21st century. And it's about looking at people and not seeing color, but seeing people.

Today there are many African Americans who seem to think If you study hard, and you work hard—and you're black—then you're not authentically black, you're actually acting white. Blacks need to have a little more of a dignified discussion that respects a range of opinion, and stop saying to those with whom they don't necessarily agree, "You're somehow acting white, you're not authentically black."

Jack Kemp never talked to black people like black people. He talked to people like people. That's very different from those politicians who would say, "Oh, we have to have an African-American outreach; let's see, let's talk about crime, let's talk about drugs, let's talk about housing reform." No, let's talk about lowering taxes, let's talk about national security issues, let's talk about issues all Americans care about.

One of the issues Jack Kemp talked about a lot is free enterprise and the poor. Free enterprise matters because of the poor. The Catholic cardinal of Chicago, Francis George, was talking to a large group of his biggest donors, millionaires giving a lot of money to the church for causes to help people in poverty. He said, "The poor need you, but you need the poor too. You know why? Because the poor are going to keep you out of hell."

Capitalism to be relevant needs the poor. Rich people don't need free enterprise very much because rich people have the system pretty wired. In America today, if you've got everything in a row, and you have powerful friends in government, you don't need free enterprise that much. The people who need opportunity most are the ones who need the warriors who believe in the free enterprise system.

When today's 50 year olds were kids, poverty was something that was really far way—sub-Saharan African poverty, the kind of poverty one saw in National Geographic—and there was nothing we could do, it was an insoluble problem and nothing was ever going to happen.

Think about the difference between then and now. Today, compared to 1970, the percentage of the world's population living on a dollar a day or less has declined by 80 percent. About 70 percent of American think that hunger is up around the world. They're wrong. There has been an 80 percent decline in starvation level poverty since 1970. Why? Some people might guess it's because of the United Nations or U.S. foreign aid. No. Those are not the reasons.

There are five explanations, with a sixth added on: Globalization, free trade, property rights, rule of law, and entrepreneurship. And add to that the strength of the American military, which has kept peace in places around the world that had never seen it before and facilitated trade. That's what has cut starvation level poverty by 80 percent. You did it, and you didn't even know it. That was the free enterprise system at work.

It was the American free enterprise systems spreading itself around the world. Modes of communication exploded, changing the ways people get information; and that meant that people around the world were able to throw off the chains their poverty and the chains of their tyranny so they could live like us.

That's a miracle. That's the greatest antipoverty achievement in the history of mankind. It happened in the last few decades. And you built that. What an extraordinary achievement.

That's why free enterprise matters. It matters so we can continue to do that around the world and right here at home. And if we don't talk about that, and if we're not warriors for the poor every single day, then free enterprise simply has no any moral content and it doesn't matter.

So how do these five principles apply in the domestic political context, where we see especially among minority children just despairing levels of persistent poverty? They are the people who could benefit most from the principles of free enterprise; how can upward mobility and the power of capitalism reach them? And how can conservative politicians take that message to them?

Conservatives have a relatively high level of difficulty in penetrating communities who actually need, or could benefit the most from the principles of free enterprise. Why is that? The answer is because, face facts, people think that conservatives don't care about the poor. The data suggests that only 16 percent of Americans think that conservatives care about the poor.

No one will ever vote for or support or even be remotely sympathetic to any candidate they think doesn't care about people like them. That was the only thing you needed to know in the 2012 election. Which candidate cared more about people like you? But before you dismiss the question because it sounds unduly emotional, ask yourself whether you would vote for anybody who doesn't care about people like you. Why would you?

There is a long history here, but the biggest reason that people, particularly people who are poor, think that Republicans/conservatives don't care about people like them is because they've talked as if they don't.

What is the Republican brand? The Republican brand is fighting against things, and it has been for a long time. What was Ronald Reagan's product line? His product line was basically fighting again five things: the sprawling big government, regulation, taxes, deficits and debt. But that actually didn't matter, because a product line is ephemeral. A company's product line changes from year to year depending on the exigencies that the market presents. What doesn't change over time is our purpose, and that's what matters. Purpose shouldn't change, and purpose comes before product.

The magic of Reagan was something very different. In liberal-democratic households in the 1980s, on Monday/Wednesday/Friday Reagan was evil, and on Tuesday/Thursday/Saturday and Sunday he was stupid…. and nobody could make up their mind. But the one thing that everybody knew was that Reagan loved this country, and Reagan loved the people who lived here.

Do you know what Jack Kemp's magic was? He loved people and he believed in them. That's the secret. The Republicans have lost their way because they are fighters against things. It's time for them to be warriors for people.

There is no issue where you can't twerk it from being against things to being for people. Who are you fighting for, and how are you going to get there? Don't fight against teachers' unions, fight for children. Don't fight against a licentious culture, fight for the good life that comes from faith, family, community and work—not because you're a puritan but because you're a Good Samaritan.

There is also a way to reach people and there is a way not to. Consider the outreach to college campuses. Politicians and others who visit campuses to "talk to" the students may be missing the opportunity to have a dialogue, which implies some measure of discourse and dissent. There needs to be as much listening as "talking to."

For example, recently Senator Rand Paul visited Howard University. There was no pre-talk, which is to say he didn't meet with the president, the provost, or any university officials. He showed up on campus, got in front of some students that he probably assumed would be hostile (because Howard has a reputation as a liberal campus) and talked to them from that preconception. He misquoted who the first black US senator was and a few things like that. They forgave him for that; they corrected him out loud. (For those who may be interested, C-SPAN taped the entire thing.)

The students listened, then asked a number of very appropriate questions. "Senator, you voted such and such, why? Can you explain?" The theme of their questioning was that he seemed to be against things; and if that is the case, "give us an explanation as to why we should come join you. What is the opportunity you would create for us?" He had difficulty articulating an answer, especially for kids who do not come from a system where their parents may have owned small businesses or were in the higher echelons of corporate America. It's critical to be able to speak to kids whose parents are public servants and explain that they can have other and different opportunities when they graduate, that free enterprise is all about creating those opportunities.

The students also brought up the question of voter ID and the Voting Rights Act and so forth. Senator Paul did not have a firm position to show them how they could get from point A to point B. They are not living the same struggles of the civil rights era. The opportunity for that dialogue was there and was missed.

The point is, political leaders who want to reach young people need to find an approach that embraces some type of a dialogue. That requires that they do some homework, and be willing to get feedback about what they care about. We make assumptions about what kids like those on the Howard campus want; but it's not at all clear that they are all liberal Democrats. Unfortunately, they have little exposure to any conservative type of leaning because no one is approaching them from that point of view. Even a U.S. senator who is interested in running for president comes to campus without having done his homework.

The lack of a Republican or conservative presence on many campuses is another missed opportunity. Just imagine the discourse at the cafeteria table where students can have somebody with the same background, but a different opinion, having a discussion about ideology.

Sadly, most university campuses today are not as open minded as they should be to dissent and discourse. Look at this commencement season. The number of people who have declined to speak or have had to be disinvited speaks to that problem. Today some colleges regard certain individuals as having a point of view that is "too conservative" or "too liberal," and say, "we don't want you on our campus." That's wrong.

Political leaders for their part need to have to have a principled position and be able to articulate that principled position. Most of the very hot political issues are the proxy for a lot of other history. These are such hard things to navigate that politicians often just try to avoid them. They pivot off and talk about whatever they want to talk about.

One of the reasons Republicans tend do so poorly in these cases is not because they have the wrong positions. To be successful in things where reasonable people can disagree requires two characteristics: to be principled and tolerant. The problem is that a lot of Republicans look unprincipled and intolerant. "I go this way on abortion, that way on abortion, this way, and then that way, but I do know that whatever position I am taking today

I hate everybody else." That has sort of become the Republican way and it's a real problem.

Politicians can go into a community that disagrees with a lot of their policies if they're tolerant, they're interested in what other people have to say, they entertain opposing points of view in a reasonable way, and they're highly principled about their point of view. Do these things, and people will listen.

Too often Republicans make the mistake of parachuting in, right around election time, saying how inclusive they are and how important it is that we're all together—and then they disappear for another four years. Contrast what Paul Ryan has been doing for the last year, going to twelve different cities talking to twelve different communities on a listening tour. It would behoove the conservative movement to listen as opposed to talk, to listen as opposed to waiting to talk, and then to have a dialogue.

One panelist recounted that he was watching the news one day when one of his very young sons asked, "Why did the president mess up the economy?" He was surprised—the boy was only 5 or 6 years old—so he asked, "What do you mean, 'messed up the economy'?" and his son engaged him in a dialogue about the fact that President Obama messed up the economy. As far as that child is concerned, there's a president of the country and that president needs to do a good job for him and the rest of the country. The fact that Mr. Obama was black (like the little boy) didn't give him a free pass.

For today's children, the next time they see a white person in the White House will be the first time that they can fully grasp that there's a white president. It's important to keep in mind that minorities, especially younger people, look at the political world from that perspective. This is the new society that we live in as a result of Mr. Obama's presidency.

With respect to "un-messing up the economy" and expanding opportunities for everyone, there are short, medium and long-range policy challenges.

To start, conservatives—along with everyone else—need to declare peace with the safety net. The social safety net provided by the government is one of the greatest achievements of our society. It's one of the singular things that free enterprise brought to the United States, which no other economic system in the history of mankind has been able to accomplish.

In order to secure the safety net, we need to declare war on policies that are going to bankrupt it for the truly indigent, the elderly, and those with disabilities. For example, entitlement reform is needed because, as an empirical matter, societies that have not gotten their entitlement programs under control (such as the periphery nations in Europe) have become insolvent. Insolvency in turn leads to austerity. And austerity always and everywhere affects the poor and not the rich.

If you care about poor people, you need to declare war on out-of-control entitlements. That's how you protect the safety net. In other words, to be for the poor, you better be a rock ribbed fiscal conservative. There is no other way out of this conundrum.

Next, in order to stop the bleeding in the economy in the short term, you have to be a jobs hedgehog. We need an energy policy that brings jobs, a regulatory policy that brings jobs, tax reform (corporate tax reform in particular) that brings jobs and so on. Why?

Jobs are the source of meaning and dignity in people's lives. There are two kinds of people: those who think that work is a punishment or those who think that work is a blessing. Everybody falls into one of those two categories. Those two categories cut across ideological boundaries. There are Republicans, for example, who want to punish the poor by making them work for their food stamps; there are other Republicans who want to bless the poor by saying "you need to work in order to get your food stamps."

If you believe that work is a blessing, which most Americans do on both left and right, then you need a jobs policy that blesses people and does not call anything a "dead end." Most of us started with a "dead end" job in some way shape or form. The social compact with the population says that if you work and play by the rules you deserve to be able to make a living.

Medium term is the need for human capital development. That's the reason that education matters. That's the civil rights struggle of our time. We need education reform to make school systems work for the benefit of children not adults. Think about this. If a company were run for the benefit of the employees as opposed to the benefit of the mission it's trying to achieve, it would deserve to go out of business and it would. No other industry bridals against both choice and innovation and stays in business and grows. Yet that's what happening with our education establishment today.

In the long term is culture and the issues of faith, family, community, and work. These elements of culture are the most concentric forces to a life of happiness and prosperity, and these are the things that are escaping the poor more and more.

Republicans often seem to believe that people on welfare don't want to work. That's a very strong behavioral assumption that turns out to be empirically incorrect. According to public opinion data, the vast majority of people who are not working would much prefer to have their children see them earning a pay check as opposed to getting a welfare check. If you believe the best about people and give them hope, then people will respond largely in a very constructive way. But if you assume the worst about them, then they will assume that you are hostile, they'll assume that you're racist, they'll assume you don't care about people like them, and to a certain extent they won't be wrong.

Today, the District of Columbia spends more per capita per student than any other municipality or state in the country, yet ranks 51st in achievement. In part that's due to a culture now that says that having the value of an education is somehow not cool, you're not "authentic." That's wrong. If a young person can't at least graduate high school and master the basics in science and mathematics and English, how are they going to get a good paying job? It's fine to talk about opportunity and empowerment, but if coming out of the starting blocks young people lack even the foundation of an education, then the game is over before they start.

We need to do a much better job of explaining why our vision of empowering people starts with fixing failing schools, which in turn starts with parents instilling an understanding in their kids why an education is important. Our parents and grandparents didn't go through all of the struggles with integration—the rocks, the batons, the water cannons—just so kids today can go to school and say "yeah, I don't care, I'm not interested." We need to honor the legacy of the opportunity that we have been given and build on it.

Entrepreneurship is another part of the equation. Students today don't necessarily want to go work in a traditional circumstance for corporate America. They want to create their own opportunity, their own jobs, the new market that they envision.

There's a chartered middle school on Howard's campus focused on math and science. Based on a lottery, they admit kids that typically preform a grade below standard levels. Of their first graduating class from that cohort, 95 percent of them went to college, 50 percent of those in the STEM fields. Why was this so successful? Because these kids were on a college campus in a focused environment of math and science, where they were given and taught how to use laptops (probably the first in their homes), and they saw that people cared. This created an opportunity for them to empower themselves.

A cartoon may help illustrate this point. Three people are looking over a fence at a baseball game, one is particularly short, the other just tall enough to see over the fence, and the last one very tall. Equality is giving each of them the same sized box for them to stand on. But if the box is too short, the shortest person never sees over that fence. Justice, by contrast, is giving the shortest guy two boxes so he can see over the fence. Balancing equality verses justice is part of what some of these policies have to demonstrate.

Questions and Answers

Q. How have you changed your views on social and economic issues over the past 30 years? Most of us don't believe the same things we did thirty years ago, what would you say has made a change in your mind and heart?

A. One significant change has been an expansion of the social safety net over that period, and how caring about people is reflected in public policy. One of the least fortunate things that Reagan did was to go after the welfare queen in the pink Cadillac, which helped foster a stigmatized concept of the undeserving poor person who really does not want to work, as opposed to somebody who finds themselves in an unfortunate situation and is looking for a way up. I think that there are far more people that are like the recent immigrants who you see gathered on that corner looking for day work, any job in order to get off that corner. It's fair to ask whether today's

Republican Party is still talking about the welfare queen in the pink Cadillac, or is it talking about helping people to find a way up that ladder of upward mobility?

At the same time, I have come to understand that intolerance on the left that can be far greater than the intolerance that would come from the Archie Bunker character on the right pointing at the guys on the corner and saying "those guys are a bunch of bums and drug dealers and I don't care about them." In fact, there is a lock on how the Left thinks at times, saying "oh, you have to simply spend more, the programs that exist now are good programs" without paying attention to the reality of persistent poverty, family breakdown, failure of the larger educational structure, and being open to real change to improve these failing systems.

Q. Back in one of my early books in the 1980s, I said that if the inner-city family broke down, the result would be the creation of a welfare state to take care of women and children and a police state to take care of the boys. All this talk of liberal compassion totally breaks down when it comes to boys. A third of black young men are either in jail, on the lam, or out on probation. That's how we solve the crime problem, and it is an outrage. It's not a defensible solution to put a third of the boys in jail and give all sorts of subsidized jobs to the women, yet this is what liberalism has done. What is the breakdown at Howard University now of girls to boys?

A. On the undergraduate campus, 70 percent of the undergrads are females, 30 percent are males. (It's great for the boys, as you can imagine.) A couple of points, though. In 2000 there were more black males in our penitentiary system than in our higher education system. That's not the case today. There are twice as many black males in our higher education system as in our penitentiary system; we've made a significant shift. In two-year institutions, there are more black females than white males enrolled.

So the pipeline of our education system is being primed well; but there is still a difference in opportunity at the end of that. When you look at two-year institutions, and their output in terms of job placement, the picture is not great. That brings us back to the need for policies that would help enable these now educated young men and women to get jobs. We need an outlet in our country to get these people into systems that would allow them to participate and diversify our workforce. And I think this is where our policies are going to let us down if we don't do something about them.

Arthur Brooks, Wayne Frederick, Juan Williams, Ron Christie

Some people say that government is not the answer; rather it is the problem. We do have to be careful in terms of the role that government plays. And it doesn't need to be sprawling to succeed.

But let's be honest. When we look at opportunity, we look through a certain prism that is not always a clear prism. Based on what we see in the young men and women who come to a school like Howard from all over this nation, and from over 44 countries, that opportunity isn't being delivered on their doorstep; but when they get it, they do some magical things with it. It would be good to find a way to deliver opportunity to their doorstep.

Q. When it comes to enabling opportunity and upward mobility, I'm hungry for courage and boldness from our political leaders. We don't see enough of that today; rather the only courage and boldness we see is in service to partisan politics and that's a sad thing. What is it going to take to break through this partisan stranglehold and embolden or empower political leaders?

A. I think that you are absolutely right. Many members of Congress for example are focused more on appeasing their political constituencies so they don't lose their next primary elections as opposed to doing what's right for the country. We as citizens have an obligation to tell them, "This is wrong. We didn't elect you to go to Washington and represent a caucus or represent a party. You may have a partisan affiliation, but you represent the American people."

KEYNOTE ADDRESS

On the Future of the American Idea

Garry Kasparov

For the last few years I have been working on a book project that I have yet had time to finish. Its central theme is the shift in American values over the past 40 years, how Ronald Reagan's shining beacon on a hill of my Soviet youth has slowly moved away from the values of individual freedom, sacrifice, risk taking and faith, both domestically and in foreign policy. Those traditional American ideals have been gradually replaced with those of security over risk, of equivalence over excellence, of comfort over sacrifice, and hyper-partisanship over unity.

The working title of the manuscript is a little shocking to some: "Un-American." But it's perfectly accurate. Of course, I'm myself "un-American." Also, I like to say that I was born in the deep South right next to Georgia. No, it's a fact of my biography that I was born in the capital city of Azerbaijan, in Baku, in the deep South of the USSR right next to the Republic of Georgia. And, through growing up with some outspoken uncles and a die-hard communist grandfather, I was exposed to political theory at a tender age—almost as early as chess.

But the title "un-American" comes directly from the dictionary: "Adjective; not characteristic of or consistent with American customs, principles or traditions." In my opinion, there is much about America of today that fights this description far too well. And this is tragic not only for Americans, but for the entire world that has depended on and learned from the United States in its economy, its military, its technology and its moral leadership for over a century. This also means that America's challenges are the world's challenges. And, for all the talk about the multipolar world, the G-20's, G-0, the rise of China, and the new Cold War with an oil rich dictator in charge of the Kremlin, America cannot be so easily replaced.

As Jack Kemp said, "there are certain fundamental concepts about human dignity and the rights of man, which if not defended by America, will not be successfully defended by anyone else." If there is any doubt on that, ask the people of Syria, or the people of Ukraine. These American values are based on believing that human freedom is of maximum value both at home and around the world. It is not only the United States that is criticized, but the system that made America and the world so successful. And by system, I do not mean democracy, although the rise of China and the arrogance of dictators like Putin and Assad in the face of weak Western opposition has allowed the superiority of democracy to be questioned.

An even more dangerous delusion is the increasing attack on the free-market concept itself, attacks on the principles of capitalism that have created unprecedented standards of living. On one hand, the critics are correct. It's important to talk about the ills of the society. For example, poverty was Jack Kemp's signature issue; the free-market approach instead of a welfare approach. He also understood that capitalism had to mean more than the acquisition of money. In another excellent phrase, he said: "Democratic capitalism is not just the hope of wealth but the hope of justice."

Justice. It's a very powerful word. The power of this phrase—it's economic justice to the poor, to the citizen of the communist country, to those living in totalitarian regimes. Many have forgotten that the American regime was not just to get rich. Immigrants did not come to the American shores just because they thought the streets here were paved with gold—maybe some did—but the American Dream for many was for their children to have a better life.

The immigrants came because in America they would be rewarded for their hard work and if they got rich, okay, that's a side effect; no one objects to that. And, in recent years, the attacks on capitalism have increased as the attacks on inequality have increased. It's a logical correlation, but also a false one. Thomas Picketty's new book Capital of the 21st Century has become the rare economics best seller (although I'm not sure how many people who bought the book are actually reading it). But, I believe that it is not capitalism that has failed us; I believe it's us who failed capitalism.

If we go back to this word justice, and if we look at the classics such as Adam Smith, correct me if I'm wrong, but, I never read anything in Adam Smith's works about the size of the corporation offering immunity against bankruptcy. And, if a small business in North Carolina is bankrupt and goes belly up, so must go Goldman Sachs. When the state steps in deciding which companies live or die, things have gone terribly wrong.

I agree with the concept of a small government, but before we move into the size of the government, we have to agree that government should not intervene in the economy. I think that this element has been missing in the debate. I think that the GOP is yet to make its position clear in anticipating the role of the government before talking about the size; and making clear that everyone is equal before the law and will be judged by the market without government officials, even with the best of intentions, deciding which company survives and which company goes under.

Today we are more and more using the stock market as a substitute for everything else. But less and less does the market represent the health of the nation, let alone its values. And, just when the market is about to do its real job of cutting the weak, the government steps in.

When you base your policies on principles, there is no room for "but." This is a very short but critical word. We believe in the free market, BUT... trouble. We will defend democracy and freedom and human rights, BUT not in Ukraine ... trouble. Rising inequality is a defining problem, but it comes from decades of moving away from the principles of excellence that had created the richest society in history by the end of the 1960s.

It's obvious that after two long engagements in Afghanistan and Iraq, the American people are not eager to hear about America's global responsibilities, about the importance of standing up for freedom around the world. Syria is far away and there are very few good guys. Let's just let bad guys kill each other. Ukraine is far away, and Putin is too strong, he is a tough guy with lots of oil.

But when you betray the notion that freedom is worth defending everywhere, you begin a very dangerous path for America and the world. The U.S., Europe and other democracies thrive with stability. Dictators like Putin, especially ones who depend on energy resources and high prices for oil and other energy resources, thrive with instability.

America generally wants to resolve the Middle East crisis with Iran without a major explosion. Putin is dreaming about any war in the Middle East that could help oil prices to rise. Economic growth requires stability, which cannot exist when Putin can annex a chunk of Ukrainian nation with impunity, and launch a paramilitary invasion of eastern Ukraine while diplomats differ.

It's time not just to react to Putin's immediate reactions but to start thinking about long-term strategy.

Harry Truman, in my view, was a great president not because he saved West Berlin, not because he saved South Korea and Taiwan, not because he had the idea of the Marshall Plan that saved Western Europe from communism, but because he laid down the foundation for the future victory in the Cold War. He came up with institutions like NATO, CIA, and Voice of America that eventually played a pivotal role in the victory forty years later.

It's time to start thinking long term. I still believe there are great opportunities that could be offered by this country. What we're lacking today is leadership—leaders willing to stand up to dictators who only respect strength.

Ronald Reagan did not need Truman's track record to command the respect of the Soviet leaders. They knew he cared vitally about human rights in the Soviet Union and elsewhere because he was never afraid to bring it up with them. They knew Reagan was not afraid to act, which usually meant he did not have to.

Reagan had two things that recent Free World leaders lack: principles and the credibility only principles can provide. Assad and Putin jumped over Obama's redline against chemical weapons in Syria and Assad is still in power, still murdering people. As I wrote at the time of this crisis, the brotherhood of dictators was watching Syria closely, and if Obama had acted there, I believe that we would not be hearing stories about Russian troops in Ukraine.

Each time we show weakness, the next crisis will be worse and costlier. The price to resolve this crisis will go higher. The Cold War was not won just because of American technology, or the disastrous communist economy. It was also values, what the whole world called, or used to call, and some people still call, American values.

For those of us behind the Iron Curtain, when you people outside genuinely cared, then we in Soviet Union, in Eastern Europe, were not alone. Individual liberty was for all, not just for those who were lucky enough to be born into it.

Just for a minute, I will slide into a more academic note. Think of three fundamental documents that establish in writing our definition of modern civil society. The English Bill of Rights, 1689. The American Declaration of Independence, 1776. And the French Declaration of the Right of Man, 1789. So, how many times is the word "democracy" mentioned in these three documents? The answer is zero, because the method by which leaders were chosen was not yet a relevant issue. The fundamental rights that define the relationship between the government and the people—that is what mattered, and that is still true today.

Central among those rights is individual freedom, the unifying theme. Individual freedom is the basis for the free-market system of all successful economies. It's the basis of our foreign policy that says freedom for others is as important as oneself. Individual freedom is the core of the American rights and values that, in my opinion, have been under attack and in decline with the United States for over 30 years. Origins of these values shifted from the 60s to today. Risk, excellence, sacrifice, faith, unity are American values that are good for the world, and good for the American economy. Not coincidentally, these are also values of innovation and entrepreneurialism, of new technology, new industries and new jobs.

Since roughly the 70s there has been a shift away from those values and toward their opposites, as I mentioned at the start. A shift toward security, equivalence, comfort, cynicism and hyper-partisanship. In the span of one generation, the world's greatest entrepreneurs and capitalists convinced themselves that they could get reward without risk. It's a time to wake up from this dangerous delusion built on a mountain of debt. It's time to dream again of exploration excellence and everything else that made and makes America great.

I'll employ a familiar anecdote about a Democratic president, since Jack Kemp was proud to be a bipartisan politician.

Risk means taking on big challenges and aiming high. Its physical expansion was always a very important part of American dreams, conquering the West's vast territory, going up to the skies, or just down into these deep oceans.

There is a reason people return again and again to the 1969 moon landing as a crowning achievement of American ambitions and ingenuity. This incredible feat must also be considered one of the least practical endeavors ever attempted. President John F. Kennedy admitted as much when exhorting the American people to support the cause during his famous "We choose to go to the moon" speech at Rice University in Houston on September 12th, 1962. The speech's most famous line is in fact the plain statement that America chooses to go to the moon because it was hard, not because it was easy. I think any other politician today would be impeached if he said that. It would have been easy for Kennedy to play the Cold War card more heavily in his speech, and to emphasize the strategic military importance of the space program. Instead he relied on the grandeur and difficulty of the challenge itself to inspire the audience and the American nation.

Kennedy believed in the power of great dreams to change the world despite or because of its impracticality. He was also enough of a politician to mention the number of jobs that the manned space program would bring to Houston. He also discussed the cost, something that was forgotten, and he mentioned that it would cost $5,400 million, because at that time Americans didn't understand the concept of a billion. And he mentioned that this amount—a huge amount by the standards of the early 60s—was less than what Americans paid for cigarettes and cigars every year.

Amazingly, it worked. People accepted the sacrifice, embraced the dream, and the challenge. It's hard to imagine that in 1969, when Americans landed on the moon, 3,500 IBMers worked for this project, and we could see the pictures of these rooms filled with the massive computers, the entire computing power of NASA was the size of one iPhone.

Keynote Speaker Garry Kasparov

Imagine the power and the creativity of people who could come up with not just the concept, but with the real implementation of something that nobody thought would be possible to achieve, using 120 kilobytes to write a software that could bring man to the moon and back safely. When I hear stories that today "Oh, we already did everything so what else could be done?" we do not appreciate the fact that with this little device in the pocket we have immense power. It's up to us to restore the great dreams, and to look up to the skies or down to the oceans and recognize that there are still the huge territories for us to conquer.

To finish, I'll come out of the stars, and out of the clouds, and dreams, and oceans, and talk about the reality of democracy—elections.

I'm running now for the President of International Chess Federation, which is the fight against another Russian who has been there for 19 years and who has effectively turned this organization into a massive KGB money laundering machine. I have 176 votes, from the United States to Palau, 1 country 1 vote, and that's why I live in the plane just traveling around, hoping that eventually we can take it out of Putin's hands.

You also have elections here in 2014. And, of course, everybody's concerned about winning elections, and about short term perspectives, next fall's midterm, the presidential elections. Maybe again since I'm un-American, I can afford to be more critical and try to look at the big picture. Because sometimes it can work tactically, but eventually it will fail strategically. I believe it's time for the GOP to come up with a long-term vision. I do understand that sometimes long-term vision may hurt short term calculations, but eventually you win, and the country wins, and the world wins, because everybody will be better off.

There are two historic examples that are probably quite relevant. One of them is from the British Empire. Benjamin Disraeli in 1867, due to the reshuffling of the party, has become prime minister, the title he coveted for his entire life. He could play it safe and stay prime minister to survive elections; instead he pushed for the reforms and new voters that were so important in his calculations to build the new Tory Party. He pushed his reform bill, but because it went against the interest of many voters, he lost the last elections in 1868 to Gladstone and was in opposition for six more years. But in 1874, he came back triumphantly because the coalition he created, the coalition of aristocracy and the working class, brought him into power. Looking at the history of the Tory Party of the 20th century, one could say it reflected Disraeli's grand vision. Two of the greatest Tory leaders in the 20th century, Winston Churchill and Margaret Thatcher, had the heritage on the one side of the Duke of Marlboro, and on the other the heritage of a town grocer. So it worked out.

The second brings us back to the United States soil, and some painful memories for some in this room: the 1964 elections, the worst electoral defeat in memory. But this defeat laid down the base for the Reagan Revolution because with Goldwater's demise, there was a rise of a new star in the Republican Party. Ronald Reagan made his name by this great speech just a few days before the elections, and that was the beginning of the Reagan Revolution, and the core of the modern Republican Party, so well represented by Jack Kemp, and it lives today here in this room.

SPEAKER BIOGRAPHIES

FRED BARNES is executive editor of *The Weekly Standard*, which he cofounded in 1995. From 1985 to 1995, he was senior editor and White House correspondent for the *New Republic*. He covered the Supreme Court and the White House for *The Washington Star* before moving to the *Baltimore Sun* in 1979. He served as the national political correspondent for the *Sun* and wrote the "Presswatch" media column for the *American Spectator*. Barnes appears regularly on the Fox News Channel. From 1988 to 1998 he was a regular panelist on the McLaughlin Group. He has also appeared on Nightline, Meet the Press, Face the Nation, the News Hour with Jim Lehrer. Barnes graduated from the University of Virginia and was a Neiman Fellow at Harvard University.

ARTHUR C. BROOKS is the president of AEI. Until 2009, he was the Louis A. Bantle Professor of Business and Government Policy at Syracuse University. He is the author of eight books and many articles on topics ranging from the economics of the arts to applied mathematics. His most recent books include *The Road to Freedom: How to Win the Fight for Free Enterprise* (2012), *The Battle: How the Fight between Free Enterprise and Big Government Will Shape America's Future* (2010), *Gross National Happiness* (2008), *Social Entrepreneurship* (2008), and *Who Really Cares* (2006). Before pursuing his work in public policy, Mr. Brooks spent twelve years as a professional French hornist with the City Orchestra of Barcelona and other ensembles.

RON CHRISTIE is founder and CEO of Christie Strategies, LLC and former special assistant to President George W. Bush and deputy assistant to Vice President Dick Cheney. He is the author of three books, including his most recent book *Blackwards: How Black Leadership is Returning America to the Days of Separate but Equal*. Prior to Christie Strategies, he served as vice president of a full-service issues management firm. He was also executive vice president and director of global government affairs at a leading private public global government affairs at a leading private public affairs firm and of counsel at the D.C. law firm Patton Boggs, LLP. Prior to joining Vice President Cheney's staff, he briefly served as counsel to former U.S. Senator George Allen, and as senior adviser to former House Budget Committee Chairman and current Ohio Governor, John Kasich.

WAYNE FREDERICK is a scholar, surgeon, researcher and respected administrator. He is President of Howard University where he previously served as Provost and Chief Academic Officer. Prior to Howard University, he served on the faculty at the University of Connecticut and was the Associate Director of its Cancer Center. Frederick attended Howard University at age 16 and eventually earned his Bachelor of Science and his medical degree at age 22. After a surgical residency at Howard University Hospital, he completed a post-doctoral research fellowship and a surgical oncology fellowship at the University of Texas MD Anderson Cancer Center. He was named a "Super Doctor" by *The Washington Post* and listed on *Ebony Magazine's* Power 100 in 2010. He was named one of America's Best Physicians by *Black Enterprise* magazine.

GEORGE GILDER is a co-founder and Senior Fellow at Discovery Institute where he directs Discovery's program on technology and public policy and the Center for Wealth, Poverty and Morality. He attended Harvard University and served as a speechwriter for several prominent officials and candidates, including George Romney and Richard Nixon. He is the author of books such as *The Party That Lost Its Head* (1966); *Men and Marriage* (1972); *Microcosm* (1989); best seller *Wealth and Poverty* (1981) and most recently *Knowledge and Power* (2013). Mr. Gilder has served as Chairman of the Lehrman Institute's Economic Roundtable and as Program Director for the Manhattan Institute. His is a frequent writer for *The Wall Street Journal*, *The Harvard Business Review*, *The American Spectator*, and other publications.

GARRY KASPAROV was a chess grandmaster at age 17. He is widely considered to be the greatest chess player of all time. He holds records for the all-time highest chess rating, the most consecutive chess tournament victories, the most Chess Oscars, and the longest time as the top rated chess player in world history. In 2004, Kasparov helped to found the Committee of 2008, a group of Russian freedom advocates and organizations seeking fair, democratic elections. Kasparov retired from chess in 2005 to devote himself full time to writing and human rights advocacy. An outspoken critic of Russian President Vladimir Putin, Kasparov created the United Civil Front, a social movement with a mission to prevent Russia from returning to totalitarianism. His activism has drawn the ire of the Russian government, and he has been beaten and arrested several times. Kasparov's keynote lectures, seminars, and articles on strategic thinking, achieving peak performance, and tech innovation have been acclaimed in dozens of countries. In 2009, he began working with Silicon Valley pioneers Peter Thiel and Max Levchin on technological progress. He is a contributing editor of *The Wall Street Journal* and a frequent contributor to *The New York Times*, *The Financial Times*, *The Daily Beast*, and various other publications. He is the chairman of the HRF's International Council.

WILLIAM KRISTOL is editor of *The Weekly Standard*, which, together with Fred Barnes and John Podhoretz, he founded in 1995. Kristol regularly appears on Fox News Sunday and on the Fox News Channel. Before starting The Weekly Standard, Kristol led the Project for the Republican Future. Prior to that, Kristol served as chief of staff to Vice President Dan Quayle during the Bush Administration and to Secretary of Education William Bennett under President Reagan. Before coming to Washington in 1985, Kristol taught politics at the University of Pennsylvania and Harvard's Kennedy School of Government.

RICH LOWRY graduated in 1990 from the University of Virginia, where he studied English and history. He edited there a conservative monthly magazine called the Virginia Advocate. He went on to work as a research assistant for Charles Krauthammer, then as a reporter for a local paper in northern Virginia. He joined National Review in 1992, after finishing second in an NR young writers contest. He became NR's Articles Editor before moving to D.C. in the summer of 1994 to cover Congress. He was named editor of National Review in 1997. He has written for *The New York Times, The Washington Post, The Wall Street Journal, The Los Angeles Times*, and a variety of other publications. He is a syndicated columnist and a commentator for the Fox News Channel. His book, *Legacy: Paying the Price for the Clinton Years* was a New York Times best seller.

PEGGY NOONAN is a columnist for *The Wall Street Journal* whose work appears weekly in both OpinionJournal.com and the Journal's Weekend Edition. She is the author of eight books on American politics and culture. The most recent, *Patriotic Grace*, was published in October 2008. Her first book, the bestseller *What I Saw at the Revolution: A Political Life in the Reagan Era*, was published in 1990. She was a special assistant to the president in the White House of Ronald Reagan. Before that she was a producer at CBS News in New York. In 1978 and 1979 she was an adjunct professor of journalism at New York University.

BOB SCHOULTZ graduated from Stanford University in 1974 with a BA in Philosophy, and was commissioned an ensign in the US Navy. He served as a Naval Special Warfare (SEAL) officer for the next 30 years and commanded Navy SEALs in multiple capacities all over the world. He retired as a Captain in July, 2005 and then served as the Director of the Master of Science in Global Leadership program at the University of San Diego until November 2011. He has been married for 34 years and has three grown children. He is currently a speaker, consultant and coach for Fifth Factor Leadership.

AMITY SHLAES is chairman of the Calvin Coolidge Memorial Foundation, based at the birthplace of President Coolidge in Plymouth Notch, Vt. She is author of *The Forgotten Man/Graphic*, a full length graphic version of her bestseller about the Great Depression, *The Forgotten Man*. She is also author of Coolidge, which debuted at number three on the New York Times bestseller list. Miss Shlaes writes a column for *Forbes*, teaches at NYU's Stern School of Business, and has served, over the years, as a columnist at The *Financial Times* and *Forbes*. She knew Jack Kemp in the 17 years she served at *The Wall Street Journal*.

JUAN WILLIAMS is contributor and co-host of Fox News Channel's "The Five" and serves as FNC's political analyst. In addition to a more than 10-year career with NPR, Williams spent 23 years at *The Washington Post*. Mr. Williams won an Emmy Award for television documentary writing and has received widespread critical acclaim for numerous projects, including the documentaries "Politics: The New Black Power" and "A. Phillip Randolph: For Jobs and Freedom." He is the author of six books including *Eyes on the Prize: America's Civil Rights Years, 1954-1965* and *Thurgood Marshall: American Revolutionary*. Williams has also contributed to many national magazines, including: *TIME, Fortune, The Atlantic Monthly, The New Republic, Ebony* and *GQ*.

DEBORAH WINCE-SMITH is President & CEO of the Council on Competitiveness and president of the Global Federation of Competitiveness Councils. She has over 20 years of experience as a senior U.S. government official as the first Senate-confirmed Assistant Secretary for Technology Policy in the Department of Commerce and Assistant Director for International Affairs in the Reagan White House. She also serves on the board of NanoMech, Inc., the Smithsonian National Board and the Secretary of State's International Economic Policy Advisory Committee. She is the vice-chair of the World Economic Forum's Global Agenda Council on Competitiveness and the Women Corporate Directors, and a member of Japan's STS Forum.

INDEX

ABM Treaty, 171
Afghanistan, 90, 172, 227, 228, 267
Africa, 19, 20, 33, 34, 35, 36, 37, 38, 39, 40, 41, 42, 85, 109, 169, 172, 203, 216, 250
Alexis de Tocqueville Institution, 28, 41
American Century, 7, 27, 32, 44, 45, 181, 189
American Idea, 1, 3, 4, 5, 6, 7, 9, 10, 13, 14, 15, 17, 18, 20, 109, 147, 148, 150, 173, 175, 176, 187, 189, 190, 191, 195, 197, 198, 199, 200, 201, 202, 205, 206, 207, 211, 217, 219, 220, 221, 226, 249, 265
American Revolution, 9, 110, 167, 168, 195, 216
anti-Semitism, 27, 144
balanced budget, 73, 102, 155
Bennett, William, 206, 277
Bosworth, Barry, 80
Brown v. Board of Education, 249
Brown, Tony, 154
Buffalo, 23, 93, 144, 149, 153
Bunche, Ralph, 155
Burke, Edmund, 93, 190
Butler, Stuart, 117
Capa, Robert, 219
capital gains tax, 70, 77, 137, 138, 177, 185, 245
Caribbean Basin Initiative, 20, 22
Carter, Jimmy, 147, 149, 150, 157, 204, 228
Central America, 172
China, 23, 28, 221, 229, 230, 234, 235, 237, 238, 241, 266
Christianity, 87, 89, 91
Churchill, Winston, 49, 57, 104, 272
civil rights, 52, 98, 106, 116, 145, 153, 154, 155, 164, 252, 256, 258
Clausen, A. W., 19

Clinton, William (Bill), 30, 35, 37, 51, 58, 63, 64, 68, 69, 70, 73, 74, 77, 83, 134, 135, 137, 138, 141, 173, 184, 278
Club of Rome, 18, 78
Cold War, 31, 34, 44, 48, 49, 109, 119, 183, 222, 266, 268, 270
communism, 28, 74, 77, 81, 104, 106, 119, 172, 174, 183, 226, 268
compassion, 5
Constantinescu, Emil, 28
Contract with America, 174
Coolidge, Calvin, 231, 251, 279
Crimea, 223, 224
culture war, 133, 141
Cuomo, Mario, 112, 125, 173
Davidov, Yuri, 15
Declaration of Independence, 90, 93, 98, 99, 100, 121, 123, 124, 131, 148, 172, 190, 195, 216, 269
democratic capitalism, 8, 18, 35, 42, 56, 74, 75, 78, 81, 84, 92, 109, 110, 131, 138, 178, 249
Democratic Party, 141, 147, 155, 161, 163, 164, 174, 184
Democrats, 80, 111, 115, 147, 148, 155, 156, 157, 159, 161, 163, 173, 175, 213, 237, 244, 250, 256
developing nations, 18, 38
dignity, 5, 11
Disraeli, Benjamin, 272
Dole, Robert (Bob), 181, 182, 183, 184
Douglass, Frederick, 140
Eastern Europe, 27, 29, 30, 31, 41, 109, 110, 123, 269
Edison, Thomas, 232
education, 22, 27, 74, 102, 111, 114, 118, 134, 137, 164, 174, 177, 178, 203, 212, 239, 240, 246, 247, 249, 250, 251, 252, 258, 259, 261, 262

Education, 102, 171, 176, 197, 206, 249, 250, 277
El Salvador, 22
Eliot, T.S., 92, 131
Engler, John, 177
Enterprise Zones, 70, 117, 137, 163, 169
entitlements, 236, 242, 258
entrepreneur, entrepreneurial, 16, 59, 114, 185, 195, 234, 245
Erhad, Ludwig, 17
federal deficit, 236
Federal Reserve, 24, 67, 157, 158, 159, 193
Feulner, Ed, 110, 176
fiscal policy, 60, 103, 193
football, 143, 144, 145, 148, 243, 249
foreign aid, 13, 253
Foreign Operations, 13
Founding Fathers, 14, 16, 97, 232
Franklin, Ben, 232
free trade, 15, 22, 23, 33, 36, 37, 40, 60, 61, 72, 80, 81, 253
Free Trade Agreement, 50, 72
freedom, 5, 6, 11, 277
Freedom House, 28, 41
Friedman, Milton, 68, 234, 236
George, Francis, 252
Germany, 15, 16, 29, 31, 83
Gilder, George, 10, 56, 89, 119, 135, 231, 234, 276
Gilman, Sid, 144
Good Shepherd, 100, 145, 179, 186
Gorbachev, Mikhail, 109
Gray, Bill, 163, 164
Gray, Kimi, 111
growth, 5, 11
Guatemala, 21
Hamilton, Alexander, 121, 172, 205
Havel, Vaclav, 179, 225
Heritage Foundation, 109, 135, 173, 174, 176, 204
Hesburgh, Ted, 185
homeless, 118, 153

homelessness, 110, 123, 125, 139
Homeownership, 116, 162
Hong Kong, 19, 20, 60, 90, 91, 92
hope, 5
housing, 111, 114, 115, 116, 118, 119, 126, 132, 136, 137, 158, 162, 169, 177, 185, 203, 252
Howard University, 245, 250, 255, 256, 260, 261, 262, 276
human capital, 221, 258
Hungary, Poland, 30, 31
immigration, 20, 185, 246, 247
infrastructure, 17, 219, 220, 232, 233, 236, 242
inner-city, 117, 138, 161, 163, 169, 177, 261
Internal Revenue Service (IRS), 66, 85, 185, 195, 198
International Monetary Fund, 30, 37, 39, 49
Iran, 229, 268
Iraq, 50, 51, 52, 267
Jackson, Andrew, 213
Jackson, Jesse, 156
Jacob, John, 153, 157
Japan, 15, 16, 17, 20, 57, 58, 80, 92, 113, 221, 230, 279
Jasinowski, Jerry, 63
Jefferson, Thomas, 90, 98, 102, 121, 122, 168, 169, 190, 195, 197, 199, 205
Jordan, Payton, 143
Jordan, Vernon, 153, 158, 250
Judeo-Christian values, 14, 148
Kahn, Alfred, 157
Keflezighi, Meb, 220
Kemp-Garcia, 163
Kemp-Kasten, 162
Kemp-Roth, 82, 192, 196
Kennan, George, 15
Kennedy School of Government, 55, 173, 277
Kennedy, John F., 41, 157, 204, 270

Kennedy, Ted, 97, 100, 101, 102, 103, 106
Keynes, John Maynard, 16, 38
Keynesian, 16, 79, 80, 201
King, Martin Luther, Jr., 8, 95, 106, 107, 145, 164, 183, 200
Kotlowitz, Alex, 132
Kuttner, Robert, 111
Lawrence Livermore National Laboratory, 241
Leader of the Free World, 14, 172, 223
Leadership, 129, 164, 219, 223, 275, 278
Leading from behind, 223
Lekachman, Robert, 80, 157, 159
liberalism, 83, 175, 179, 261
Lincoln, 5
Lincoln, Abraham, 3, 5, 8, 10, 29, 48, 82, 110, 111, 121, 122, 123, 124, 125, 126, 127, 136, 137, 140, 145, 148, 155, 170, 181, 183, 199, 205, 209, 211, 212, 213, 214, 215, 216, 217, 219, 230, 249, 251
Lindsey, Lawrence, 113
Locke, John, 97
low-income housing, 115
Madison, James, 196, 206
Marshall, Thurgood, 250, 279
Marx, Karl, 88, 109
Marxism, 81, 101, 103, 109, 169
Maybury, Richard, 90, 91
Middle East, 23, 47, 230, 268
Mondale, Walter, 157, 158, 159, 160, 164
monetary, 16, 23, 24, 30, 36, 39, 41, 50, 55, 65, 68, 69, 71, 77, 80, 85, 159, 192, 193
moon landing, 270
Mora, Jim, 143
moral relativism, 103, 104, 131, 134
More, Sir Thomas, 95, 96
NAACP, 149, 156
NAFTA, 50, 85
NASA, 270

National Urban League, 153, 156
NATO, 224, 268
NFL, 143, 195
Novak, Michael, 20, 92, 131
Obama, Barack, 195, 201, 204, 222, 228, 236, 251, 257, 268
O'Neill, Tip, 163
opportunity, 5, 6, 11, 187
Paul, Rand, 249, 255
politics, 5, 11, 277, 278
Popper, Carl, 233
population growth, 20, 67, 79
power of ideas, 232
private sector, 34, 66, 71, 72, 158, 235, 240, 241
product liability, 245
productivity, 40, 66, 67, 74, 77, 85, 112, 114, 203, 235, 240
property rights, 36, 215, 241, 253
protectionism, 15, 23, 24, 31, 36, 155, 198
public housing, 116, 162
Putin, Vladimir, 222, 223, 224, 225, 228, 266, 267, 268, 272, 277
quantitative easing, 244
Raspberry, William, 116, 132
Reagan, Ronald, 13, 20, 32, 64, 65, 68, 77, 78, 79, 80, 81, 82, 84, 86, 103, 104, 105, 106, 109, 112, 119, 147, 152, 168, 169, 172, 173, 176, 183, 186, 187, 195, 196, 197, 198, 199, 203, 204, 221, 223, 225, 228, 231, 254, 255, 260, 265, 268, 273, 277, 278, 279
recession, 65, 67, 77, 92, 158, 243, 249
Republican Party, 9, 34, 83, 111, 140, 141, 147, 151, 153, 154, 155, 156, 157, 164, 165, 199, 223, 249, 261, 273
Romania, 28
Ronald Reagan, 278
Roosevelt, Franklin, 84, 173
Roosevelt, Theodore, 251
Rostenkowski, Dan, 163

Rowan, Carl, 163
Russell Kirk, 139
Russia, 30, 31, 223, 228, 229, 277
Ryan, Paul, 178, 249, 257
Sakharov, Andrei, 225
Samuelson, Paul, 16
Schultz, Theodore, 19
Sherraden, Michael, 136
Smith, Adam, 16, 23, 36, 56, 89, 90, 110, 119, 133, 267
Sochi, 223
Social Security, 73, 85, 118, 173, 245
Socialism, 136, 183
Solzhenitzyn, Aleksandr, 129
Soviet Union, 15, 25, 44, 105, 109, 148, 172, 223, 225, 268, 269
Sullivan, Leon, 33, 34, 39, 42, 164
supply-side, 19, 112, 201
Syria, 221, 222, 266, 267, 268
tax code, 17, 66, 69, 70, 83, 85, 178, 197
tax credits, 22, 118, 207
tax rates, 16, 17, 24, 36, 38, 39, 41, 58, 65, 66, 72, 78, 82, 85, 114, 115, 117, 139, 157, 158, 161, 177, 192, 196, 204
tax reform, 41, 65, 118, 161, 258
technological innovation, 57, 61
Thatcher, Margaret, 174, 203, 272
Third Way Movement, 83, 84, 85
Third World, 61, 104, 113, 114, 138, 150, 159
Thompson, Tommy, 177
Tocqueville, Alexis de, 28, 29, 40, 41, 83, 84, 101, 189, 193
Tory Party, 272
trade restrictions, 22, 37
Truman Doctrine, 14
Truman, Harry S., 30, 221, 268
Ukraine, Poland, 30, 223, 224, 228, 266, 267, 268
United Nations, 17, 45, 46, 47, 48, 50, 88, 191, 253
University of Virginia, 102, 275, 278
Vietnam, 28, 115
Volcker, Paul, 157
von Hayek, Friedrich, 80
Wallenberg, Raoul, 27, 28, 29, 31, 32
Wassily Leontief, 19
Whitman, Christie Todd, 177
Will, George, 206
Wirtschaftswunder, 17
Woodson, Robert (Bob), 117, 137
World Bank, 17, 19, 39, 45, 176
Zola, Emile, 27

APPENDIX

THE AMERICAN IDEA: A NATIONAL SURVEY

The American Idea
A National Survey

April 2014

Executive Summary

"The American idea was never that everyone would be leveled to the same position in 'life.' The American idea was that each individual should have the same opportunity to rise as high as his effort and initiative and God-given talent could carry him. If you were born to be a master carpenter, or a mezzo-soprano—or even a pro football player—here in America you could make it... America was founded on this sense of boundlessness."

Jack Kemp GOP Convention speech, 1980

"For the first time in history, a government was established, not with the power to bestow happiness—or withhold it—but to create the climate in which each individual, guided by Judeo-Christian values, could pursue his or her own happiness."

Jack Kemp GOP Convention speech, 1980

- When asked to describe what is unique about the American way of life, the resounding answer among Americans is freedom.

- More than three-quarters of Americans believe hard work can pave the way to success in the United States including 72% of immigrants who share this view.

- More than three-quarters of Americans, 78%, believe people as individuals, not government, should take more responsibility for themselves.

JACK KEMP
FOUNDATION

Executive Summary (continued)

"All around the world, despite the resistance of the old guard, freedom and free markets, democracy and capitalism are increasingly on the march. From Eastern Europe and Latin America to Africa and Asia and even the Soviet Union, people are dreaming of freedom and democracy after decades and even centuries of oppression, poverty, despair, and debt."

—Jack Kemp, 1990

"Government must be established to protect the rights of each individual, and the rights of the community as a whole. Beyond this, the proper scope of government is a matter for continual debate. But government itself must be limited so that it does not threaten the rights with which it is entrusted."

—Jack Kemp, 1983

- Most Americans believe the United States is a model of freedom and opportunity for people around the world.

- In fact, a majority of Americans believe the best days for the U.S. are still to come.

- More than two-thirds of Americans want to see the country's political leaders work to create a smaller government. But, they divide over whether there should be greater emphasis on the free market or on cutbacks to existing programs.

The American Way of Life

What do people see as most important about the American way of life?

In a word, *Freedom*.

What one word or phrase would you use to describe what you think of as most important about the American way of life?

Freedom Opportunity OffTrack Independence Equality Liberty HardWork Economy God Christianity Constitution Jobs Good Family FreedomtoChoose FreedomofSpeech Morality PersonalFreedom Compassion SmallGovernment RestoreEthics Selfish Integrity Happiness FreeEnterprise Rights PutU.S.First Great Democracy Free Inequality FreedomofReligion Medicare Money Ambition EqualOpportunity Education Loyalty Progress Constitution Comfortable Security Honesty Diversity PersonalResponsibility Crazy

JACK KEMP FOUNDATION

A Model for Freedom

Three-quarters of Americans believe the U.S. is a model of freedom and opportunity for other nations.

Because of the United States' history and its Constitution, do you think the U.S. is a model of freedom and opportunity for other countries around the world, or don't you think so?

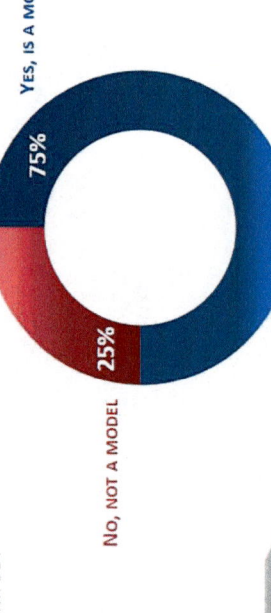

YES, IS A MODEL 75%

NO, NOT A MODEL 25%

Digging Deeper

Most Americans, regardless of age, education, or gender, see the U.S. as a model for other countries. 83% of African Americans, 77% of whites, and 71% of Latinos share this view. 81% of Democrats, 77% of Republicans, and 72% of independents agree. Other groups of note include 79% of adults between the ages of 45 and 59, 79% of Americans who earn $50,000 or more, and 79% of immigrants to the U.S. have this opinion.

Glory Days

58% of Americans believe the best days for the U.S. are yet to come.

Overall, do you think the best days for the United States are:

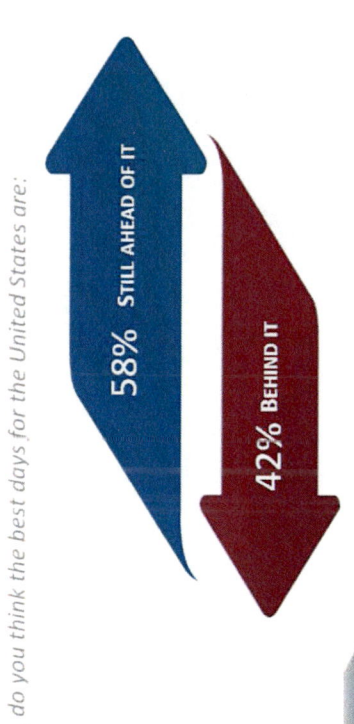

58% STILL AHEAD OF IT

42% BEHIND IT

Digging Deeper

There are partisan differences. 69% of Democrats are optimistic about the future of the United States while a slim majority of Republicans, 52%, are concerned. Interestingly, there is little difference on this question when it comes to age, gender, or income.

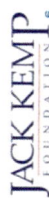

The Power of One

Most Americans believe individuals should take greater responsibility to provide for themselves, not government.

Which comes closer to your view:

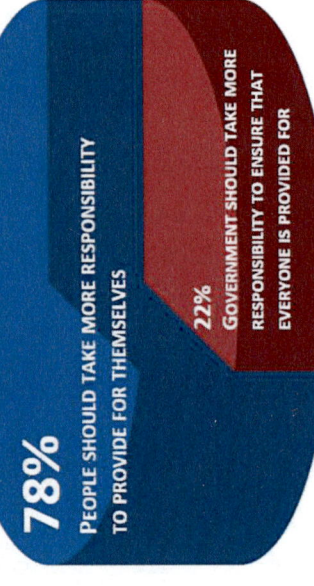

78% PEOPLE SHOULD TAKE MORE RESPONSIBILITY TO PROVIDE FOR THEMSELVES

22% GOVERNMENT SHOULD TAKE MORE RESPONSIBILITY TO ENSURE THAT EVERYONE IS PROVIDED FOR

Digging Deeper

Despite a strong consensus among most Americans on this issue, there are partisan differences. 96% of Republicans, 78% of independents, and 63% of Democrats agree in individual responsibility. 37% of Democrats, 22% of independents, and just 4% of Republicans think government should take a primary role in providing for people.

The American Dream

Most Americans believe hard work can pay off in the United States. Fewer than one-quarter say that diligence and determination are no guarantee of success for most people.

Which comes closer to your view:

76%

MOST PEOPLE WHO WANT TO GET AHEAD CAN MAKE IT IF THEY'RE WILLING TO WORK HARD

24%

HARD WORK & DETERMINATION ARE NO GUARANTEE OF SUCCESS FOR MOST PEOPLE

Digging Deeper

Success through hard work is at the core of the American Dream and most Americans, regardless of age, gender, or education, agree. 89% of Republicans, 75% of independents, and 67% of Democrats share this view. In addition, 82% of Latinos believe hard work is the way to get ahead compared with 77% of whites, and 69% of African Americans.

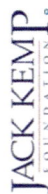

Priorities for the Nation's Success

More than seven in ten Americans point to the ability of the individual to be free to control their own destiny as a top priority for the future of the United States.

When thinking about the future of the United States, is each of the following a top priority, important but not a top priority, or not a priority to the future success of the United States:

47%* GROWTH OF FREEDOM & DEMOCRACY IN THE WORLD

50%* HEALTH OF PRIVATE ENTERPRISE

62%* PEOPLE WHO ARE ACTIVE AND ENGAGED AS CITIZENS

64%* FAITH & MORAL VALUES

72%* THE ABILITY OF EACH INDIVIDUAL TO BE FREE TO CONTROL THEIR OWN DESTINY

* Presents percentage reporting 'top priority'

Digging Deeper

There are differences along party lines.
Faith and moral values in our daily lives resonates with 77% of Republicans followed by the ability of individuals to control their own destiny with 75%, and the health of private enterprise with 65%. For Democrats, 66% point to individual freedom with an active and engaged citizenry in second with 63%. The ability of the individual to be free tops the list for independents with 73%.

JACK KEMP FOUNDATION

Leadership for the Future

Most Americans want political leaders who will work to create a smaller government. But, they divide over whether there should be greater emphasis on the free market or on cutbacks to existing programs. One-third of Americans want government to support individuals.

Thinking about the kind of political leadership the United States needs today, which of the following comes closest to your view:

Digging Deeper

60% of Democrats believe the U.S. needs leaders who want government programs that support individuals. This contrasts with Republicans and independents who divide between leaders who rely on the free market with limited government and leaders who will cutback current government programs and spending.

34% THE U.S. NEEDS LEADERS WHO WILL CUTBACK GOVERNMENT PROGRAMS AND SPENDING

34% THE U.S. NEEDS LEADERS WHO RELY ON THE FREE MARKET WITH A LIMITED GOVERNMENT

33% THE U.S. NEEDS LEADERS WHO WANT GOVERNMENT PROGRAMS THAT SUPPORT INDIVIDUALS

JACK KEMP FOUNDATION

Crisis in Confidence

Americans lack confidence in today's political leadership to guide the country. Only 36% have faith in the country's leaders to create policies which will generate economic opportunity. 63% of Americans do not share this view.

Do you have a great deal of confidence, a good amount, not very much, or no confidence in the political leadership in the United States to create policies which will grow economic opportunity for all Americans?

36%
GREAT DEAL,
GOOD AMOUNT
OF CONFIDENCE

63%
NOT VERY MUCH,
NO CONFIDENCE
AT ALL

Digging Deeper

A slim majority of adults under 30 (52%) and a similar proportion of Democrats (53%) have a great deal or a good amount of confidence that the country's political leaders will be able to grow economic opportunity for all Americans. Only 21% of Republicans, 29% of independents, and 32% of Americans 45 years of age or older agree.

STUDY METHODOLOGY

Methodology Statement

- This survey of 1,212 adults was conducted April 7, 2014 through April 10, 2014 by The Marist Poll and sponsored by The Jack Kemp Foundation. Adults 18 years of age and older residing in the contiguous United States were interviewed by telephone using live interviewers.

- Both landline and cell phone telephone numbers were randomly selected. Landline telephone numbers were randomly selected based upon a list of telephone exchanges from throughout the nation from ASDE Survey Sampler, Inc. Selection was done to ensure that each region was represented in proportion to its population. To increase coverage, this landline sample was supplemented by respondents reached through random dialing of cell phone numbers from Survey Sampling International.

- The two samples were then combined and balanced to reflect the 2010 Census results for age, gender, income, race, and region. Respondents in the household were selected by asking for the youngest male. Results are statistically significant within ±2.8 percentage points. The error margin increases for cross-tabulations and split samples.

- Please note that some totals may not add to 100% due to rounding.

Contact Information

(202) 452 6224

info@jackkempfoundation.org

The Jack Kemp Foundation is a 501(c)(3) organization committed to advancing the universal values of the American idea of growth, freedom, democracy and hope. Each of our programs is intended to foster the spirit of leadership that Jack Kemp demonstrated, expand the impact of powerful ideas on public policy, and prepare a new generation of leaders who can translate principled ideas into action.

(845) 575 5050

themaristpoll@marist.edu

Founded in 1978, The Marist College Institute for Public Opinion (MIPO) is a survey research center at Marist College in Poughkeepsie, New York. The Marist Poll has conducted independent research on public priorities, elections, and a wide variety of social issues. Through the regular public release of surveys, MIPO has built a legacy of independence, reliability, and accuracy. Its results are featured in print and electronic media throughout the world.